FLORIDA
BREWERIES

GERARD WALEN

STACKPOLE
BOOKS

0 11557 01214 9

To Grace,

*Your smile infects me. Your mind inspires me. Your soul gives me hope.
You're a great homebrewing assistant, my dear daughter,
and I'm looking forward to sharing a pint or two with you
on your twenty-first birthday in 2024. I love you.*

Copyright © 2014 by Stackpole Books

Published by
STACKPOLE BOOKS
5067 Ritter Road
Mechanicsburg, PA 17055
www.stackpolebooks.com

The author and the publisher encourage readers to visit the breweries and sample their beers and recommend that those who consume alcoholic beverages travel with a designated nondrinking driver.

Printed in the United States of America

10 9 8 7 6 5 4 3 2

FIRST EDITION

Cover design by Tessa J. Sweigert
Labels and logos used with permission of the breweries

Library of Congress Cataloging-in-Publication Data

Walen, Gerard.
    Florida breweries / Gerard Walen. — First edition.
        pages   cm
    ISBN 978-0-8117-1214-9
    1. Breweries—Florida—Guidebooks. I. Title.
TP572.W53   2014
663'.4209759—dc23

                                                            2013046641

Contents

Central Florida

Tampa Bay Area

Foreword

Standing in the hallway of a flophouse in Ybor City, the "rough part" of Tampa, with a pickax slung over my shoulder, I was thinking to myself, "What has my overly ambitious brother gotten us into this time?" It was May 1996, and my brother Johnny had promised me and the rest of my family that if we built this place, we would have a seemingly endless supply of good beer. So like any good beer drinker, I started swinging my pickax, and nine months later we had built one of Florida's pioneering brewpubs: Tampa Bay Brewing Company. Since then, Florida has seen an incredible transition from a beer wasteland to a major player in the craft beer movement.

When Tampa Bay Brewing Company first hit the scene, we were greeted with comments such as "Well, obviously you guys are going to brew light beer, right?" or "Of course we love IPA, but that beer style won't fly down here." Good old Anheuser-Busch even tried infiltrating our little haven for the craft beer lover by offering my now-broke family some enticing incentives to get one of their products in the door. We just kept our heads down, brewed aggressive beers, and trucked along, having confidence that there were others like us who needed to quench their palates' longing for a more flavorful beer. Boy, were we right!

Witnessing the emergence of the Florida craft beer community has been an amazing experience. What was once a small collection of ragtag homebrewers strewn throughout the state has grown into a relevant segment of the multibillion-dollar craft beer industry. Back then the community consisted of McGuire's, Dunedin Brewery, TBBC, and a few others that were scattered across the state fighting the good fight and holding down the fort; today powerhouses such as Cigar City Brewing are leading an assault to put Florida on the U.S. craft beer map. It has been an incredible two decades, and I am fortunate to have been a founding member of this grassroots movement made possible by a bunch of people who simply wanted better beer.

Today Florida is recognized as an epicenter of craft beer growth. We are experiencing a massive wave of bold new breweries opening, from large-scale, well-financed production breweries to nanobreweries started by homebrewing hobbyists who grew frustrated with the daily grind of their regular jobs and finally made the leap of faith into the entrepreneurial and rewarding world of craft beer. As I reflect on my eighteen years in this incredible industry, I think to myself, what a ride. Then I realize the ride is just beginning!

This is a great time to be a Floridian, and we also welcome visitors to come and experience the diversity of our craft beer scene—Jim over at Florida Beer Company pumping out great Florida brews on his 90-barrel brewhouse, Bob at Saint Somewhere Brewing crafting artisanal Belgian ales on his 7-barrel system, the husband-and-wife team of Southern Brewing and Winemaking carving a unique niche with their homebrew shop coupled with a 1-barrel brewery and biergarten, and all the other breweries described in this book, as well as new ones to come. We welcome you to explore our wonderful beer state, filled with plenty of fun under the sun and beers crafted by passion. Cheers and always remember, Beer Is Your Friend!

David Doble
Past president, Florida Brewers Guild,
head brewer at Tampa Bay Brewing Company,
and one of the founding members of Tampa Bay Brewing Company

Acknowledgments

Shortly after I started as a copy editor at the *Sarasota Herald-Tribune* in 1999, I began hearing some of my colleagues throw around terms and acronyms unfamiliar to me: "ABV," "IBU," "imperial stout," "mash tun," and such. Soon I learned that they were talking about beers, not the fizzy yellow lagers I had been consuming for years, but "craft beers." I had heard about "microbreweries" and had eaten meals at some of the so-called "brewpubs" that had popped up in Florida a few years before. But passion about beer, something that I bought by the twelve-pack for NFL Sundays and consumed without thought, had not yet entered my consciousness.

Like any introverted nerd, I wanted to be one of the "cool kids." (Though "cool kids" on a newspaper copy desk has a different meaning than in the rest of the world.) So I started exploring this strange, new world of craft beer. Researching it. Drinking it. It quickly hooked me, and I soon was using those now-familiar terms in my own conversations and eschewing the watery swill I had been drinking in favor of the Sierra Nevadas, Dogfish Heads, and Stones, when I could find them.

Now I'm writing about craft beer—sometimes getting paid to do so—running two blogs on the subject and spending way too much at the beer store. So thank you, guys—Alan Shaw, Erin Banning, Gerry Galipault, Alec Rooney, Dave Wisor, and Eddie Robinette—for opening that door. Also thanks to Sheri Wallace House, who allowed me to run her newly launched Road Trips for Beer website shortly after I left the newsroom in 2009. That indirectly led to my writing this book.

About a year after I started as editor of the site, I received a review copy of *Indiana Breweries*, by John Holl and Nate Schweber. Though I had not reviewed books on the site, it seemed like a good idea, seeing as how it directly related to the overall theme of beer travel. But to review it meant that I had to read it, and I immediately became gripped by the stories of the brewers and breweries in the Hoosier State. Subsequently, I reviewed more beer travel books, including another from the Stackpole Books Breweries Series, *Ohio Breweries*, by Rick Armon.

In the meantime, I had launched a blog called Beer in Florida to chronicle the rising craft beer scene in the Sunshine State, and I started thinking that there were enough breweries in the state to warrant such a guidebook. So I reached out to John Holl, whom I had met at the inaugural Beer Bloggers Conference in Boulder, Colorado, in 2010. He happily offered me tips on pitching the book and has remained a phone call away to advise me when I run into roadblocks or have stupid questions. Kyle Weaver, now my extremely helpful, talented, and patient editor at Stackpole, accepted the pitch, and I soon had a contract to write *Florida Breweries*. So thank you, John and Kyle.

But I didn't come out of the womb fully formed as a writer. Ever since I learned to string words together, I've been endlessly amused by what I put down on paper—or later, on the computer screen. I had some fine teachers in my life, but I wanted to give shout-outs to Katy Megahee, my high-school English teacher whose notations on my assignments made me think that I might have some degree of talent; Nancy White, my journalism teacher at Hillsborough Community College, who pushed me toward journalism; and Rick Wilber and Randy Miller, journalism professors at the University of South Florida who helped me learn how to write in journalese, so that I could get a job.

Once I started actually working at newspapers, I met many editors to whom I am grateful for being mentors and providing inspiration, and I apologize if I miss any, but in no particular order, they are Sherri Lonon, Dave Loverude, Dee Maret, Dave Szymanski, Kyle Booth, Matt Sauer, Robert Eckhart, Jay Goley, and Rosemary Armao. Special gratitude also goes to Leigh M. Caldwell, my all-time best editor and cheerleader, to whom I was married for a while.

And now that I've completed *Florida Breweries*, I have to give thanks to all of those at the breweries who took the time to sit down and talk with me about their craft—even on those occasions when I showed up unannounced. I appreciate what all of you have done, both in helping with the book and in driving the Florida craft beer scene to unprecedented levels of quantity, quality, and respect.

Many people deserve my gratitude for their help during the research stage of this book, by passing along contacts, making introductions, sharing inside tips, volunteering as a designated driver, or giving me a place to stay for a few days. Again, apologies to those whom I may have left out, and in no particular order, thanks go to Alan Shaw (his second mention!), Sean Nordquist, Tom Scherberger, Bill Presswood, Bob Lorber, Bill Tabone, Patricia Jimenez, Mike Jurewicz, Tom Barris, Gary Ryan, Terry Ryan, Regina Heffington, Todd Carpenter, and Cesar Vazquez.

Thanks also to Fran and Donna Copp, for making me feel at home in your little brewery in my new hometown, being a sounding board, and sharing your knowledge about making beer and running a brewery.

And of course, to the Friday Night Big Deck Monkey Club at Copp Brewery, for helping keep what sanity I have left.

I would be lax in not thanking Deirdre 2, my GPS device. Disregarding that time in South Florida when you tried to kill me (I admit that I make you recalculate far too often), I'd still be lost somewhere in the Panhandle without you.

Finally, there's my family. Dad, you taught me that strength comes through perseverance and humility. Mom, I know you never made much money at writing, but your thrill when you did get a piece published was inspiring. I miss you both. And, of course, my eight older brothers and two sisters (take a breath), Greg, Peter, Paul, Gary, David, Tommy, Mary, Linda, Jim, and John, thank you for the encouragement, support, and love throughout my life.

Introduction

Welcome to the Sunshine State! Common lore says that Spanish explorer Juan Ponce de Leon sought to drink from the Fountain of Youth during his explorations of the peninsula in 1513. If he had waited five hundred years, he could have enjoyed plenty of hand-crafted beer from the nearly seventy breweries in Florida today. If you live elsewhere, you might be surprised that the number is so high.

For many years, the rest of the country considered Florida a craft beer wasteland. It was. Though the state had a handful of brewpubs, and even fewer production breweries, including the Anheuser-Busch plant in Jacksonville and a Yuengling brewery in Tampa, the craft beer renaissance in California, Colorado, the Pacific Northwest, and New England had not yet arrived. A variety of factors led to the current livelier state of affairs, but describing how that happened first requires a little geography and history.

Florida is not a small state. It ranks twenty-second of the fifty states in total area, with 58,560 square miles. It has 1,197 miles of shoreline, of which 663 are beach. Driving from the southernmost brewery in the state, Kelly's in Key West, to Pensacola Bay Brewery in the Panhandle is, according to Google Maps, an 834-mile trek by the shortest route. The Beer Institute, a national trade organization, ranked Florida third in shipments of beer in 2012, with 12.9 million barrels being distributed. We're a thirsty bunch.

As is the population of the United States in general, dating back to the early colonists. It is said that the Pilgrims landed the *Mayflower* at Plymouth Rock rather than sail farther south because their supply of beer had reached dangerously low levels. The exact motivation remains a mystery. It may have had more to do with the weather, but a diary entry from one of the colonists confirms that the beer certainly was a factor: "We could not now take time for further search or consideration, our victuals being much spent, especially our beer, and it being now the 19th of December." Regardless, the history of the United States, at least the version written by Europeans and their descendants, drips with beer.

A Brief History of Brewing in the United States

I don't want to spend too many words recounting the entire history of the country's love affair with beer, because it's not what this book is about. It's a story that's been told many times before, and you can find countless versions in other books, magazine stories, and blogs. So I will make this as brief as possible.

Breweries of early colonial days were mostly found in personal kitchens, and the brewers usually were the women of the households. Another fermented beverage, cider, served as the drink of choice for the Founding Fathers and other colonial subjects of the English monarchy. Then the Revolutionary War made them all citizens of the newly birthed United States of America, and immigration to the country kicked into high gear. Sure, some little breweries were tucked here and there, but it wasn't until the mid-1800s, with an influx of German immigrants who brought with them their centuries-old traditions of brewing clear, crisp pilsners and lagers, that the beverage became part of the culture. Some of those German immigrants bore names that you still see on the shelves at the beer store: Busch, Miller, and Schlitz. By 1900, the country had somewhere around two thousand breweries.

Things were going along just fine. Some of the breweries had gotten pretty big, but the market still had plenty of room for everybody. Then in 1919, the Eighteenth Amendment to the U.S. Constitution was passed, and the "Great Experiment" of Prohibition outlawed intoxicating alcoholic beverages. The experiment failed, and in 1933, the Twenty-first Amendment ended it. But by that time, the vast majority of breweries had shut down, leaving only the largest, for the most part.

Fast-forward to 1979. After years of consolidation, mergers, and takeovers, only forty-four brewing companies still operated, and many of those were in danger of closing. But a couple of things had happened shortly before that would change the course of brewing in the United States.

In 1965, Fritz Maytag had purchased controlling interest in the struggling Anchor Brewing in San Francisco because he didn't want to see the tasty local beer that he favored go out of production. By the late 1970s, Anchor was in full swing. Then in October 1978, President Jimmy Carter signed a bill into law that lifted federal prohibitions against the brewing of small amounts of beer for personal consumption. Homebrewing must have been easy in those days, because seemingly overnight, thousands of people across the country emerged with the knowledge, some with bottles of homebrew ready to drink. Or maybe they had been brewing beer anyway.

In fact, two years before, one of those homebrewers, John "Jack" McAuliffe, had quietly started the modern craft beer revolution by incorporating New Albion Brewing in Sonoma, California, cobbling together brewing equipment from dairy tanks and fabricating parts using skills he had picked up servicing submarines during his navy career. New Albion didn't last long, however. Jack couldn't raise the financing to continue, and he shut the doors in late 1982. But during those years, he hosted visitors at the brewery who soon started their own small breweries, Ken Grossman of Sierra Nevada Brewing Co. in Chico, California, for one.

Side note: After selling his equipment to the Mendocino Brewing Company, a newly minted brewpub not far from New Albion, Jack helped assemble it and brewed there for a while, before essentially dropping out of sight for a few decades. A few very limited revivals of his ales happened over the years at other breweries; some he was involved with, others not. Then in 2012, Jim Koch, a fellow craft-brewing pioneer who founded the Boston Beer Company on the other coast in 1984, brewed and released nationally New Albion Ale with Jack's blessing and help. He used not only the original New Albion recipe, but also the original yeast strain, which the University of California–Davis had preserved. The release was a onetime thing, with all profits going to Jack. But as of this writing, Jack and his daughter Renee M. DeLuca had reached an agreement with Mendocino Brewing to brew Jack's recipes under the New Albion label. She said it should be on shelves in 2014.

Anyway, after those early days, a steady growth in small, independent craft breweries continued. The 1990s saw a brief boom as investors and businesspeople sought to jump on the bandwagon. Unfortunately, unrealistic dreams of rapid expansion and, in some cases, not very good beer saw many of them go out of business within just a few years. Still, in 2000, more than fifteen hundred breweries operated in the United States.

Then, starting in 2005, economic and market forces conspired to create another growth spurt in the industry that shows no sign of abating. According to the Brewers Association, a trade and advocacy group for small brewers, as of June 2013, there were 2,538 total breweries in operation and an additional 1,605 in planning.

Florida's Beer History

The Sunshine State's love affair with beer was defined for many years by iced coolers stuffed with cheap, mass-produced lagers or imported Mexican yellow beer with a lime on the bottle's rim. This is partly because Spain, whose explorers "discovered" Florida five centuries ago, does not have the beermaking heritage of the British and German immigrants who flocked to the northeastern and midwestern states.

But though it may not be as storied, Florida does have a history of brewing. Sean Nordquist, a beer writer and blogger based in the Tampa Bay area, was able to summarize most of it in just two paragraphs from a presentation he did, which he later posted on his Beer for the Daddy blog:

> The oldest brewery on record in Florida was the aptly named Florida Brewing Company. It was opened in 1896 by a group of cigar industrialists in Ybor City. In fact, the brewery they built still stands, and is the tallest building in Ybor to this day. The Florida Brewing Company made La Tropical Ale and Bock, and was the leading beer exporter to Cuba in the U.S. At their peak, they were producing over 80,000 barrels of beer a year.
>
> Up in Jacksonville, Jax Brewing opened up in 1913. Their "Jax Beer" was described in advertising as "tangy and zestful," "smooth," "mellow," as well as "fine," "full-bodied," and "refreshing." I guess they wanted to cover all of their bases! At their peak, Jax Brewing was putting out over 200,000 barrels annually, and were distributed well through the South.

Jax eventually closed in 1956 and sold the naming rights to Jackson Brewing in New Orleans. The Florida Brewing Company decided to deal with Prohibition by ignoring it and continuing to brew beer until 1927, when federal agents raided the brewery and shut it down. It reopened after Prohibition's repeal under new ownership and was renamed Tampa, Florida Brewery Inc. It closed for good in 1961.

Other breweries came and went over the years. In the late 1950s, Anheuser-Busch and Schlitz opened plants in Tampa, with AB opening its Jacksonville brewery in 1969. The miniboom of the 1990s reached Florida, with a slew of breweries and brewpubs opening, and most closing. Among the survivors are Tampa Bay Brewing Company, Dunedin Brewery, Sarasota Brewing Company, McGuire's Irish Pub, and Titanic Brewing Company.

It wasn't until 2001, when then-governor Jeb Bush signed a bill that repealed an old law on the books that had effectively barred nonstandard sizes of beer containers—such as the 750-milliliter and 22-ounce bombers popular with the country's craft brewers—that the craft beer revolution swept into Florida. Beers from now-storied breweries such as Stone from California, Dogfish Head out of Delaware, and Oregon's Rogue Ales began showing up on store shelves, eagerly snapped up by local beer geeks who had been denied too long. And the homebrewers began to get ideas.

Around 2005, new breweries and brewpubs started opening in the state. Saint Somewhere Brewing Company in Tarpon Springs opened in 2006, as did Orlando Brewing. Franz Rothschadl's Lagerhaus Brewery came into existence in 2007, and plans were under way for others. Then in 2009, Cigar City Brewing opened its doors and almost immediately received national recognition for the boundary-pushing beers that came from head brewer Wayne Wambles. The floodgates opened.

When I first signed the contract for this book in the summer of 2012, Florida had nearly fifty breweries producing beer on the premises. A year later, the number had jumped to sixty-six, with only two closing in that time. Another forty-plus are on their way, many of them poised to open within weeks or months of this writing (see Breweries to Come on page 183). Florida no longer can be called a craft beer wasteland. Instead, it's become a major beer tourism destination. And that defines this book's purpose.

About the Book

Over the course of about a year, I traveled to all of the state's breweries to speak with a brewer, owner, or manager and sample the beer. Each brewery has a chapter in which I tried to tell the most compelling story I found. Sometimes the story is about the beer; sometimes it's about the brewer; sometimes it's about the building; and sometimes it's about how perseverance, mixed with a bit of good luck, resulted in success.

I divided the state into four regions that made the most sense, but because Florida still contains a lot of large areas of nothing but swamp and palmetto scrub, all but one of those regions—the Tampa Bay area—cover wide swaths of real estate. Draw a horizontal line across the state below Tallahassee, and above that is the North Florida region, which basically encompasses the I-10 corridor, running from Pensacola in the west to Jacksonville in the east. Draw another west-to-east line from Sarasota to Port St. Lucie, and everything below that falls into the South Florida region. The Tampa Bay area, currently the hotbed of craft breweries in the state, merits its own section, encompassing Pasco, Pinellas, and Hillsborough Counties. The "most gerrymandered region" title goes to Central Florida, which is the rest of the state.

Each region is introduced with a bit of its history, some interesting things to do in addition to brewery visits, and some of the more noteworthy places to sleep or eat, with an emphasis on locally owned establishments. The brewery chapters include basic information about each brewery and a list of beers currently available there at the time of this writing, along with my Pick for the best one to try. I understand it may not be everyone's favorite, so don't please don't crucify me on social media if you don't like it. In some of the chapters, I've also mentioned nearby establishments of interest to the beer traveler. Some of these I've visited; others I relied on trusted sources to recommend. Wherever possible, I've included the contact information for them. I hope you enjoy reading each brewery's unique story, but I would advise that you take a tour or sit down in the tasting room and listen to the folks there tell it themselves.

BREWERY LOCATIONS

2 Aardwolf Pub and Brewery

1 A1A Ale Works

3 Alligator Brewing Co.

2 Anheuser-Busch InBev

4 Barley Mow Brewing Co.

5 Big Bear Brewing Company

6 Big River Grille & Brewing Works

7 Big Storm Brewing Co.

2 Bold City Brewery

8 Brewzzi Boca Raton

8 Brewzzi CityPlace

6 Cask & Larder Southern Brewery & Kitchen

9 Charlie & Jake's Brewery Grille

10 Cigar City Brewing

10 Cigar City Brewpub

10 Cigar City Brewpub, Tampa Airport

9 Cocoa Beach Brewing Company

11 Copp Winery & Brewery

4 Cycle Brewing at Peg's Cantina

10 D. G. Yuengling & Son

12 Darwin Brewing Company

8 Due South Brewing Co.

4 Dunedin Brewery

2 Engine 15 Brewing Co.

4 Florida Avenue Brewing Company

9 Florida Beer Company

13 Fort Myers Brewing Co.

5 Funky Buddha Brewery

8 The Funky Buddha Lounge & Brewery

2 Green Room Brewing

23 The Hourglass Brewery

2 Intuition Ale Works

15 Kelly's Caribbean Bar, Grill & Brewery

4 Lagerhaus Brewery & Grill

16 Lagniappe Brewing Company

5 The Mack House

17 McGuire's Irish Pub, Destin

18 McGuire's Irish Pub, Pensacola

14 Miami Brewing Co.

1 Mile Marker Brewing

19 Momo's Pizza Market Street Brew Pub

16 Mount Dora Brewing and the
   Rocking Rabbit Brewery

20 Naples Beach Brewery

5 Organic Brewery

6 Orlando Brewing

18 Pensacola Bay Brewery

21 Pinglehead Brewing Company

19 Proof Brewing Company

17 Props Brewery & Grill

4 R Bar

2 Ragtime Tavern & Seafood Grill

4 Rapp Brewing Company

2 River City Brewing Company

22 Sailfish Brewing Company

4 Saint Somewhere Brewing Company

12 Sarasota Brewing Company

4 Sea Dog Brewing Co.

2 Seven Bridges Grille & Brewery

4 7venth Sun Brewery

10 Southern Brewing & Winemaking

3 Swamp Head Brewery

5 Tampa Bay Brewing Company
   Coral Springs Tap House

10 Tampa Bay Brewing Company

8 Tequesta Brewing Co.

10 Three Palms Brewing

14 Titanic Brewing Company

The Big Boys

For many years, Florida beer drinkers had little choice other than what was produced by the big brewers—Anheuser-Busch, Miller, and Coors— but only one of the "Big Three" currently operates a brewery in the state. That would be the Anheuser-Busch InBev plant in Jacksonville, which opened in 1967. The company once operated another brewery in Tampa, built in 1957, around which the Busch Gardens theme park arose. The company closed the brewery in 1995, though it still operated a smaller system on the property until shortly after AB was acquired by the multinational brewing company InBev in 2009. The smaller brewing system ended up being purchased by local startup Florida Avenue Brewing Company.

Hard-core craft beer geeks pooh-pooh the international conglomerate's products and marketing, calling the former tasteless and the latter campaigns that employ scantily clad women and dim-witted frat boys to appeal to the lowest common denominator of beer-drinking consumers. Whether there's truth to those accusations or not, there's no denying it works. AB InBev controls nearly 50 percent of the U.S. market share and puts a lot of people to work. As part of my research, I visited and toured the Jacksonville plant, and I now recommend that every craft beer lover in the state do so as well, if for no other reason than to gain perspective. All of the people I spoke with there were enthusiastic, talented, intelligent, and proud of their work.

The other large brewery in Florida belongs to a big regional brewery based in Pennsylvania. D. G. Yuengling & Son started brewing in Tampa in 1999, taking over the plant from Stroh's. When it first opened in 1958, it was a Pabst brewery and has changed hands several times over the years.

Yuengling bills itself as "America's Oldest Brewery," having been operating continuously since founder David G. Yuengling opened its predecessor, Eagle Brewery, in 1829 in Pottsville, Pennsylvania. The name was changed in 1873 after David's son, Frederick, became a partner. Though none of the Yuenglings work out of the Tampa brewery, the employees there are not afraid to boast of their pride at working at the family-owned operation. Although it's been modernized, touring the brewery still offers a fascinating glimpse into how breweries operated half a century ago.

Anheuser-Busch InBev

Anheuser-Busch

111 Busch Drive, Jacksonville, FL 32218 • (904) 696-8373
www.budweisertours.com/z01/index.php/jacksonville/overview

Seasoned beer tourists can become jaded about brewery tours. The process is basically the same whether it's a 5-gallon, 50-barrel, or larger system. Entire breweries are often visible behind a glass wall. But to tour the Anheuser-Busch InBev brewery in Jacksonville is to walk among giants. Tremendous mash tuns, fermenters, and tanks tower above your head, and the rows stretch nearly as far as you can see. Then you're told there are four more floors above you.

To brew American pale lagers at multiple facilities across the United States and have each come out with a consistent taste requires an abundance of laboratory process and quality control. Many of the employees at the brewery are engineers or have a food science background, according to Michael Anderson, who served as head brewmaster there for about three years until leaving for another brewing company in late 2012.

There are two ways to tour Jacksonville's Anheuser-Busch InBev brewery. The first is a free self-guided tour in which you walk past large windows where you can see the various stages of beermaking. A large wall sign next to each window explains what is going on down on the brewery floor, and various historical photos and items are displayed. But I recommend the second way. The Beermaster Tour takes groups of visitors, provided with safety glasses and earplugs, down through the brewery with a guide. There you visit the brew hall, primary fermentation cellar, lager cellar, packaging facility, quality assurance, and finishing cellar. The tour includes tasting samples drawn directly from a finishing tank.

The in-depth tour drives home the sheer scale of the brewery relative to its smaller craft brethren. Instead of 50-pound sacks of malted barley and other grains, they are delivered via railcars. The brewery's control room resembles an airport control tower, rather than a panel of switches,

Beers brewed: Budweiser, Bud Light, Budweiser Select, Budweiser Select 55, Michelob Ultra, Michelob Ultra Amber, AmberBock, Shock Top Belgian White, Land Shark Lager, Natural Ice, Natural Light, Busch, and Busch Light.

The Pick: Budweiser. You won't taste a fresher, better Bud than straight from the tap in the tasting room.

buttons, and lights nestled in a single brewhouse. The two pasteurizers are the size of small houses. And you can anecdotally confirm that it might be true that a macrobrewery spills more beer in one day than many smaller breweries make in one year. (Stay behind the yellow line, and your shoes will remain dry.)

At the time of this writing, the cost for the Beermaster Tour was $25 for visitors age twenty-one and older, and $10 for ages thirteen to twenty; check the website or call for current prices. Children under age thirteen are not allowed on the tour. Reservations are generally required, but sometimes last-minute openings are available. Both tours end in the Tour Center's hospitality room, where visitors twenty-one and older can taste two samples of the brewery's products along with complimentary pretzels.

The key to brewing beer with a consistent taste lies in the water. But how does one do that when the company's breweries are scattered from one coast to the other? In Jacksonville, the brewing cycle starts 950 feet deep in the Floridan Aquifer, the porous layer of limestone on which Florida lies and which provides most of the state's drinking water. Pumped through a well, the water is treated through nanofiltration, similar to reverse osmosis, to filter out undesirable elements and minerals that would taint the brewing process.

The treatment yields usable water at a rate of 86 percent. But the rest, laden with solids and minerals, does not go to waste because the brewery operates with a dedication to conservation. "The other 14 percent goes directly to our land application to our farms," Anderson told me. The water runs through pipelines to two nearby sod farms run by the brewery. One of them, directly behind the brewery, consists of 500 acres, 320 of which are irrigated. The other, 1,500 acres about 15 miles away, has 685 acres that are irrigated. The drought-resistant sod grown at the farms goes to the Florida Department of Transportation to be used for landscaping highways.

The plant also strives to keep its energy use as low as possible. Fifteen percent of its electricity is generated on-site with a 12,000-horsepower turbine engine powered in part by methane gas produced in the brewing process. The company's overall recycling rate hovers just below 100 percent. Even the famous beechwood chips used during fermenting are ground into mulch after they outlive their usefulness.

With nearly 10 million barrels of beer produced annually, the three canning lines, three bottling lines, and one kegging line run twenty-four hours a day. A lot of the packaged brew doesn't even make it to the warehouse area to be stored. Fifty percent of the beer goes straight onto the trucks for distribution. The rest goes on the next round of trucks.

In common with breweries of all sizes, quality control is key. Not only do the brewmaster and other sensory experts taste each batch of beer at different stages of brewing, but they also taste the water. And not just the water for brewing, but also the water used to rinse the tanks before they are filled. About the only H_2O that doesn't pass over a palate is that destined for sinks, toilets, and landscaping.

The brewmaster and sensory experts keep detailed notes. "We record all of our information in these binders so we have a history of that particular beer during that particular time," Anderson said. "Every single batch." Even after the beer is packaged, the tasting continues. "Every shift, we're going to taste some of the packaged beer and make sure the pasteurizer, the filler, everything that's going on in that process is tested as well."

The brewmaster's private tasting room, not open to the public, shows the attention to detail. Containers from each step of the process, from water to finished product, and clean tasting glasses line the shelf along three walls. A large conference table in the center provides the work space where the sensory experts ply their trade and make notes in the aforementioned binders. "We need to understand what's going on," Anderson said, "and make recipe adjustments if necessary."

Anheuser-Busch InBev

Opened: 1969.

Owner: Anheuser-Busch InBev.

Brewers: Aaron Vaughn and several assistants.

System: Expansive; no set classification.

Annual production: 10 million barrels per year.

Hours: Monday through Saturday, 10 a.m. to 4 p.m.

Tours: Free self-guided tour; Beermaster Tour by appointment.

Parking: Free on site.

Takeout beer: Bottles and cans in gift shop.

Special considerations: Handicapped-accessible.

Extras: Beer School daily on first-come, first-served basis.

D. G. Yuengling & Son

11111 North 30th Street, Tampa, FL 33612
(813) 972-8529
www.yuengling.com/breweries/tampa

Tour guides at D. G. Yuengling & Son in Tampa eagerly share the history of the brewery while they shepherd visitors through the sprawling complex on 62 acres in the north side of the city. Among the facts revealed is that World War II U.S. Army Air Force pilots once trained there, when the acreage was known as Hillsborough Army Air Field. The plant first opened in 1958 as a Joseph Schlitz brewery. During the subsequent decades, through acquisitions and brewery trades, it bore the names of Stroh's, then Pabst, then Stroh's again, before the Yuengling family took it over in 1999. Richard "Dick" Yuengling Jr., president of the family owned and operated Yuengling, rehired many of the Stroh's employees, and a good many of those continue to work at the brewery.

Yuengling actually started many years before, in 1829, when David G. Yuengling emigrated from Germany and opened a small brewery in Pottsville, Pennsylvania, naming it the Eagle Brewery. This is why an eagle is emblazoned on Yuengling's beer label. As the guides point out, this is not to be confused with the "other one" used by Anheuser-Busch InBev, which is a bit ironic because you can see the tops of roller coasters at nearby Busch Gardens from the property.

The tour starts with a look at the 260-barrel mash tuns and goes through the packaging line. (The new, larger brewhouse is now part of the tour.) The guide explains each step of the process along the way. There you will learn that the plant gets its water from 277-foot-deep wells, that two to three railcars filled with grain arrive each week, that 825 to 850 bottles per minute are filled on the bottling line, that the canning line fills about 1,000 cans every minute, and that when the brewery first opened in 1999, it filled 500 kegs a week. It now spits out 400 an hour. The tour also includes a stop in the lab, where the chemists and technicians will take time to discuss the more esoteric, microbiological nuances of the craft of beer. Questions are welcome, though sometimes an

Beers Brewed: Year-round: Traditional Lager, Premium and Porter. Seasonals: Oktoberfest and Yuengling Bock.

The Pick: The Yuengling Porter is a fine example of the British style.

enthusiastic beer geek may dominate that part (guilty). The last stop of the tour is the tasting room, in which each participant is allowed two 7-ounce samples of Yuengling beer. The décor exudes the essence of a British pub, with dark wood accents, no barstools at the bar itself, and a few scattered tables.

On occasion, brewmaster John Houseman makes an appearance behind the bar. He was one of the Stroh's employees whom Yuengling rehired after buying the plant. Houseman had been hired as a senior brewer in 1997 after sixteen years at the G. Heileman Brewing Company in Baltimore, eleven of which he spent there as brewmaster. When the Stroh plant closed in January 1999, Houseman contemplated moving back to Baltimore, but his wife enjoyed living in Florida so much that it wasn't an option.

Then, while Houseman was preparing his Baltimore house to sell, Dick Yuengling called. "He said, 'How would you like to be my brewmaster?'" Houseman recalled. "My wife wasn't even going to move to Baltimore—I knew she didn't want to move to Pottsville." After Yuengling told him the job was in Tampa, Houseman realized that Yuengling had bought Stroh's. "He said, 'When can you be here?' I said, 'I'll be there tomorrow.' I got on my phone, got my airplane tickets the next day, and I was there the next day."

D. G. Yuengling & Son

Opened: 1999.

Owner: Richard "Dick" Yuengling Jr.

Brewer: John Houseman.

System: 675-barrels.

Annual production: Estimated 1.2 million barrels in 2013.

Hours: Tours and gift shop, Monday through Friday, 9 a.m. to 3 p.m.; gift shop only, Saturday, 10 a.m. to 2 p.m.

Tours: Free. Times vary by date. Reservations recommended for groups of fifteen or more.

Parking: Free on site.

Takeout beer: None.

Special considerations: Tour not handicapped-accessible, but a PowerPoint presentation is available for disabled visitors.

Other area beer sites: Mr. Dunderbak's, 14929 Bruce B. Downs Blvd., Tampa, FL 33613, (813) 977-4104, www.dunderbaks.com.

Container Laws

Across most of the country, in states that allow it, breweries with taprooms can sell growlers, reusable jugs filled with fresh beer from the tap, for customers to take home and enjoy. Usually, it's a 64-ounce growler, the equivalent of a full 4 U.S. pints, an ideal size for a couple to drink with dinner or to take to a bottle-share tasting. You can buy growlers in Florida at locations with the proper setups and licensing, but in only two sizes: 32 or 128 ounces (a quart or a gallon). To learn why the popular 64-ounce size is unlawful in the state, we have to go back to the 1960s.

The story goes that Florida was in the running for a new Miller Brewing Co. brewery, but the company decided to build it in Georgia instead. Infuriated, the legislature struck back. At the time, Miller sold a popular 7-ounce "pony bottle." So legislators passed a bill in 1965 that restricted individual containers of "malt beverages" sold in the state to 8, 12, 16, or 32 ounces. To account for bulk packaging, such as kegs, sales in containers of 1 gallon or more were allowed. By the way, the "Miller motivation" has never been proven, but it's pretty widely accepted as truth.

In later years, attempts were made to change the law, but the state's wholesale beer distributors fought against it fiercely. In the late 1990s, opposition to the restrictions grew stronger after craft brewers in other states started shipping 22-ounce and 750-milliliter "bomber" bottles, and foreign breweries imported their brews in a plethora of metric containers. Beer distributors, most of them Bud or Miller houses, said their business would be adversely affected because they would have to add warehouse space and more employees, brewers would have to retool bottling lines to put their products in similar containers, and retailers would have to increase shelf space.

Eventually, government studies and reports commissioned by the legislature blew holes into those specious arguments, and on November 1, 2001, Gov. Jeb Bush signed the amended law allowing any size of malt beverage container up to 32 ounces or greater than 128 ounces.

Nobody really thought about growlers at the time, not until more small breweries opened and the proprietors realized they were outlawed from selling the popular half-gallon jug.

Efforts have been under way for a few years to eliminate the "doughnut hole" in the container size law. A bill to amend the law was introduced to and passed by a senate committee in the 2013 legislative session, but a companion bill in the house never even made it to committee, quashed through the efforts of lobbyists hired by the Florida Beer Wholesalers Association, which represents the state's Anheuser-Busch InBev distributors. Interestingly, other beer distributors in the state did not oppose the law, among them the Beer Industry of Florida group, which mainly represents MillerCoors distributors.

In reality, it all boils down to the three-tier system of beer distribution, established after the repeal of Prohibition, which effectively prevents manufacturers of alcoholic beverages from distributing directly to retailers or consumers, though exceptions have been made, such as wineries being able to sell bottles to customers. The lobby opposing the changes claims such a move would threaten the three-tier system, though it doesn't seem to have much affected distributors in states where 64-ounce growlers are sold. Small breweries say that being allowed to sell the half-gallon containers would be convenient for customers and more economical. Because the container size is more prevalent in the country as a whole, manufacturers can sell them cheaper than the other sizes. That would free more funds for expansion and hiring.

The issue is expected to return in the 2014 legislative session. In the meantime, when you read in this book that a brewery or brewpub sells growlers, realize you won't be able to buy a half gallon to go of any one beer. Unless you buy 2 quarts.

North Florida

There's an old saying in Florida, "It's the only state where the farther north you go, the farther south you get." There's more than a ring of truth to that, as Florida as a whole isn't really considered the Deep South. Across the Panhandle to Jacksonville, though, you'll hear thicker drawls, drive through more small rural towns, and not have to worry about whether the greasy spoon you stop at for breakfast serves grits. It does.

The Western Panhandle

Pensacola, the westernmost city in the Panhandle and in Florida, is nicknamed the City of Five Flags because five governments have controlled it since the arrival of Europeans: Spain, France, Great Britain, the Confederate States of America, and the United States of America. Just outside the city is Naval Air Station Pensacola, called the "Cradle of Naval Aviation" because of its long history. The U.S. Navy first arranged to build a navy yard here in 1825, and the first permanent naval air station was opened on the site in 1914. You might be entertained by aerial acrobatics performed by the navy's Blue Angels team, which is stationed there, as it practices maneuvers.

The city's metropolitan area anchors the west end of what is billed as the Emerald Coast—and what some folks refer to as the "Redneck Riviera," though you probably won't see that nickname in official tourist brochures. It's the area of the Gulf Coast stretching about 100 miles from Pensacola Beach to Panama City. The beaches boast some of the whitest, most sugarlike sand in the world and are a popular destination for tourists and spring breakers.

Other attractions and events in the area include *The National Naval Aviation Museum* (www.navalaviationmuseum.org), with its overwhelming array of actual aircraft both inside and out, as well as flight simulators and accompanying exhibits and presentations. The best part—the admission, parking, and guided tours are all free, though donations are accepted. You will need valid identification to get onto the Naval Air Station Pensacola property, where you also will find the **Pensacola Lighthouse and Museum** (www.pensacolalighthouse.org). You can climb the 177 steps to the top of this beacon for a panoramic view of the surrounding beaches and landmarks. The U.S. government built the first lighthouse here in 1824; the current structure was first lit in 1859. **Gulfarium Marine Adventure Park** (www.gulfarium.com) is the state's oldest still-operating marine park, first opened in 1955. It's now home to exotic animal encounters, daily dolphin and sea lion show, interactive exhibits and more. Throughout the area, you'll also find countless opportunities for **water sports** such as swimming, snorkeling, waterskiing, parasailing, boating, fishing—just about anything you can think of to do at a beach.

As with pretty much anywhere in Florida, it's easy to find hotels associated with major chains from budget to luxurious throughout the Emerald Coast. Here are a few places unique to the area: Solé Inn and Suites, 200 N. Palafox St., Pensacola, FL 32501, (850) 470-9298, www.sole innandsuites.com; WaterColor Inn & Resort, 34 Goldenrod Circle, Santa Rosa Beach, FL 32459, 850-534-5000, www.watercolorresort.com; and Sandestin Golf and Beach Resort, 9300 Emerald Coast Parkway, Miramar Beach, FL 32550, (800) 622-1038, www.sandestin.com. For more information check with the local visitors bureaus: www.visitpensacola .com and www.emeraldcoastfl.com.

Tallahassee

The Western Panhandle, as you'll find out, is home to fewer breweries and craft beer bars than the rest of the state, so when it's time to move on, you'll likely get on I-10 and head east to Tallahassee. If you're not in a big hurry, there are other, smaller highways that will get you there, but it will be a significantly longer drive. The first few miles on I-10, you'll see thick stands of trees on either side of the highway. That's pretty much what you'll see the entire drive. There's no other way to put it—it's a visual bore.

Tallahassee is the state capital, so it's full of politicos, lobbyists, and government workers. It's also a college town, home to Florida State University (FSU) and Florida A&M. Its population is a bit more than 180,000, but that number swells for sixty days beginning in early March, when both the legislature and schools are in session. The big game in town is the FSU Seminoles, especially the football team. Unless you're a fan, however, it's best to stay out of town on game day.

Two breweries currently call Tallahassee home, but here are some other things to do while you're in Florida's capital city. The **Florida Capitol Complex** (myfloridacapitol.com) in downtown Tallahassee includes the twenty-two-story state capitol building and several other government buildings. On the grounds, you'll also find the Old Capitol, built in 1845 and restored by volunteers. It is now open to visitors as the **Florida Historic Capitol Museum** (www.flhistoriccapitol.gov) and has the classic dome, cold marble, and all the other cool, old stuff you'd expect. The **John G. Riley Center/Museum of African American History & Culture** (rileymuseum.org) was the former home of John G. Riley, who served as principal of the first black high school in Leon County. Built in 1890, it is now a storehouse of exhibits and educational material about the state's African American culture and history. **Edward Ball Wakulla Springs State Park** (www.floridastateparks .org/wakullasprings) is one of the world's largest and deepest freshwater springs, where you can swim, hike the nature trails, or take a guided riverboat or glass-bottom boat tour. It has been designated a national natural landmark. Some nice places to stay in this area include the Governors Inn, 209 S. Adams St., Tallahassee, FL 32301, (850) 681-6855, thegovinn.org; the Little English Guesthouse, 737 Timberlane Rd., Tallahassee, FL 32312, (850) 907-9777, littleenglishguesthouse.com; and Cabot Lodge, 1653 Raymond Diehl Rd., Tallahassee, FL 32308, (850) 386-7500, www.cabotlodgethomasvilleroad.com. For more information on the area, see www.visittallahassee.com.

Jacksonville

The next stop on the I-10 trail through North Florida is Jacksonville and St. Augustine. This is where the excitement really begins on your beer tour. Over the past few years, the Jacksonville–St. Augustine area has grown into one of the state's craft beer hotspots, with twelve operating breweries and brewpubs in the metro area at the time of this writing.

Jacksonville lays claim to being the largest city by population in Florida and the largest city by land area in the Lower 48. That might have something to do with the fact that it consolidated with Duval County in 1968, thereby extending the city limits to the county line. The city is home to a major shipping port and two navy bases—Naval Air Station Jacksonville and Naval Station Mayport—as well as a U.S. Marine Corps base and a Coast Guard base. The Florida Air National Guard's home base is Jacksonville International Airport. Jacksonville is well defended.

The St. Johns River, Florida's largest and one of the few in the country that flow from south to north, bisects Jacksonville. It flows west to east through the city, dividing the town into what residents call the Northside and Southside. The Northside of Jacksonville consists of the city's urban core, large tracts of undeveloped land, and industrial areas. The Southside is in the midst of revival, with modern lifestyle centers, older neighborhoods being restored, and newer subdivisions, some built around golf courses. On the Atlantic Ocean side of Jacksonville, you'll find the coastal communities of Mayport, Atlantic Beach, Jacksonville Beach, Neptune Beach, and Ponte Vedra Beach.

Because of the port, rail lines, proximity to the interstate system, and the airport, Jacksonville is headquarters for some major corporations, such as the railroad giant CSX; Fidelity National Financial, a financial services conglomerate; and the southeastern grocery store chain Winn-Dixie. But by far the largest employer is the military, with a yearly impact of more than $6 billion on the local economy.

Jacksonville hosts several minor-league sports teams and the Jacksonville Jaguars of the National Football League. Before it was awarded the NFL expansion team, which started playing in the 1995 season, area college football fans knew Jacksonville as the host of the annual game between the University of Florida Gators and the University of Georgia Bulldogs. The traditional battle on neutral turf, nicknamed the "World's Largest Outdoor Cocktail Party" because of the huge tailgating crowds, has been held in Jacksonville nearly every year since 1933. The city also has hosted the postseason Gator Bowl since 1946.

Jacksonville is home to two craft beer–based tour companies: *Jax Brew Bus*, (904) 352-0982, www.jaxbrewbus.com, with a tour of local breweries every Saturday; and *Play Harder Tours*, (904) 910-7009, playhardertours.com, with local, national, and international craft beer tours, most based around pro sports games. In such a metropolis, other activities also abound. Here are just a few of them: *Jacksonville Zoo and Gardens* (www.jacksonvillezoo.org) is a top-notch place to take the family, providing up-close encounters with a wide variety of exotic animals and botanical garden integrated among the animal exhibits. You can hike, bike, kayak, or just sightsee at the 46,000-acre *Timucuan Ecological & Historic Preserve* (www.nps.gov/foca/index.htm), which offers a glimpse of Florida's natural past, with an expanse of protected critical coastal wetlands, as well as the restored Kingsley Plantation and Fort Caroline, a relic of the short-lived French presence in sixteenth-century Florida. At *Crazy Fish* (www.crazyfishjax.com), you can dine on seafood, rent a kayak, or take a tour on the *Dolphin Limousine* or an airboat to see wildlife that lives in and around the local waters, including dolphins, manatees, alligators, marsh birds, and bald eagles. Places to stay while you're in the area include Aloft Jacksonville Tapestry Park, 4812 Deer Lake Dr. W., Jacksonville, FL 32246, (904) 998-4448, www.aloft jacksonvilletapestrypark.com; One Ocean Resort & Spa, 1 Ocean Blvd., Atlantic Beach, FL 32233, (904) 249-7402, www.oneoceanresort.com; and Seahorse Oceanfront Inn, 120 Atlantic Blvd., Neptune Beach, FL 32266, (904) 246-2175, www.jacksonvilleoceanfronthotel.com. For more information, see www.visitjacksonville.com.

St. Augustine

Less than an hour's drive down the coast is the oldest continually occupied European-established city in the continental United States: St. Augustine. Spanish explorer Juan Ponce de Leon first landed in the area in 1513, claiming it for the Spanish crown, and Spanish admiral Pedro Menendez de Aviles founded the city in 1565. Tourism is St. Augustine's lifeblood, especially in the Old Town district, where tour trolleys run along the cobblestone streets among historic structures of the city's various eras. Haunted pub tours are popular, and so many fascinating attractions exist that you could likely spend a week exploring the area and still not see everything.

A few of the more notable sites include *Castillo de San Marcos* (www.nps.gov/casa/index.htm), the oldest surviving masonry fort in the United States, dating from 1672 and designated a national monument in 1924. Drinking from the freshwater spring at *Ponce de Leon's Fountain of Youth Archaeological Park* (www.fountainofyouthflorida .com) will not make you younger, but legend has it that Ponce de Leon sought such a fount when exploring the area. The park's shows, exhibits, and reconstructed historical buildings will give you a sense of what life was like at various periods in the region's history. First opened in the late nineteenth century, *St. Augustine Alligator Farm Zoological Park* (www.alligatorfarm.com) is now a fully operating zoo, with plenty of Florida's state reptiles, their toothy cousin crocodiles, and other native flora and fauna. Places to stay during your visit include Casa Monica Hotel, 95 Cordova St., St. Augustine, FL 32084, (904) 827-1888, www.casamonica.com; and St. Augustine Island Inn, 894 A1A Beach Blvd., St. Augustine Beach, FL 32080, (904) 471-1440, www.staugustineislandinn.com. For more information, see www.floridas historiccoast.com.

Aardwolf Pub and Brewery

1461 Hendricks Avenue, Jacksonville, FL 32207
(904) 301-0755 • aardwolfbrewing.com

As Michael Payne explained to me, naming a new brewery does not happen easily. The brewer and co-owner of Aardwolf Pub & Brewery took a lot of factors into consideration. "About seven years ago, I decided I wanted to get into opening a brewery," he said. "One of the things I learned along the way is that naming things can be a real challenge. Especially for the name of your brewery, where you want to have something that's defensible from copyright and trademark standpoints. Everything you can think of has been used. Wineries count, and wineries will basically trademark every name they can think of. Maybe they'll use it and maybe they won't."

Every time he thought of a good name, a Google search showed him that it wasn't original. Finally, he went back to Latin. The scientific name for hops, *Humulus lupus*, roughly translates into "earth wolf," which in turn loosely translates into "aardwolf" in the Afrikaans/Dutch language. That became the brewery's name. "Aardwolf" is also the name of a hyenalike insectivorous mammal native to parts of Africa. Payne didn't know that at first. "I didn't realize it was an actual animal right off the bat," he said. "I figured that out by the time we opened here." An aardwolf, the critter, was incorporated into the logo.

Not only did the name arrive a bit circuitously, but so did the brewer. Payne went to school for ceramic art and continued in that field for several years after college, but he started second-guessing that career. "It became clear that the only viable career path with that was going back to school and teaching, which I didn't want to do," he said. "It kind of came down to go to law school or try something else that might be more viable than ceramic arts, so I decided to start brewing."

His beermaking journey began as a homebrewer, then he attended brewing school and worked at a few breweries, including Terrapin Beer Company in Athens, Georgia, and Brewer's Pizza (now Pinglehead Brewing Company), just outside Jacksonville city limits, in Orange Park. With his hands-on experience and education from Chicago's Siebel Institute and Doemens Academy in

Beers brewed: To be determined, but likely big hoppy and sour beers will predominate.

Munich, Payne decided to leave Brewer's Pizza in 2011 and open the brewery he had dreamed about. He partnered with Preben Olsen, who was a beer buyer for local bottle shops and had a lot of connections in the beer community.

They found their space in an 11,500-square-foot warehouse on the edge of downtown, a vast shell of a building that in the past had served as the municipal icehouse for the former city of South Jacksonville. The icehouse, according to Payne's understanding, serviced both the city and the Florida East Coast Railway, which had a depot across the street. In the 1950s, it was sold to a tile company, which added on to the building.

The bar in the tasting room is covered with brushed stainless steel, and much of the furniture is built from reclaimed wood. Antiquities uncovered during the conversion to a brewery are displayed on the shelves behind the bar, including a pair of ice tongs that one of the plumbers had found when he worked for the tile company as a teenager. Presumably, they came from the building's icehouse days.

The carpenter who worked on the renovation added even more history to the space in the form of some refurbished wood he used for decorative paneling. Only after it was installed did Payne find out its background. "He told us that wood came from the Apollo Theater. And we were like, does he mean *the* Apollo Theater or an Apollo Theater? I'm sure there's more than one," Payne said. "But he said it was the one in Harlem. In the nineties, they did some restoration and that wood was salvaged."

When I visited Aardwolf, it was still a work in progress. Though its doors had been open for a few months, the only Aardwolf beers served were those brewed in collaboration with other breweries, though other craft beers flowed from the twenty taps. The brewhouse was in place, and Payne was brewing. Delivery of a walk-in cooler was expected any day.

The community's anticipation became evident at a soft opening in late March 2013. Payne and Olsen told no one about it but a few friends, but it leaked on social media. "We had three of our collaboration beers on tap," Payne said. "This place was standing room only. It was crazy. In one Friday night, we did what we do in about a week now."

The customers continued to come in to quench their thirst. "The neighborhood needed a beer bar, more than anything," Payne explained. "Even though we don't have much of our own beer on tap yet, people are coming in and drinking what we can get. We tried to get a selection that was representative of things we might make. We've been very happy with the turnout so far."

Though the first phase was not complete, Payne looked ahead to the future. "I want to develop a barrel program to a greater extent than anyone else in the area has done," he said. "I'm going to put a dedicated barrel cooler there in the warehouse to keep barrels at a regular temperature year-round. The only way you're going to do a sour barrel program in this part of the country is to at least keep it below 60 during the summer. Once that starts taking off, we'll probably start doing some small-scale bottling. It may be quite a while, if ever, before we get to the point of actually sending bottles out into the world, but we will do some here."

Aardwolf Pub and Brewery

Opened: 2013.
Owners: Michael Payne and Preben Olsen.
Brewer: Michael Payne.
System: 15-barrel Allied Beverage Systems.
Annual production: Estimated 1,200 to 1,500 barrels.
Hours: Wednesday through Saturday, 3 to 11 p.m.; Sunday, 2 to 10 p.m.
Tours: None.
Parking: Free on site.
Takeout beer: Growlers.
Special considerations: Handicapped-accessible.

A1A Ale Works

1 King Street, St. Augustine, FL 32084
(904) 829-2977 • www.a1aaleworks.com

Fans of old horror movies might feel a stirring of familiarity when they walk into A1A Ale Works. The historic 1880 building on the edge of St. Augustine's Old Town district once was occupied by Potter's Wax Museum, where much of the filming took place for *House of Wax*, the 1953 thriller starring Vincent Price. Potter's has since moved to another locale in the oldest continuously occupied European-established city in the continental United States, but that doesn't mean there's not still a bit of creepiness lingering about the place. In fact, according to general manager Phil Maddox, the building was constructed over a cemetery.

"I've talked to some of our A/C repair guys, and they've seen some crazy things," he said. "There is a cemetery under the building. We had a maintenance guy who went under the building to repair some stuff, and he told me he had to crawl over headstones. There is a plaque a street over that shows where the church sat, and it's right where this building was built. I don't know how they got around building on top of a cemetery, but there's one down there." No wonder, then, that the frequent ghost tours and haunted pub crawls often end up at A1A Ale Works for a final toast to the ghosts.

A1A Ale Works sits on the edge of St. Augustine's historic district, which is usually packed with tourists meandering through its narrow, cobblestoned streets, snapping pictures and learning about what is sometimes called the "Ancient City." Trolley tours continuously wend their way past the historical buildings and sites. Directly across Highway A1A from the two-level brewpub and restaurant are Matanzas Bay and the historic Bridge of Lions, finished in 1927 and guarded on the west end by a pair of statues of the king of the beasts, designed by the sculptor Romanelli of Florence, Italy. The bridge is on the National Register of Historic Places, and the brewpub's

Beers brewed: King Street Light Lager, Porpoise Point I.P.A., Bridges of Lions Brown Ale, Red Brick Ale, and A. Strange Stout, plus various seasonals.

The Pick: The Bridge of Lions Brown Ale has its roots in England, but Mount Hood hops adds a bit of spice to the caramel and chocolate flavors from the malt.

second-floor dining balcony offers a panoramic view of the bridge and a marina.

Inside, the age of the building is evident in the natural stained oak trim, iron balustrade accents, exposed brick walls, and pressed-tin ceiling tiles. Downstairs are a small bar and dining areas; another bar is up the stairs, along with more tables for diners. Two separate banquet rooms are available for large parties, wedding receptions, and such.

The brewpub has a full range of liquors and other beers, but the creations of brewer Doug Murr are available throughout. As with the other brewpubs in the CraftWorks chain, some of the recipes are handed down through corporate fiat, while Murr has free rein with other taps. The brews' names reflect local history and nature, King Street, Porpoise Point, and Bridge of Lions among them. The restaurant component bustles along with the brewery, specializing in Caribbean-influenced dishes and fresh seafood.

Being smack-dab in one of the most popular tourism destinations in world means that visitors to the city make up a good portion of the clientele—about 80 percent, according to Maddox. "A lot of locals try to get down here, but parking is a problem. This is one of the best tourist cities in America."

But is the pub actually haunted? Maddox told me that although some staffers have reported seeing strange things, he's never had any sort of paranormal experience there. But "when you close it down at night and the lights go out in the kitchen and you're walking out," he said, "it crosses your mind."

A1A Ale Works

Opened: Mid-1980s.

Owner: CraftWorks Restaurants & Breweries Inc.

Brewer: Doug Murr.

System: 10-barrel DME.

Annual production: 880 barrels.

Hours: Sunday through Thursday, 11 a.m. to 11:30 p.m.; Friday and Saturday, 11 a.m. to midnight.

Tours: None.

Parking: Difficult. Nearby paid street and lot parking.

Takeout beer: None.

Special considerations: Handicapped-accessible.

Extras: Second-floor balcony seating.

Bold City Brewery

2670-7 Rosselle Street, Jacksonville, FL 32204
(904) 379-6551 • www.boldcitybrewery.com

Unfamiliar faces at Bold City Brewery are asked, "Is this your first time here?" If the answer is yes, that customer is treated to a free tasting tray of all the Bold City beers on tap at the time. The reasoning behind this, bartender Kevin Miller explained, is that the brewery wants its taproom to be more of a marketing tool so that its customers will spread the word about Bold City beer. That way, when folks who can't make it to the brewery see the beers at other venues and in stores, they'll be more likely to purchase it. "We do our best to not compete with our retailers," he said.

Bold City Brewery is a family affair. Kevin's mother, Susan, and a brother, Brian, opened the venture in October 2008. Brian is the head brewer. Other family members fill various positions in the business.

The vast majority of the space is dedicated to the brewery and storage. Tour guides take visitors through the brewing process, from grain to bottling and kegging. The kegs remain the primary method of distribution outside the brewery, but Bold City has recently started releasing some of its brews in cans. The brewery has grown over the years, with more and bigger tanks, added cold storage areas, and walls knocked down to expand into the space next door. And recently, Bold City announced another expansion—into the 14,000-square-foot building behind the brewery—which will double its capacity.

The taproom takes up just a small part of the space in the old warehouse, but despite the marketing focus, it buzzes with activity. Customers of all ages drink and talk at the red brick–faced bar, elbows resting on the heavily shellacked wood top. Others occupy a few tables topped with conversation lamps crafted from growler and bomber bottles, enjoying pints, while a steady stream of folks line up to have their growlers filled for

Beers brewed: Killer Whale Cream Ale, Fritz's Hefeweizen, Duke's Cold Nose Brown Ale, Mad Manatee IPA, Chinook IPA, 1901 Red Ale, and Archie's Rhino Rye Pale Ale. Seasonals: Big John's Apricot Wheat, Bold English Ale, and Smokey Porter.

The Pick: The 1901 Red Ale, named in recognition of a disastrous fire that destroyed 146 city blocks that year, is a filling, full-flavored red ale, thanks to the roasted barley malt used in brewing.

enjoying elsewhere, even though it's early afternoon on a Saturday. Hungry patrons are welcome to bring in their own food, but from 4 to 10 p.m., local business Jolly Mon Catering grills burgers, wings, brats, and other beer-friendly food for purchase.

Bold City Brewery

Opened: 2008.

Owners: Brian and Susan Miller.

Brewers: Brian Miller and Cody Cassidey.

System: 20-barrel Stainless.

Annual production: 6,000 barrels.

Hours: Thursday and Friday, 3 to 11 p.m.; Saturday, 1 to 11 p.m.

Tours: Most Saturdays from 2 to 5 p.m.

Parking: Free on site.

Takeout beer: Growlers.

Special considerations: Handicapped-accessible.

Other area beer sites: Just Brew It (homebrew supply store), 2670-1 Rosselle St., Jacksonville, FL 32204, (904) 381-1983, justbrewitjax.com.

Engine 15 Brewing Co.

1500 Beach Boulevard #217, Jacksonville Beach, FL 32250
(904) 249-BEER • Engine15.com

ENGINE 15
★ *Brewing Co.* ★

One of the questions Sean Bielman is most frequently asked about Engine 15 Brewing Co. is, "Are you guys firefighters?" The short answer is no. The longer story behind the brewery's name has to do with the 1962 Ford fire truck partner Luch Scremin owns. "We used it for tailgates," Bielman told me. "We'd throw the kegerator in it, and couches and all that onto the back of it, and go tailgating with it. When it came time to name the bar, we were sitting at his house and his wife comes in, and we were hemming and hawing about names, and she asks, 'What are you guys doing?'" They told her, and she suggested, "Why don't you name it after that fire truck you have?" The men decided it was perfect. "It kind of stuck," said Bielman.

But the name incorporates an old-school attitude as well, said Bielman, who, along with homebrewing buddies Scremin and Andy Price, turned the dream of opening a brewery into reality. "We just thought that it fit our motif of strength and will, of doing things yourself, and kind of old-school engineering and technology and that sort of thing," Bielman explained. "We bring that into the brewing process enough. Our brew system is sort of a Franken-system, with parts and pieces from here and there. If it breaks, we fix it ourselves. That's kind of our mentality around here." At the time of this writing, Luch Scremin is the only one of the three partners with any sort of training or experience in commercial brewing, having completed the Master Brewer Program at Chicago's Siebel Institute.

Though Engine 15 serves its own beer, it also holds a reputation as one of the area's top beer bars. With five to ten of its house-brewed beers on tap and fifty-some draft lines, there's plenty of room for taps from other local, national, and foreign breweries. In fact, the bartenders poured

Beers brewed: Old Battle Axe IPA, (904) Weissguy Hefeweizen, Rye of the Tiger, and Nut Sack Imperial Brown Ale, plus a unique small batch beer released every Thursday. Seasonals: Pumpmaster Pumpkin Ale, Chupacabra Oak-Aged Russian Imperial Stout, and Blueberry Wheat.

The Pick: The Nut Sack Imperial Brown Ale is a tasty brew, but be careful—the prominent nutty and caramel flavors help camouflage that it can pack a wallop, with a higher-than-normal ABV of 7 percent.

only those guest beers while the owners worked through some kinks to get their own beers on tap. The bar side was open and a one-barrel system was in place, nearly ready to go, Bielman explained, and the city said that the brewery would have a natural gas line installed within a month of opening. "So we said, 'OK, we'll buy a natural gas boiler; we'll get it all set up to do that.'" Instead, it took almost eight months to get the natural gas line in place. "We were in a holding pattern. We couldn't close up the shop—we'd already started the buildout. We'd already had plans to have other taps, so it wasn't that rough for us."

Housed in two units of a nondescript strip center in the community of Jacksonville Beach, next to a credit union branch, Engine 15 enjoys a thriving business. A long shotgun-style bar stretches along one wall of the first unit, in front of a small kitchen where a cook prepares bar food with a twist: a barbecue Cuban sandwich, Frito pie with a beer queso topping, or a Snicker dumpling dessert. The other side is where the brewing happens. There's limited seating, but people can hang out there and chat with the brewers about all things beer, at least when they're on a break from making beer.

One of the more unusual activities at Engine 15 is that customers can brew their own beers. Brew sessions start at $98, plus bottles, and each brew yields 10 gallons of beer for the customer to bottle and take home. "We have all the recipes, we have all the ingredients, we take them through the whole process, they come back in three weeks and it's ready to bottle," Bielman said. There's a long waiting list, so planning ahead is essential.

For those who want to delve deeper into the world of brewing, Engine 15 has partnered with the University of Florida to offer a Craft Beer 101 course. "It's everything from where beer styles came from to the entire brewing process, through packaging, flavors, proper glassware—you name it, we try to cover it. It's five Mondays five weeks in a row, for two to three hours," Bielman said. "It's a continuing education kind of thing, which is nice because you don't have to be a college student to take the class."

The brewery draws an eclectic crowd whose only motivation comes from a desire for good brews and good conversation. "We have tons and tons of regulars, we've got a lot of first-timers every day, we've got a lot of people who've never brewed a beer in their lives, and probably don't care to, but just enjoy a good beer," Bielman told me. "We have the homebrew club come in, and they really enjoy the fact that there's a place fairly local where they can get a variety of beers, and we're always changing over taps and getting new stuff in."

Because of the restaurant aspect, a good number of families are among the regulars, as evidenced by the high chairs stacked against the wall. "I think I take the most pride in knowing that almost any day of the week, except a late Friday or Saturday night where it's just packed, our regulars are just good people that will start up a conversation with most anyone who walks in the door—and most of them do—so you feel welcome," Bielman said. "People really love it and respect it; they're so happy to have what they have and want to keep it that way. It's a good scene, for sure."

Engine 15 Brewing Co.

Opened: 2010.

Owners: Luciano ("Luch") Scremin, Andy Price, and Sean Bielman.

Brewer: Luch Scremin.

System: 5-barrel Price Schonstrom steam-fired brewhouse.

Annual production: 1,100 barrels.

Hours: Monday, 4:30 p.m. to midnight; Tuesday through Sunday, 11 a.m. to midnight.

Tours: On request, if a brewer is available.

Parking: Free on site.

Takeout beer: 32-ounce growlers of Engine 15 beers only.

Special considerations: Handicapped-accessible.

Extras: Outdoor seating; brew-it-yourself classes.

Green Room Brewing

228 Third Street North, Jacksonville Beach, FL 32250
(904) 201-9283 • www.greenroombrewing.com

A "green room" in a theater or television studio is where performers and guests not required on stage at the moment can relax, perhaps noshing on snacks or even sipping beer or wine while waiting their turn. A "green room" in surfing vernacular refers to the inside curve, or "barrel," of a totally gnarly wave in which the surfer is bathed in the green tone of sunlight filtered through the surrounding seawater.

If you want to know which one Green Room Brewing turned to for its name, just walk in and take a look around at the surfboard-shaped tap handles and the boards, gear, and art around the taproom and it becomes clear. Not to mention the sea breeze that wafts from the Atlantic Ocean three blocks away from the brewery's front door.

Co-owners Eric Luman and Mark Stillman, to no one's surprise, love to surf, and they were determined to plant their business at the beach. "It was always in the plan to be in the beaches area," said Luman, who is also the head brewer. "That was highly built into our business plan. Both Mark and I are avid surfers and fishermen—that's what we do. We both live out here at the beach. We wanted to keep it local to our areas that we like. There are some industrial areas out here near the beach that we were looking at where the rent's a little cheaper, but we decided to bite the bullet and go for a high-visibility, great location on A1A, right off the beach. It's been well worth it."

The "green" might also refer to Luman's love of hoppy beers, which he cultivated during his years in Florida's brewing scene, starting in 2001 at the now-defunct Jacksonville location of Southend Brewery & Smokehouse and then at some of the chain's other southeastern U.S. stores, then moving on to Seven Bridges Grille & Brewery, where he brewed for five years. All the time, he nurtured a long-term plan of opening his own brewery, and finally he got serious about it after partnering with

Beers brewed: Head High IPA, Pablo Beach Pale Ale, Double Overhead Double IPA, Undertow Barleywine, Shaka Oatmeal Stout, and Diamond Belgian Style Wit, plus many one-offs and seasonals.

The Pick: Pablo Beach Pale Ale is a refreshing American-style pale ale that clocks in at 5 percent ABV, but it has enough hops bitterness that it could be considered a "gateway IPA."

Stillman, who is also Luman's uncle and had a business and finance background, and getting him excited about the concept of combining their talents in the venture. So the two finished the business plan and arranged financing, and after about a year, they opened the doors.

Luman and Stillman strongly support the local beer, business, and arts communities at the brewery. Of Green Room's sixteen taps, eight to twelve are for beers brewed on the premises, and the rest are from other Florida breweries. They use local businesses for necessary printing and other services. And on the walls of the taproom hang works by local artists, creating what is essentially a small gallery. "We let anyone who's local come put their own art up," Luman explained. "If it sells, they keep all the money. We don't do a commission or a gallery fee or anything like that. It's straight between the buyer and the artist; we don't get between that. We just want to put cool local art on the walls."

Unlike the businesses in most beach communities in Florida, Green Room and other Jacksonville Beach enterprises are not deeply dependent on tourism. "We get tourists, but Jacksonville Beach isn't a really touristy area," Luman said. "There's not much seasonality or anything out there. We don't see spring break or summer break or any of that kind of tourism. Unless your family lives here, you don't really travel here, for whatever reason. We're not Daytona or any of those other places. We have the city of Jacksonville, which is huge, right next to us, but we're like a small town out here, which we really like."

Green Room Brewing

Opened: 2011.

Owners: Mark Stillman and Eric Luman.

Brewer: Eric Luman.

System: 7-barrel IDD.

Annual production: 2,000 barrels in 2012.

Hours: Tuesday through Thursday, 4 p.m. to midnight; Friday, 4 p.m. to 1 a.m.; Saturday, noon to 1 a.m.; Sunday, 2 to 10 p.m.

Tours: On request, if someone's available.

Parking: Free on site and on Second Avenue North.

Takeout beer: Growlers.

Special considerations: Handicapped-accessible.

Extras: Dog-friendly and just a few blocks' walk to the beach.

Intuition Ale Works

720 King Street, Jacksonville, FL 32204
(904) 683-7720
www.intuitionaleworks.com

A sort of race took place in early 2012 among three of Florida's craft breweries: Which would be the first to put its beer into cans? Intuition Ale Works won, canning its flagship People's Pale Ale just a few days ahead of Tampa Bay Brewing Company. Cigar City Brewing followed shortly after.

Ben Davis, Intuition's founder and owner, never even considered bottling, "mainly because [a can is] better for the beer, a better container for beer," he said. "I also think that in Florida, in Jacksonville, it's better for our lifestyle. Cans are right for being at the beach, being on the water, the pool, golf courses." Davis wanted to make a statement as well: "Canning your beers when you're a young brewery in a state like Florida that people always looked at as being kind of a beer wasteland, it kind of says, 'Whoa, these guys are serious. They're taking some risks.'"

The Jacksonville-area beer scene, including St. Augustine, has exploded in just the past few years, going from five small brewpubs to eleven craft breweries by the time of this writing. Intuition, which opened in 2010, was one of the first in the new wave.

Davis took a different path than most other small brewers. In 2002, the Jacksonville native moved to the vineyard-covered hillsides of Sonoma County, California, to work at wineries. Eventually, he started producing wine under his own label, Tallulah. He lived, though, just five minutes from Lagunitas Brewing Company in Petaluma and was a big fan of its beers. In 2008, he sold the business and moved back to Florida with his wife, also a Jacksonville native.

"I decided to get into brewing after some buddies kind of talked me into it," he told me. "I started taking brewing classes at the Siebel Institute up in Chicago. I started their diploma program and I completed a couple of modules, but it was

Beers brewed: People's Pale Ale, I-10 IPA, Jon Boat Coastal Ale, King Street Stout, Riverside Red, and Triad Tripel, plus lots of seasonal and one-off releases.

The Pick: With a hoppiness that borders on IPA territory, the citrusy People's Pale Ale is a real thirst-quencher, especially during the hot and humid Florida summer.

tough for me to be able to finish the whole program. I ended up finding this location that we're currently at in April of 2010, then signed a lease in May, started build-out in July of 2010, and we brewed our first batch in October."

Though winemaking and brewing are two different animals, Davis discovered similarities in the more esoteric aspects of palate, perspective, and balance when creating a recipe, as well as in the process and equipment. And a difference in the potential dangers to life and limb. "Brewing is a lot more dangerous than making wine," he said. "There's no real danger in winemaking, but in brewing you can get burned—there's carbon dioxide that can blow tanks up."

Intuition, housed in a warehouse that was once home to a doughnut factory, lies in the Avondale-Riverside district of South Jacksonville. The traditionally warehouse-industrial area is slowly gentrifying into a historic neighborhood of restored homes, funky cafés and shops, and trendy restaurants and pubs. "This area is one of the more unique pockets of Jacksonville," Davis said. "It's got a lot of history and culture to it."

The brewery's taproom, in a part of the building originally built in the 1920s, evokes the feel of a German beer hall, with long community tables where customers can converse over a pint. According to Davis, the clientele is as eclectic as the neighborhood. "It's kind of all over the place. A lot of regulars come here after work, then typically as it gets later, the crowd gets a little bit younger. It will be the beginning of the night for some people—they'll have a few beers, then go off. We sell a lot of cans out of our taproom, a lot of growlers. There's people coming in to buy beer, then taking it home to drink."

Patrons can find not only the flagship Intuition brews on tap, but also a wide variety of special releases and one-offs. "We typically try to have twenty beers on tap," Davis said. "We brew a lot of different styles. People expect a new beer on tap every week. We can't do that, but we try to brew a lot of different stuff."

Unfortunately, as much as Davis loves the neighborhood and the thriving business, trouble with a few neighbors has forced him into considering a move, even though he lives close enough to ride his bike to work and his lease still has a couple of years to go. Noise complaints during popular events, primarily from one particularly vocal resident, have brought sheriff's deputies and code enforcement officers to the premises enough times that he had to pay a large fine.

Many of the events raised thousands of dollars for local charities, which were able to use the space free of charge and brought much-needed business during what might otherwise have been slow times.

Hundreds flocked to the festivals and celebrations, where the brewery would open the doors in its loading docks, allowing attendees to gather and purchase beers at an open-air bar near the brewing equipment. The brewery chose to end the events rather than continue to deal with the politics involved, however. "Sadly, the obstacles to operating a unique, mixed-use business in our historic district have proved insurmountable at our King Street home," the brewery posted on its Facebook page. Regardless, until a move is made, the brewery will continue to operate at its current address.

Intuition Ale Works

Opened: 2010.

Owner: Ben Davis.

Brewers: Ben Davis and Andrew Cattell.

System: 10-barrel Premier Stainless.

Annual production: Estimated 6,000 barrels in 2013.

Hours: Tuesday through Friday, 3 to 11 p.m.; Saturday, 1 to 11 p.m.

Tours: Tuesday through Friday at 3 p.m. by appointment

Parking: Free on site.

Takeout beer: Growlers, kegs, cans, and occasional special-release bottles.

Special considerations: Handicapped-accessible.

Extras: Food trucks; occasional beer and brewing seminars.

Other area beer sites: Kickbacks Gastropub, 910 King St., Jacksonville, FL 32204, (904) 388-9551, www.facebook.com/kickbacksgastropub; Dahlia's Pour House, 2695 Post St., Jacksonville, FL 32204; www.dahliaspourhouse.com.

McGuire's Irish Pub, Destin

33 East Highway 98, Destin, FL 32541
(850) 650-0000 • www.mcguiresirishpub.com

McGuire's Irish Pub in Destin is far more than a restaurant—it's a warren of nooks and crannies bursting with funky antique wall hangings, photos, paintings, beer, and whiskey signs. I would hate to have to inventory that stuff! In keeping with the tradition started at the original McGuire's in Pensacola, dollar bills cover pretty much every available space on the walls, ceilings, and beams. Room upon room with different themes are part of the exploration, including the Notre Dame Room, adorned with authentic felt panels and autographed photos of some of the great Fighting Irish teams through the years. Then there's the brewery, with its wooden-clad tanks and a crew of brewers in matching coveralls, any of whom will be happy to chat with you if they aren't too busy making beer.

That's just on the inside. Outside, hallways and sidewalks connect to a gift shop full of Irish-themed merchandise, books, and beer; an area where you can watch the butchers prepare the restaurant's freshly cut meats; the Grand Hall, for special events; a barrel room that specializes in wine; and a pizza joint. The whole block is owned by McGuire Martin and his family.

And there's another brewery in the works, separate from the restaurant, where plans call for brewing for distribution, possibly packaging in cans. Currently, McGuire's does some contract brewing at Florida Beer Company in Cape Canaveral for limited distribution. "We've got a spot down the building, and we're going to put a microbrewery in there, a 15-barrel brewhouse," head brewer Tom Anderson told me. "Our plan is to ultimately do our contract ourselves once we work through the legality of being able to do that."

The complex has expanded since it first opened, he said, but went through a growth spurt starting around 2008. "It grew the most over probably the last five years, through an oil spill here and through a recession," he explained, referring to the disastrous April 2010 explosion

Beers brewed: Light Ale, Irish Red Ale, Wild Irish Raspberry Wheat, Porter, and Irish Stout, plus various seasonals and specials.

The Pick: Guinness is often the choice in an authentic Irish pub, but for an even better experience, try the house-brewed Irish Stout. Poured from a nitrogen draft system, it's just as dark as Guinness but even fuller-bodied, with just a hint of a hops bite.

on the Deepwater Horizon oil rig in the Gulf of Mexico that sent nearly five million barrels of crude oil billowing into the water. Some of that oil washed up on area beaches, and tourists stayed away in droves for a while.

Though the crowd ebbs and flows somewhat with the various tourist seasons, the local traffic keeps things busy through the year. "It's hands down the busiest restaurant in Destin, bar none," Anderson said. "It's so accessible to people to come in here and get a great meal, sit at the bar, and feel like you're part of the family."

The restaurant draws customers from all walks of life. Families flock there, as do young professionals, hipsters, and airmen from nearby Eglin Air Force Base. Because it fronts busy U.S. 98, right across the Miracle Strip Parkway from Fort Walton Beach, people on their way back from a day on the sand often stop for a bite or a cold beer on the way home. "It's an Irish pub. It's accessible to everybody," Anderson said. "It's not too pretentious, and it's not too fine dining, even though our food is phenomenal. We're a great steak restaurant, and we've got some of the biggest burgers you've ever seen."

McGuire's Irish Pub, Destin

Opened: 1997.
Owner: McGuire Martin.
Brewers: Tom Anderson and Gary Essex.
System: 7-barrel custom.
Annual production: 1,200 barrels.
Hours: Seven days a week, 11 a.m. to 2 a.m.
Tours: On request or call ahead for group tours.
Parking: Free on site.
Takeout beer: Growlers and bottles.
Special considerations: Handicapped-accessible.

McGuire's Irish Pub, Pensacola

600 East Gregory Street, Pensacola, FL 32502
(850) 433-6789 • www.mcguiresirishpub.com

It's customary for a new business to hang one of its first dollar bills on the walls. Sometimes, especially in pubs, customers might add more bills next to the original. That's what happened at McGuire's after cofounder Molly Martin tacked her first dollar tip to the wall behind the bar. But the plastering never stopped. Almost every square inch of the walls and ceilings is covered in multiple layers of bills, most of them with written messages or signatures. The last time the Martins did an estimate, there were more than a million. Among the bills tacked to the ceiling are other mementos—women's brassieres. The unofficial word is that bras are legal tender for a shot from the full-liquor bar. Several moose heads are mounted on the wall, and another McGuire's tradition is that customers are encouraged to kiss them for good luck.

McGuire's first opened in 1977 in a strip mall, then moved to its current location in 1982; the owners installed the brewing system in 1989. This McGuire's—there's another east of it in Destin—is housed in Pensacola's original 1927 firehouse, but it's now themed as a New York Irish saloon from around the turn of the twentieth century. "It really wasn't set up for a brewery; there are tons of small rooms and narrow hallways," said head brewer Mike Helf. "It's all part of the charm of McGuire's bars."

The pub's menu offers traditional Irish fare, but McGuire's has also earned a reputation as a place for fresh seafood and top-notch steak—"One of America's Great Steak Houses" says a sign on the front. This boast is backed up by a slew of awards over the years, including Steak House of the Year from the National Beef Council in 1998. The customers are mostly local, Helf told me, and the pub tends to fill quickly most days. "I tend to brew in the very early hours because the pub gets so crowded," he said.

The dining area is divided into themed rooms, such as the Pipers Den, Notre Dame Room, and Irish Links Room, all decorated eclectically with old beer signs, photographs, and miscellaneous

Beers brewed: Light Ale, Irish Red Ale, Wild Irish Raspberry Wheat, Porter, and Irish Stout, plus various seasonals and specials.

The Pick: The Wild Irish Raspberry Wheat pops with subtle tartness from the 84 pounds of raspberry puree used in each batch, and at only 4.8 percent ABV, it's a refreshing thirst-quencher during a hot summer day.

antiques matching the particular theme. Brass plaques on the bar top bear the names of those patrons named "Customer of the Month" over the years, and Irish homilies hang on the walls.

McGuire's ran into a bit of controversy in 2007 because of its restroom signage. For years, the gender signs on the doors were reversed as a joke. Female patrons not in on the joke would often walk into the men's room, and vice versa, though a smaller sign on the door pointed to the correct restroom. Then a customer claimed that a man walked in on his fifteen-year-old daughter and filed a complaint with state regulators. The state cited the restaurant and said it must change the signs or risk being shut down. Eventually, a compromise allowed McGuire's to keep the signs, but it had to install a second swinging door that bore the proper gender behind the first one.

McGuire's Irish Pub, Pensacola

Opened: Pub in 1977, brewery in 1989.

Owner: McGuire Martin.

Brewer: Mike Helf.

System: 6-barrel.

Annual production: 1,000 barrels.

Hours: Seven days a week, 11 a.m. to 2 a.m.

Tours: On request.

Parking: Free on site.

Takeout beer: Growlers.

Special considerations: Handicapped-accessible.

Other area beer sites: Hopjacks Pizza Kitchen & Taproom, 10 S. Palafox Place, Pensacola, FL 32502, (850) 497-6073, hopjacks.com.

Mile Marker Brewing

3420 Agricultural Center Drive, Suite 8, St. Augustine, FL 32092
(904) 217-4294 • www.milemarkerbrewing.com

Sometimes seemingly coincidental events coalesce into a result that makes those random occurrences appear to be part of a grand plan. It's called synchronicity, and you might believe it helped bring Mile Marker Brewing to its space in a warehouse park not far from I-95 in St. Augustine.

In 2010, Vance Joy and his business partner Mike Fierro had been seeking both a place to lease and used brewing equipment to open a brewery, but they had a limited budget and little luck in either quest. "This was about the tenth building I looked at, and when I walked up, a mockingbird had its nest on the ground and it was flying by me because I got too close to its eggs," Joy said. "So as they were opening the door, I'm thinking about this bird. They opened up the door and I walked into this building, and I'm staring at a 7-barrel brewhouse, three 14-barrel fermenters, seven 7-barrel grundy tanks, a filtration system, all the brewing hoses, pumps, and filters needed to have a brewery. That all came from a Hops restaurant in Ocala that had closed." He negotiated a lease for the equipment and space, and Mile Marker was on its way. "I don't know 100 percent if we would be in business if I hadn't walked into the building and started staring at a brewing system," Joy said.

And though you might wonder whether the partners considered naming the brewery Mockingbird Aleworks, they already had their brand. The name comes from the little rectangular green signs with white numerals that mark each mile along the interstates and major highways. They are especially important in the Florida Keys, where the locations of businesses and landmarks are often referenced by the nearest mile markers on U.S. 1. Key West is where you'll find Mile Marker 0 at the southern terminus of the highway, and where Fierro and Joy hoped to open their brewery.

In fact, the initial name they had in mind was Mile Marker Zero. But places in Key West cost too

Beers brewed: Mile Marker Zero Blonde Ale, Mile Marker 1565 Ancient City Red Ale, Mile Marker 82 Islamorada IPA, Mile Marker 1513 Pecan de Leon Nut Brown Ale, and Mile Marker 70 Palm Beach Coconut Porter, plus various seasonals and one-offs.

The Pick: The Mile Marker 82 Islamorada IPA has distinct citrus and floral notes from Columbus and Sterling hops, but not the overpowering bitterness of some IPAs. It's a perfect IPA for someone just beginning to explore the style and pretty damn thirst-quenching in the Florida heat.

much, Joy said, "and the water quality down there was terrible for brewing beer. We happened to live here in St. Augustine, so we cut the 'Zero' off of the name, called it Mile Marker Brewing, and now we name our beers after different mile markers around the state." The idea of Mile Marker Zero didn't go away completely, though—it's now the name of the brewery's flagship blond ale, on tap at many places in the Keys.

Landing the equipment and the space was not enough to open the doors, however. A lot of work still needed to be done. "We built everything in here ourselves," Joy said. "Every single nut, bolt, and wire was done ourselves over about nine months. We really put our sweat equity into this place." The hard work resulted in a funky, blue-light-tinted taproom and a large seating area in the warehouse next to the brewing tanks. Customers are welcome to bring their dogs, and eclectic music wafts through the space as people chat and laugh over hand-crafted beers. "People like it," Joy said. "They say it's like hanging out in your friend's garage."

The brewery's eye-catching sea turtle logo is plastered all over the place. Designed by local graphic artist Mark Mueller, a friend of the partners', it has garnered a lot of praise from customers. "I'm so proud of what our turtle logo looks like and our artwork," Joy said. "Our branding, I think, is top-notch."

Mile Marker Brewing

Opened: 2011.

Owners: Vance Joy and Mike Fierro.

Brewers: Vance Joy and Dennis Grune.

System: 7-barrel brewhouse PUB.

Annual production: 2,500 barrels.

Hours: Tuesday and Wednesday, 4 p.m. to midnight; Thursday and Friday, 1 p.m. to midnight; Saturday and Sunday, noon to midnight.

Tours: On request.

Parking: Free on site.

Takeout beer: Growlers.

Special considerations: Handicapped-accessible.

Extras: Dog-friendly; cornhole tournaments; charity events.

Momo's Pizza Market Street Brew Pub

1410 Market Street, Tallahassee, FL 32312
(850) 412-0222
momospizza.com/market-street-brew-pub

Momo's Pizza Market Street Brew Pub breathes comfort. After you walk under a stucco and wood archway and through the front door on sunny North Florida afternoon, and let your eyes adjust to the dimmer light, you'll notice that the eclectic décor and well-used equipment feel like the proverbial old shoe. From the dings and dents on the pizza oven doors to the scratches and scars on the wooden bar, Momo's is the sort of place that you know sees a lot of regulars come through for slices of pizza advertised to be "As Big as Your Head." They are.

It's one of those joints where it looks like someone decorated it by buying this and that at yard sales and thrift stores, then finding nooks and crannies to display the pieces, with some loose sense of grouping. You'll see a few dusty action figures here, some novelty postcards there. A Guinness mirror hangs next to a black-and-white print of a post–World War I dirigible, which is next to a poster of John Belushi's Bluto character from *Animal House*, which is next to a photo of the Rat Pack loitering around a billiard table. And so on.

Momo's has three separate areas in its shopping plaza space on Market Street, and you've only been in the first one. Go through the glass door and weave through the tables and chairs on the popular outdoor deck to the other inside space, where you'll find another bar, more tables, and the place where brewmaster John Larsen plies his trade.

Larsen has been brewing at Momo's since the brewery section opened in 2011, but he's been stirring mash for a bit longer. He started as a homebrewer about twenty-five years ago and opened a homebrew supply store in 1993. Though his store, Homebrew Den, has called a couple of locations home over the years, its latest incarnation has done business right next door to Momo's for the past five or so years. "It's just a nice location, even before the brewing side here opened. It was nice to be close to a pizza place," he said with a chuckle.

Larsen's judged beer competitions as a member of the Beer Judge Certification Program, and he's been active in the local homebrewing community

Beers brewed: Varies. Usually a dark, a light, a double IPA, and one or two others.

The Pick: Go for the double IPA, if available. The hoppy goodness complements the fresh and robust pizza toppings.

for decades. Momo's is his first commercial gig. A few years after moving his homebrew shop next to Momo's, he and the restaurant's owner, Don Dye, started discussing adding the brewery. "We talked to the owner here, developed an interest on both sides to open a brewpub, and here we go," he said. So far, it seems to be a good fit; after all, pizza and beer have gone together since pizza was invented (beer came first). "We make suggestions when a new beer comes out for the staff to suggest to patrons which pizzas would go well with the beers that we're making," Larsen said.

His brewing philosophy is grounded in the classics: "We do a little bit of playing around with big IPAs and spiced beers and those kinds of things, but I'm not a beer experimenter," he said. "I like to expose people to the classic beer styles. We make some very standard beer styles—I think they're very well made. There's a reason classic beer styles are classic: they've been around a long time, and they taste really good. So we make brown ales, porters, stouts." First- and second-place Best of Show medals in the 2013 Best Florida Beer Championships, for Moose and Squirrel Nut Brown Ale and Big Papa Porter, respectively, attest to the quality of Larsen's beer.

Momo's has another location in Tallahassee, at 1416 West Tennessee Street, but though it has a wide selection of craft beer on tap and in the bottle, the Market Street store is where the beer is crafted. At either place, though, you can order those "Big as Your Head" slices to go with your tasty brew. Just order one.

Momo's Pizza Market Street Brew Pub

Opened: 2011 (brewery).

Owner: Don Dye.

Brewer: John Larsen.

System: 6-barrel custom-built.

Annual production: 120 barrels.

Hours: Monday and Tuesday, 11 a.m. to 9 p.m.; Wednesday and Thursday, 11 a.m. to 9:30 p.m.; Friday, 11 a.m. to 10 p.m.; Saturday, 11:30 a.m. to 10 p.m.; Sunday, noon to 9 p.m.

Tours: On request, if Larsen is available.

Parking: Free on site.

Takeout beer: None.

Special considerations: Handicapped-accessible.

Extras: Outdoor seating; homebrew supply shop next door.

Pensacola Bay Brewery

225 East Zaragoza Street, Pensacola, FL 32502
(850) 434-3353 • www.pbbrew.com

Pensacola Bay Brewery resides in a state-owned building in the Historic Pensacola Village, just a few blocks north of Pensacola Bay and just south of the city's Seville Historic District. Perhaps, then, the breezes carry the essences of local folklore and seafaring, mixed with more than a touch of piracy, which seem to infuse the beer coming from the brewery's fermenters. You can see it in the décor and the names on the taps: the buccaneer-themed Black Treasure Imperial Porter and Blackbeard Stout; the Lighthouse Porter, named after one of Pensacola's most famous landmarks; and Li'l Napoleon, ostensibly made in recognition of "all short bastards," but also a nod to the French, who once owned the city. "We have a nautical theme," said head brewer Rogers Conolly. "All of our beers are tied to that in some way or at least the history, the natural history of Florida."

Co-owners Elliott Eckland and Mark Robertson opened Pensacola Bay Brewery in November 2010 to bring hand-crafted beer to a community that was more or less a vacuum when it came to being able to find a place to hoist a pint of any brew that wasn't owned by one of the multinational corporations. In other words, it sucked. But being a pioneer means sometimes standing behind the proverbial lectern. "We're still kind of in the process of educating our local population on craft beer, on what beer can be," Conolly told me. It helps that other venues, such as a World of Beer, have opened nearby and that other establishments have increased their tap count. "I think that's done a lot for us to expose people to different styles of beer, different flavors," Conolly said. "It gets them to where they can come in here and they're not intimidated by trying something that's darker than what they're used to."

Pensacola Bay Brewery certainly offers a broad enough range of styles, from Kolsch and amber ale to imperial porter and thick stout, as well as a slew

Beers brewed: Banyan Brown Ale, Black Treasure Imperial Porter, Blackbeard Stout, DeLuna Kolsch, DeSoto Berliner Weisse Ale, Lighthouse Porter, Li'l Napoleon IPA, and Riptide Amber. Seasonals: Conquistador Dopple-Bock, Pensacola Bay's ESB, Pumpkin Vanilla Porter, Sawgrass American Wheat, Treasure Grove Citra Pale Ale, and 1845 Pilsner.

The Pick: The creamy, chocolaty, 6.1 percent Lighthouse Porter is full-flavored, but with a lightness that makes it a treat no matter the season.

of seasonals throughout the year. Any craft beer fan will likely find at least one palate-satisfying brew to suit his or her taste. The brewery distributes some of its beer in bottles and kegs locally and a select few throughout the state. According to Conolly, plans include installing a less manual bottling line and increased production.

The medals hanging on the wall attest that the brewers' peers think highly of their creations. In March 2011, at its first Florida Brewers Guild Best Florida Beer Championships, an annual event in which most of the state's brewers strive for recognition, Pensacola Bay Brewery won third-place Best of Show for its Banyan Brown. The next year, it won second for the Lighthouse Porter.

The cozy tasting room and a patio paved with red bricks that reflect the historic building's façade provide enough room for visitors and regulars alike to discuss the day's topics or the day's beer. But it's the regulars who provide the word of mouth buzz that any young brewery hopes to cultivate. "Those are the people, our regulars," Conolly said, "the ones that we count on to get out there and help spread the word."

Pensacola Bay Brewery

Opened: 2010.
Owners: Elliott Eckland and Mark Robertson.
Brewers: Mark Robertson and Rogers Conolly.
System: 15-barrel Pacific Mechanical Systems.
Annual production: Estimated 3,000 barrels in 2013.
Hours: Monday through Thursday, noon to 9 p.m.; Friday and Saturday, noon to 11 p.m.; Sunday, noon to 6 p.m.
Tours: Saturdays at 3:30 p.m.; $5 charge includes one pint.
Parking: Street or nearby lots.
Takeout beer: Growlers and some bottles.
Special considerations: Handicapped-accessible.
Extras: Outdoor seating; PBBrew Running Club run Wednesdays at 6 p.m.
Other area beer sites: World of Beer–Palafox, 200 S. Palafox St., Pensacola, FL 32502, (850) 332-7952, wobusa.com/Locations/Palafox.aspx.

Pinglehead Brewing Company

14 Blanding Boulevard, Orange Park,
FL 32073 (at Brewer's Pizza)
(904) 276-5160 • www.pinglehead.com

To avoid confusion, Pinglehead is the brewery arm of Brewer's Pizza, which will be the sign you're looking for at its location in an Orange Park strip mall, just outside Jacksonville city limits. It's tucked between a Thai market and a work uniform shop. If you're still not certain you're at the right place, look for the neon "Craft Beer to Go" sign in the shape of a growler.

And one mild warning: if you suffer from coulrophobia (the fear of clowns), brace yourself, because the visage of Pinglehead, which sits atop the tap handles and appears in images around the rooms, pretty much exemplifies what most folks picture when they hear the phrase "evil clown." But the beer makes it worth it.

At first it was just Brewer's Pizza, a takeout pizza joint with a few craft beer taps that opened in 2010. "People just started coming in, wanting to just sit down and eat pizza, eat here, so we had to follow the lead and the voice of our customer," said Steve Halford, taproom and beverage manager. So the owners acquired the unit next to the original one, opened it up with tables, and started producing their own beer about a year later. The on-premises brew was initially called Brewer's Pizza beer, but once the brewery started distributing kegs to other establishments, the brewing component was redubbed Pinglehead.

The owners hired Michael Payne as brewmaster and Keegan Malone as an assistant. Payne has since gone on to open Aardwolf Brewing Company in Jacksonville, and Malone took over as brewmaster. "Before Brewer's opened up, I didn't know anything about beer," Malone said. "Michael Payne, he taught me, guided me, taught me everything he knew, and then he ended up leaving. It was like jumping into the deep end of the pool and learning

Beers brewed: Black hOPs India Black Ale, Landslide Double IPA, Mind Drive Extreme Imperial Porter, Moon Dance Oatmeal Stout, Pinglehead Imperial American Amber/Imperial Red Ale, Tribal Rite Robust Porter, Ambitious Monk Belgian Tripel, Endless Summer Blonde Ale, Rawhide Strong Ale, and Tailhook American Brown Ale, plus various one-offs and seasonals.

The Pick: The flagship Pinglehead red ale balances hops bitterness with malt sweetness to make this 7.8 percent ABV offering extremely quaffable.

to swim." The proverbial swimming has gone well, and all five Pinglehead beers entered in the 2013 Best Florida Beer Championships won medals—three gold and two silver. Since my visit, Malone moved on to another brewery, passing the head brewer's mash paddle to his assistant, Aaron Taylor.

Mike Wilson, one of the owners, used to run a software engineering company. He used his knowledge and connections to develop a tap list that shows on TV screens around the taproom and restaurant and can be instantly updated, replacing the traditional chalkboard and paper lists. It eases the workload of busy bartenders and servers, Halford said. "The minute you updated that paper tap list, three hours into the shift a beer blows, then I'd have my waitresses and waiters going around to each table saying, 'Oh, you can have everything except this, this, and this because they blew today,'" he said. "And on a busy Friday, it's hard to go back and rework the menu." The system is available on a smartphone app, so customers can download and peruse it at their leisure, even before arriving at the restaurant or when the TVs are switched to the occasional major sports event.

Oh, and why does the scary clown bear the name Pinglehead? "That was Mike's creation," Halford explained. "One of his brothers growing up made up that word. You know, kids make up names to call each other. That one happened to stick."

Pinglehead Brewing Company

Opened: 2011.
Owners: Mike Wilson and Troy Maas.
Brewer: Aaron Taylor.
System: 5-barrel Newlands Systems.
Annual production: Estimated 700 barrels.
Hours: Monday through Thursday, noon to 9 p.m.; Friday and Saturday, noon to 11 p.m.; Sunday, noon to 6 p.m.
Tours: Call ahead to make sure someone is available as a guide.
Parking: Free on site.
Takeout beer: Growlers and limited-release bottles.
Special considerations: Handicapped-accessible.
Extras: Outdoor seating.

Proof Brewing Company

1717 West Tennessee Street, Tallahassee, FL 32304
(850) 894-5638 • www.proofbrewingco.com

Fans of fantasy novels and movies are familiar with the concept of the tiny structure that's magically much bigger inside than it appears from the outside. Proof Brewing Company gives that impression, though it's accomplished by efficient use of space rather than any sort of wizardry.

Housed in a nondescript, standalone building near the campus of Florida State University, Proof is a bit of a three-headed beast. The first head, created in 2007, takes the form of a bottle and liquor shop that quickly became the go-to store for craft brew–deprived beer geeks in Florida's capital. The next head, opened in 2008, is the upstairs taproom, featuring thirty-eight brews—some rare releases—and about 150 bottles, as well as liquor. Down the stairs, a twenty-two-tap bar, the brewery (opened in 2012), and an outdoor deck complete the Cerberus-like hat trick of the beer beast that is Proof.

"We had always been into brewing beer," said owner Byron Burroughs. "We realized that Tallahassee really needed a brewery. I'm from Florida. Florida needs great breweries." The market proves Burroughs correct. Weekend nights, the crowd packs in wall to wall. And though you may find more students down the street at other nightspots, they certainly are a big part of Proof's clientele, along with the other demographic groups you would expect in a university town that also is the state's political center. You might find yourself rubbing elbows with one of the students, a professor, a lobbyist, or even a state representative. "I think that the crowd that we have, it's just an excellent cross section of what's around," Burroughs said. "It's unbelievable."

The taps boast beer from some of the top craft brewers in the world, which serve as a touchstone for the beers that come from Proof's brewhouse. "I feel that with what we carry, our beer should be as good as anything else we put on tap," Burroughs told me. "You can come in and drink Green Flash, Stone, or Cigar City, or anyone else. I hope that when you drink our beer, you're like, 'Wow, that stands up to it.'"

Beers brewed: Proof Pale Ale, Proof IPA, Proof MangoWit, Robust Porter, Cocoa Stout, and PBC Rye.

The Pick: The Proof IPA proves the brewers know how to use their hops. The dark aromas and citrusy sweet flavors hold up to any West Coast IPA.

The journey has been one of calculated experimentation and tweaking. Burroughs, born in Dade City and raised in Bradenton, said that early success helped guide recipe development. "We went down to Best Florida Beer Championships in the first six months of operations and entered five beers and won four golds and a bronze," he said. "Those are our mainstay cores. We've been hammering those, and they've turned out really well. I think we've got our process down, and the overall quality of all the beers we're putting out is about as good as it's going to get."

According to Burroughs, the brewing focus is on "big beers," not necessarily in the sense of having high alcohol content, but in that the brews are big and flavorful, so that focus also extends to the lower-ABV styles. None of them are filtered. "We try to keep everything as pure as we can, no additives or adjuncts," he explained. "Our cores are our IPA, our pale ale, our rye ale, and we have a couple of variations going of some lighter styles because inevitably, no matter how much I love to drink IPA, a lot of people need some sessionable beers." Some of those styles include a witbier, a mango version of that, pale ale, and Berliner Weisse. The brewery has plans to brew some traditional lager styles too.

Proof already distributes draft beer on a limited basis to various beer spots in the region and the state, but sights are set much higher. "For us, our goal has always been to be Tallahassee's first distributing brewery, and when we started distributing, we wanted to make sure we came and did it as well as everybody else." Now, Burroughs said, "our goal is to be a top regional brewery." Proof recently announced that it was taking the next steps in that quest by adding more fermentation capacity at its current brewery and opening a 10,000-square-foot second location with a 20-barrel brewhouse and 10,000 barrels of fermentation capacity.

Proof Brewing Company

Opened: Bottle shop in 2007, pub in 2008, and brewery in 2012.
Owners: Byron and Angela Burroughs.
Brewers: Larry Agee (head brewer), Arin Brown, and Nick DiGioia.
System: 3-barrel Premier Stainless.
Annual production: 1,000 barrels.
Hours: Seven days a week, 5 p.m. to 2 a.m.
Tours: On request.
Parking: Free on site.
Takeout beer: Growlers.
Special considerations: Handicapped-accessible.
Extras: Outdoor seating.

Props Brewery & Grill

255 Miracle Strip Parkway Southeast, No. 19,
   Fort Walton Beach, FL 32548
(850) 586-7117 • www.propsbrewery.com

A customer walking into Props Brewery & Grill might never guess that the U.S. Air Force has anything to do with it—provided that customer just arrived on this planet and had never heard of airplanes or the USAF. If the squadron insignia, historical photos, and close-cropped haircuts do not give it away, the 260-pound DC-3 propeller that doubles as a ceiling fan might clinch it.

"The military's been awfully good to us," said general manager and partner Brian Oneill. "They're definitely our bread and butter." That comes as no surprise, seeing as how the Fort Walton Beach brewery is just a few miles from Eglin Air Force Base, and its two founders, Michael Kee and Nathan Vannatter, are active-duty air force majors, flying C-130s in the Middle East, Africa, or wherever their deployments take them. It was during the downtime on such missions that the two officers and homebrewers began talking about starting a brewpub.

Kee and Vannatter were on deployment when I visited the brewery, but Oneill recounted the initial results of those conversations: "They said, 'We love brewing, we love beer, it would be great if we put together a place,' so eventually they marched forward with it. They took a chance and they threw all their money into it and started picking up used equipment, whether it was used fermenters, a used glycol machine, used mash tuns. Then they also started picking up used restaurant equipment—refrigerators and grills and all that kind of stuff. They found this location, negotiated a great lease and moved on from there."

Oneill joined the venture near the beginning, after seeing an ad for a general manager. He met the owners, they hired him, and he started planning the restaurant and the menu, which mostly consists of standard pub food—burgers, fries, chicken wings, salads, wraps, and so on.

At any given time, the pub might be hosting a party for the air force squadron, whether for a promotion, retirement, or someone leaving on or

Beers brewed: Four Kings Brown Ale, Flying Coffin IPA, Blonde Bomber Ale, Rye of the Tiger IPA, Prop Oil Porter, and various seasonals.

The Pick: Released as a seasonal, the hoppy, spicy Rye of the Tiger proved so popular that it's now a regular offering.

returning from deployment. But the military is not the brewpub's only customer base. Props occupies a corner unit in a shopping center on the land side of the U.S. 98 bridge, and drivers coming in from Fort Walton Beach can see the large "Brewery" sign on the back of the building as soon as they cross the top of the bridge. This draws in a lot of beachgoers, Oneill said, but it's the locals whom the owners had in mind when conceiving the concept. "Around here, there's the spring break season, there's the snowbird season, and then there's the tourist season in the summer," he said. "We love them all, but they're gravy to us. We really live and die by the locals. It was our goal to be steady all the time."

For those locals, Props offers a mug club with a slew of perks, including discounted beers, first crack at beer dinner and tapping party invitations, and a 15 percent discount on the entire check each Wednesday. There's also the Regulars Club. Admission requires only that the customer purchase and drink a hundred beers in sixty days, and that includes those from the ten or so guest taps. The reward for completing the challenge is a 20-ounce glass with the customer's name engraved on it, which can be refilled at the 16-ounce price. The patron can also add his or her name to a list on the wall.

Oneill said that the owners are looking toward future growth, starting with a possible expansion into the unit next door, aptly named unit B-17. Other things they're considering include more fermenters, more kegs, and a production facility.

Oh, and about that DC-3 propeller . . . one does not simply hang a 260-pound fixture with a standard ceiling fan mount. Oneill said they had to buy the hardware from a company that installs the giant video screens in sports stadiums. And it spins just fine.

Props Brewery & Grill

Opened: 2011.
Owners: Michael Kee and Nathan Vannatter.
Brewer: Michael Kee.
System: 7-barrel custom-built.
Annual production: 300 barrels in 2012.
Hours: Seven days a week, 11 a.m. to 1 a.m.
Tours: On request.
Parking: Free on site.
Takeout beer: Growlers.
Special considerations: Handicapped-accessible.
Extras: Outdoor seating.

Ragtime Tavern & Seafood Grill

207 Atlantic Boulevard, Atlantic Beach, FL 32233
(904) 241-7877 • www.ragtimetavern.com

Scott Bannester helped sow some of the seeds that grew into the current U.S. craft brewery movement. Fresh out of the University of Vermont with degrees in political science and English literature, Bannester took his newly minted knowledge to a job at a publishing house. After a year, he decided it didn't pay that well, so he pursued a longtime dream. "Not beer, but skiing," he said. "I worked at Killington ski area for six years. This was back in 1986, so the craft brewery movement really hadn't started, especially in the Northeast."

Then a guy by the name of Andy Pherson moved up to Vermont from Boston and opened Long Trail Brewing Company in 1989. "He talked me out of my cushy ski area job to go work for him as a salesman," Bannester said. "The brewer there quit, and I decided that I really wanted to learn a trade, and making beer was really interesting to me. So I stopped doing sales and started devoting myself to working all facets of the brewery."

After getting hands-on experience at the brewery, Bannester enrolled in the Master Brewers Program at the University of California, Davis. Upon completing the program and passing the exam, he didn't want to go back to cold Vermont, so he landed a job as brewmaster and quality control manager at a little startup brewery in Delaware named Dogfish Head. "I worked there four years, from 1998 to 2002. That was right when Dogfish was leaving their small location in Rehoboth Beach, Delaware, and building a really big facility in Milton," he said. "After the new brewery was built, one of my buddies from brewing school called me and asked me if I would be interested in leaving the huge brewery and working in a brewpub."

And that's how he ended up working for Big River Brewing Company, which was later folded into CraftWorks Restaurants & Breweries Inc. His first gig was as head brewer at Seven Bridges Grille

Beers brewed: Dolphin's Breath Lager, Red Brick Ale, and A. Strange Stout. Seasonals: Sweet Magnolia American Brown Ale and Westbury Wheat.

The Pick: A. Strange Stout, named after the founder's grandfather, Alexander Strange, is a robust and drinkable stout with a full-bodied mouthfeel.

& Brewery in Jacksonville. He held that position for three years. "Then they asked if I wanted to come to Ragtime," Bannester said. "I did because this place needed a lot of work and updating, so it was a challenge. But I took that on, and I've been here for seven years. So that's how I got into it. I was never a homebrewer. I was more like, came in it and rode the tide of the developing craft brewery movement."

Ragtime sprawls across three separate bar and dining areas, each with its own décor but a unifying theme incorporating dark wood and exposed brick, and with fresh-every-day seafood featured on the menu. A New Orleans Bourbon Street vibe resonates throughout the family-friendly establishment. But what it is today is not what it was in the past. "It started out very small; we've gone through three expansions now," Bannester said. "It was an old pharmacy initially. The pharmacist sold the building to the Morton family, who were the original owners of Ragtime Tavern. That's why the tavern isn't as corporate-themed as some of the other locations" owned by CraftWorks.

Bannester also serves as regional manager for three other Craft-Works brewpubs in Florida, and each has its own personality. "When you come here, you don't feel like you're at a Starbucks or McDonald's," he said. "Half the regulars who come here don't know we're owned by a corporation, so it's really nice to have that feeling. We have our own atmosphere and our own vibe that's not a corporate vibe at all. It's much more local and fun."

Ragtime Tavern & Seafood Grill

Opened: 1983.

Owner: CraftWorks Restaurants & Breweries Inc.

Brewer: Scott Bannester.

System: 10-barrel DME Ltd.

Annual production: 700 barrels.

Hours: Sunday to Thursday, 11 a.m. to midnight; Friday to Saturday, 11 a.m. to 1 a.m.

Tours: By reservation.

Parking: Free on site and nearby streets and lots.

Takeout beer: None.

Special considerations: Handicapped-accessible.

Extras: Outside seating on patio.

River City Brewing Company

835 Museum Circle, Jacksonville, FL 32207
(904) 398-2299 • rivercitybrew.com

The white tablecloths and magnificent views of the St. Johns River and downtown Jacksonville skyline might lead beer tourists to momentarily think that they may be in the wrong place. But a quick glance to the right reveals the more casual and lively Brewhouse Lounge, confirming that they have indeed found River City Brewing Company.

The restaurant and brewpub embodies multiple personalities. The fine-dining side caters to first dates, business dinners, and other culinary occasions that require a bit more elegance than found in the typical burgers-and-wings brewpub. A handful of ballrooms and salons provide the necessary ambience for the more private wedding receptions, company banquets, and cocktail parties. But the Brewhouse Lounge is where the laid-back happy hour and beer-loving crowds congregate, and where the creations of brewmaster Bob Grandstaff flow from the taps, though the beers are available throughout.

Grandstaff retired in 1994 from the Anheuser-Busch InBev brewery in Jacksonville, where he had served as manager of quality assurance. Other than brewmaster, that might be the most important job at a brewery where millions of gallons of beer are produced each year, and the beer in the bottle filled on January 1 has to taste exactly the same as the brew in the bottle filled 365 days later on New Year's Eve. It was about a year after retiring that Grandstaff took the job at River City, where he tries to maintain the same consistency in his products that he strived for at the brewpub's much bigger neighbor. "Even though we're a microbrewery and it's hands-on, it's still important for regular customers that it's going to taste the same today and two months from today," he said. "We put a lot of effort in trying to be consistent."

That doesn't always come easily, especially when working with an older system with unique quirks and a sometimes cantankerous personality. Grandstaff must deal with temperature controls that aren't as sophisticated as those he was used to, and there's little automation, making it a very manual operation. Using high-quality ingredients

Beers brewed: Jag Light, Jackson Pale Ale, Red Rooster Ale, and Riptide Porter. Seasonals: Oktoberfest, Kentucky Bourbon Ale, and Summer Wheat IPA.

The Pick: Red Rooster Ale is an easy-drinking brew with noticeable malt sweetness and just a touch of chocolate flavor.

helps overcome any technical bumps, with German malts and hops from other European countries to produce what Grandstaff describes as, predictably, European-style beers.

The polite and soft-spoken brewmaster works out of a closet-size office when he's not in the cramped, two-level brewery, but there is plenty of room to move around on the property. In addition to the 325-seat dining area, banquet rooms, and lounge, River City's outdoor venue takes up a significant stretch along the south bank of the St. Johns River. A maze of outdoor seating, stages, and bars peppered with nautical décor provides a platform from which customers can watch the pleasure boats and freighters parade by against the backdrop of tall buildings reflecting the sun's rays in various directions.

In the evening, the area bustles with families and workers who are enjoying a stroll or one of several riverfront festivals regularly held at the venue. Nights with live music on the deck draw folks in, and they frequently linger for a drink or a meal. It's especially busy around the holidays, when companies book parties at River City, often bringing in hundreds of their workers, who might enjoy the warming effects of the seasonal Kentucky Bourbon Ale. And no matter what time of the year you visit, there's always the view.

River City Brewing Company

Opened: 1993.

Owner: Anthony Candelino.

Brewer: Bob Grandstaff.

System: 14-barrel PUB.

Annual production: 275 barrels.

Hours: Lounge, Monday through Thursday, 3 to 11 p.m.; Friday and Saturday, 3 p.m. to late night; Sunday, 11 a.m. to 5 p.m.; Sunday brunch, 10:30 a.m. to 2:30 p.m.

Tours: By appointment.

Parking: Free on site for customers.

Takeout beer: None.

Special considerations: Handicapped-accessible.

Extras: Lots of outdoor riverfront seating.

Seven Bridges Grille & Brewery

9735 Gate Parkway North, Jacksonville,
FL 32246
(904) 997-1999 • www.7bridgesgrille.com

Seven Bridges Grille & Brewery bears many of the trappings of a typical casual-dining chain restaurant: TVs tuned to sports, dark wood floors and trim, a U-shaped bar at which customers gather for munchies and drinks, and a location across a vast parking lot from a multiscreen movie theater. But even though its parent has "Inc." tacked onto its name, it soon becomes apparent that this brewpub is closer to a beloved neighborhood hangout than a place to grab a quick meal on a road trip. Even the name bears witness to its local roots, referring to the seven bridges that span the St. Johns River, providing routes between the north and south banks. The towering grain silo attached to the side of the building and the second-floor brewery overlooking the main dining area clinch the fact that this is a brewpub with a distinct personality.

Head brewer Aaron Nesbit started with CraftWorks Restaurants & Breweries in 2002 as a server at one of its Gordon Biersch properties, moving up to assistant brewer for a couple years. He was offered the head brewer position at Seven Bridges, where he started in March 2011. When I asked Nesbit what his main duties are, he replied with a laugh, "Cleaning. That does not stop. You have to clean before you brew and clean after you brew. It's hard to pinpoint a schedule. You do what the beer lets you do. You can't really rush anything. I may plan on brewing two or three or four times a week, but if I don't have yeast ready, and it gets put behind . . . So the only real constant is cleaning."

Naturally, he manages to get quite a bit of brewing done in between the cleaning. As with all CraftWorks properties, there's a lineup of beers brewed with recipes provided by the company, but Nesbit has quite a bit of wiggle room when it comes to expressing his creativity. "I'm fortunate to have a couple of extra tanks and tap handles," he said. "So if I have tank space, I can draw up a

Beers brewed: Southern Flyer Light Lager, Southside Pilsner Lager, Toll Tender IPA, Sweet Magnolia American Brown Ale, Iron Horse Stout, and various seasonal and brewer's choice selections.

The Pick: The British-style sweet Iron Horse Stout delivers a full-bodied taste with just the right amount of chocolate notes. Drink it with dessert.

recipe and submit it, and then go from there and do my own thing, as long as I don't run out of house beers. I do have some freedom here, which is really nice, so I do that every chance I get. I do a few barrel-aged projects every year, none of which are corporate beers. I try to have a hand pull on every Thursday, none of which are corporate beers. It's fun. I get a lot of room to play while still doing the corporate stuff; I get a chance to do my own things, which is really nice." Nesbit also works with the kitchen, choosing brews for each course of the occasional beer dinner and matching new menu items with beer.

Seven Bridges works closely with the Jacksonville beer community. The local homebrew club, CASK, holds an annual interclub competition, and the winner brews his or her beer in the brewery. It's then served at an event in which the money raised from the beer's sale goes to a charity chosen by the homebrewer. Tied in with the fund-raiser is a pig roast, but the chefs don't just run down to the nearest butcher shop for the pig. The brewery donates its spent grain throughout the year to a local pig farmer, who in turn provides the main course. "People really love that," Nesbit said. Seven Bridges also has a mug club that regulars can join, which gives them their own mug and discounts on beers, food, and events.

Seven Bridges Grille & Brewery

Opened: 1999.

Owner: CraftWorks Restaurants & Breweries Inc.

Brewer: Aaron Nesbit.

System: 7-barrel Specific Mechanical Systems.

Annual production: 800 barrels.

Hours: Sunday through Thursday, 11 a.m. to midnight; Friday and Saturday 11 a.m. to 2 a.m.

Tours: On request.

Parking: Free on site.

Takeout beer: None.

Special considerations: Handicapped-accessible.

Extras: Two outdoor seating areas.

Other area beer sites: World of Beer–Southside, 9700 Deer Lake Court, Unit #1, Jacksonville, FL 32246, (904) 551-5929, wobusa.com/Locations/Southside.aspx; Mellow Mushroom Pizza Bakers, 9734 Deer Lake Court, Unit #1, Jacksonville, FL 32246, (904) 997-1955, mellowmushroom.com/store/Jacksonville.

Beer Chains

As craft beer continues its upward spiral into the sphere of mainstream con-sumer consciousness, entrepreneurs take note that those consumers seek watering holes where they might sample a wide variety of hand-crafted brews while sharing observations and conversation with fellow fans. In a market such as Florida, where the craft beer scene is rapidly expanding but still has large areas with few local breweries, such outlets provide nearby places where residents can find otherwise hard-to-obtain brews.

Some of these pubs and taverns in Florida have embraced good beer for a while: Mr. Dunderbak's in North Tampa (www.dunderbaks.com) and the Cock & Bull Pub (www.facebook.com/CnBpub) in Sarasota, both of which opened in the mid-1990s, come to mind. Others that opened more recently have found existing local markets eager to consume what they're providing. Still others, seeing the success of their initial endeavor, opened more outlets and became a chain. And, in some cases, chains that started in other states moved into Florida or vice versa to help supply the ever-increasing thirst for good beer. Following are descriptions of several beer chains operating in Florida.

World of Beer (wobusa.com) started in Westchase, a suburban neighborhood northwest of Tampa, in 2007. The combination of hundreds of craft beers on tap and in bottles, along with live music and special beer-centric events, proved so successful that others inquired into the possibility of opening franchises. At the time of this writing, nearly fifty World of Beer franchises were operating around the country, more than half of those in Florida.

The Brass Tap (brasstapbeerbar.com) was a three-store chain in the Tampa Bay area in 2007, each location offering more than three hundred different beers in an upscale atmosphere. Then in 2012, the operators of the Beef 'O' Brady's family sports bar chain, also based in Tampa, acquired the franchising rights to the Brass Tap and quickly got started expanding into other areas. As of this writing, the Brass Tap has eight locations in Florida, including the original three; one in Texas;

and twenty-nine additional locations set to open in the near future, including franchises in Texas, Maryland, and Ohio.

BJ's Restaurant and Brewhouse (www.bjsbrewhouse.com) is a California-based casual dining chain that first entered the Florida market in 2007 and has since added more than a dozen other locations throughout the state. Despite "Brewhouse" in its name, the restaurants in Florida brew only root beer on the premises. The "house brews" on tap are produced in six out-of-state breweries. Three are owned and operated by BJ's, and the others are contract breweries. The closest to Florida is Saint Arnold Brewing Company in Houston. Regardless, the restaurants serve a nice variety of the house beers and guest taps, along with pretty tasty food.

House of Beer is a small chain that started in February 2009 with the Dunedin House of Beer (www.dunedinhob.com). A second location, in Palm Harbor (www.palmharborhob.com), opened in September 2010, and exactly a year later, the Gainesville House of Beer (www.gainesville hob.com) came into being. Each bar has forty to fifty taps and dozens of bottles of craft beer from around the world and offers live music and other events throughout the week.

Miller's Ale House (www.millersalehouse.com) is a chain with about fifty locations in Florida. From the name, you might expect a large selection of local and national craft beers to be available at this chain. Unfortunately, though you may find Sam Adams seasonals, Rogue Dead Guy, or one or two other widely available crafts, the selection skews heavily toward mass-produced lagers and imports. But if you're happy with a bucket of macrobrews while you nosh on bar food and watch the games, you'll be just fine here.

Mellow Mushroom (mellowmushroom.com) is a pizza-and-beer joint specializing in local and national craft beers and imports, on tap and in bottles, along with its signature hand-tossed pizza. It started in a humble Atlanta storefront in 1974 and opened its first "friendchise" in 1982. Now dozens of the stores, with their unique art and décor, are spread across the country, mostly in the Southeast but as far west as Portland, Oregon. As of this writing, Florida had sixteen.

Central Florida

Let's play a quick word association game. If I say "Central Florida," what pops into your mind? Was it theme parks? Florida has plenty of them, and the biggest are clustered in the Greater Orlando area: Walt Disney World, Universal Studios Orlando, and SeaWorld Orlando. But ever since residents of the country's northern climes first came to the Sunshine State to escape their hellish winters, promoters and entrepreneurs have found ways to entertain these visitors while separating them from a bit of their money. Many of these older Central Florida "tourist traps" still exist. Some have been revived; others have seen better days.

I-4 bisects Central Florida, running west to east from downtown Tampa through Orlando, the seat of Orange County, and on to I-95 just west of Daytona Beach. The defining moment in Orlando's recent history began in the mid-1960s, when a group of newly formed companies began buying up acreage in the area. The man behind those companies was Walt Disney, and the purchased parcels became Walt Disney World. After it opened in 1971, the population of the Orlando metropolitan area boomed, other theme parks and attractions moved into the region, and tourism became its major economic driver. If you're interested in this part of Central Florida's history, *Realityland: True-Life Adventures at Walt Disney World* by David Koenig (Bonaventure Press, 2007) provides an excellent telling of the behind-the-scenes stories.

One tip if you plan on doing a lot of driving around the Orlando metropolitan area: have a lot of small bills and change on hand, because a network of limited-access toll roads weaves throughout the region. Though there are ways to avoid them, the nontoll roads are often choked with traffic, making the cost worthwhile if you dislike stop-and-go driving. The SunPass prepaid toll program sells transponders that automatically record and pay tolls, but unless you live here, it's likely not worth the cost.

Central Florida overflows with interesting little towns and communities more closely linked with the real world than are the theme parks, though Cassadaga might stretch the "reality" part a bit. This community, north of Orlando in Volusia County, is known as the "Psychic Capital of the World." A traveling medium by the name of George Colby was reportedly led to the site by his "spirit guides," and he founded a spiritualistic camp there in the late 1800s. The community's full title is Southern Cassadaga Spiritualist Camp Meeting Association, and it's technically a church and not a town. It now boasts all manner of resident psychics, mediums, and other New Age types.

The Central Florida region has several other towns of interest. Cedar Key (www.cedarkey.org) is an old fishing village in the Big Bend area of Florida, an unofficial name for the stretch where the state curves around the Gulf of Mexico between roughly Crystal River and Apalachee Bay. It still hosts an active fishing industry and retains an unspoiled charm that has attracted artists and writers who enjoy its isolation. You'll also find plenty of nature-oriented activities.

In Citrus County on the Gulf Coast, you can observe dozens of fish species and manatees in the wild from the underwater observatory nicknamed the Fish Bowl, installed in the 1940s at what is now the ***Ellie Schiller Homosassa Springs Wildlife State Park*** (www.homosassa springs.org). About thirty minutes south on U.S. 19, another 1940s private attraction turned state park, ***Weeki Wachee Springs*** (www.weeki wachee.com), lets you watch live mermaid shows from the comfort of a theater. The "mermaids" are actually humans in fishtail costumes, mostly women, who have learned to breathe underwater with the help of air hoses that dangle into the crystal-clear springs.

Mount Dora (www.visitmountdora.com) is in one of the hilliest areas of Florida, although there's not an actual mountain here. Located in Lake County, northwest of Orlando, the town of Mount Dora sits on a plateau 184 feet above sea level, providing panoramic views of the historic downtown on the shore of Lake Dora. Visitors fill the streets most weekends, visiting the plethora of antiques stores and other small businesses or enjoying one of the many outdoor festivals held there throughout the year.

Winter Park (cityofwinterpark.org) is a northern Orlando suburb founded in the late nineteenth century as a winter resort for wealthy easterners. During Prohibition, it gained a reputation as a home to speakeasies and the accompanying clientele and "proprietors," but today it's a tony community with a variety of cool restaurants, art galleries and museums, and plenty of parks.

Other Old Florida attractions found throughout the region include *Gatorland* in Kissimmee (www.gatorland.com); the *Citrus Tower* (www.citrustower.com) and the *Presidents Hall of Fame* (www.the presidentshalloffame.com) in Clermont; and *Bok Tower Gardens* (boktowergardens.org) in Lake Wales, with its 205-foot-tall art deco Singing Tower carillon. Over on the Atlantic coast, the *Kennedy Space Center Visitor Complex* (www.kennedyspacecenter.com) provides a fascinating look at the U.S. space program with exhibits of actual spacecraft, including the shuttle orbiter Atlantis, presentations, and interactive exhibits. Though the shuttle program has been shelved, unmanned rockets still launch from the center; check the website for schedules.

Long stretches of coastline bookend the Central Florida region. On the "left coast," you'll find the gentle swells of the Gulf of Mexico kissing the sands, though the actual beaches are fewer and farther between than in South Florida. Instead, you'll find a lot of kayak-friendly mangrove wetlands, waterfront parks, and fishing communities. The inshore waters are great for manatee and dolphin watching, fishing, and scalloping, when it's in season, and there are plenty of local businesses that will be happy to guide you.

The Atlantic coast, on the other hand, has seemingly endless miles of white sand beaches and pounding waves that call to surfers. Driving along the coast, you'll find extensive expanses of nearly deserted shoreline punctuated by the popular tourist destinations of Daytona Beach (daytonabeach.com) and Cocoa Beach (www.cocoabeach.com), as well as countless other small beach towns. Daytona Beach is home to the famous Daytona International Speedway (www.daytonainternational speedway.com), a haven for spring breakers, and host to motorcycle enthusiasts during Bike Week in March and Biketoberfest in October (www.officialbikeweek.com).

So though the Orlando-area theme parks certainly bring folks to the state, you'll find plenty of other things to do and see in Central Florida when you're not visiting its breweries.

Alligator Brewing Co.

10 Southeast Second Avenue, Gainesville, FL 32601
(352) 505-0990 • www.facebook.com/TallPaulsBrewHouse

10 SE 2nd ave Gainesville FL

Alligator Brewing Co. operates out of Tall Paul's Brew House in downtown Gainesville. So the first question is, just how tall is Paul Evans? "Six foot seven," he said. "Anyone taller than me gets a free pint, but I have to be here to prove it."

According to Evans, a chance meeting in Cape Cod, Massachusetts, with family friend Fred Forsley, founder of Shipyard Brewing Company, started him on the road to opening his own brewpub. "I'd always had this dream of opening a brewpub, but I didn't really know much about brewing," he said. "I knew I liked craft beer; I'd always been a big fan of that in college." So he approached Forsley for ideas. That "turned into an apprenticeship," Evans said, "where I worked in Shipyard from August of 2007 to March of 2008, doing all aspects of the brewing process from the cold room to the brewhouse to the bottling lines, and marketing and promotion." He offered to be a brewery representative for Shipyard and sister brewery Sea Dog Brewing Co., and in March 2008, he started covering the territory in Florida that encompassed Gainesville, Tallahassee, and Jacksonville. He spent two years learning the ins and outs of the local bar and beer scenes.

In 2010, Evans decided it was time to open his own bar and brewery. But first he had to find a place to do it. Among the spaces he considered was an old brick building that was constructed in 1880 as a carriage house for the Gainesville Fire Department and had been a pool hall and parking garage after that, among other things. "I found it in 2010 and ended up walking away from the building because it was so dilapidated," Evans said. "But dealing with the landlord a little bit more and getting a good twenty-year lease with a fixed rate, I was able to get some deductions based on the improvements that we made." Evans put out the word that he sought a brewmaster, and he hired Neal Mackowiak.

The renovation began, emphasizing the use of recyclable and recycled materials throughout. Transforming a 130-year-old shell of a building into a working brewery and bar meant tearing up a good deal of the concrete slab, installing new plumbing and electrical systems—and the

Beers brewed: Eight to ten Alligator brews. Styles vary.

The Pick: The offerings change, but you can't go wrong ordering whichever IPA is on tap.

brewery—and building all the interior features. The work paid off. The restoration earned Tall Paul's a 2011 Gainesville City Beautification Award.

The brewpub's location in downtown Gainesville, not far from the University of Florida, ensures a steady clientele flow of students, professors, staff, alumni, and visitors to the campus. The wall behind the long, curved bar is painted "Gator orange" in homage to the UF mascot. A large alligator preserved through the magic of taxidermy holds court from a raised platform, posed and proudly holding an orange-and-blue Gators flag. Exposed wooden beams, ductwork, and painted brick attest to the structure's age. Sturdy, hand-built wooden tables, benches, and picnic tables scattered about the space offer plenty of seating. The twenty-nine taps usually have eight to ten Alligator brews, with the rest being guest taps from other craft breweries, many from Florida.

Evans and Mackowiak were still searching for their flagship brews. "Neal is very creative," Evans said. "He's combined many styles at once. Like instead of a brown ale, a brown wheat porter and a black imperial stout that could almost be an IPA. One of our most popular beers—it won a gold medal this year—was the smoked habañero ale, which is an amber ale." Establishing the flagships will help create a base for the brewery's growth, one of Evans's goals. At the time of this writing, Evans expected a trio of recently acquired 500-liter fermenting tanks to quadruple output. But that's just a baby step. "We should be with the big boys sometime in the future," Evans said, "but on our own path."

Alligator Brewing Co.

Opened: 2011.

Owner: Paul Evans.

Brewer: Neal Mackowiak.

System: 1.5-barrel More Beer brew system with Burton Union Fermentation system.

Annual production: 200 barrels.

Hours: Monday through Saturday, 4 p.m. to 2 a.m.

Tours: On request, if someone is available.

Parking: Free, on street.

Takeout beer: None.

Special considerations: Handicapped-accessible.

Extras: Mug club; various games, including play-free classic arcade games and a giant Connect Four.

Other area beer sites: Stubbies & Steins, 9 W. University Ave., Gainesville, FL 32601, (352) 384-1261, www.stubbiesandsteins.com; House of Beer, 19 W. University Ave., Gainesville, FL 32601, (352) 376-1100, www.gainesvillehob.com.

Big River Grille & Brewing Works

2101 North Epcot Resort Boulevard,
Lake Buena Vista, FL 32830
(407) 560-0253 • www.bigrivergrille.com

It's one of Disney's best-kept secrets: a working brewpub on Disney World's property. Don't expect to see Mickey bending elbows there with Donald, though you might spy the big mouse on occasion strolling by the pub. "I see him walk down the boardwalk for weddings now and then," said head brewer Kent Waugh, which makes him stop and think about the fact he brews beer in the "Most Magical Place on Earth." "It always reminds me, here I am at work, and there's the official Mickey Mouse standing over there, in a tuxedo of all things."

Big River is owned by Chattanooga, Tennessee, based CraftWorks Restaurants & Breweries Inc. and, for the most part, operates independently of Disney in the entertainment company's BoardWalk Inn, a sprawling resort on Crescent Lake. Big River is neighbor to a variety of shops, restaurants, and clubs along the Coney Island–style boardwalk on the lakeshore and is a short walk or boat launch ride to the Epcot and Disney's Hollywood Studios theme parks.

Waugh started his brewing career as a home-brewer while living in the craft beer mecca of Colorado—in Breckenridge, specifically. "My buddy got me started," he said. "We brewed a Newcastle clone, a 5-gallon extract, then tasted it in a blind tasting and couldn't tell the difference. Here we go, I thought." His homebrewing led to a job at Boulder Beer, as one of the guys at the end of the bottling line. In his three years there, he eventually worked his way up to the brewhouse, then six or seven months later, he landed a job as head brewer at the Overland Stage Stop Brewery in nearby Longmont, where he brewed for about a year and a half until it shut down.

After that, Waugh stayed out of the brewing business for a while, taking a bit of an itinerant path in such fields as horse ranching and construction. Then his wife's job took the family to Central Florida. He wanted to open his own brewery, but

Beers brewed: Southern Flyer Light Lager, Gadzooks Pilsner, Steamboat Pale Ale, Rocket Red Ale, IPA, and various specialties and brewer's select options. Seasonals: Summer Wheat and Sweet Magnolia American Brown Ale.

The Pick: If you're lucky enough to visit the brewpub when Soleil IPA is on tap, grab it. It's a hoppy, refreshing brew that brings to mind a West Coast IPA, but with a bit more malt backbone. If it's not there, the award-winning Rocket Red would be the Pick.

then he saw an ad for the brewmaster position at Big River. "I sent my résumé on a Friday night, and they gave me the job the following Monday," he said. That was in 2010, and he's been there since.

The family-friendly brewpub provides visitors a welcome midday respite from hectic days at the Disney parks or a place to wind down at the end the day with dinner and a few cold, hand-crafted brews. Big River has a great partnership with the Disney folks, Waugh said. "It helps us by having a name at Disney, on the website; having that kind of connection with Disney, it's kind of a green light that 'They're OK. Go there and check them out.'" It's not bad for business, either. "We make more money per square foot than any other brewery in our company because, for one, we're so small, but there's also the Disney foot traffic."

As of this writing, plans were being discussed for remodeling the brewpub and possibly rebranding it as a Rock Bottom restaurant and brewery, another of the labels under the CraftWorks umbrella. No timetable had been set, but anyone looking for Big River in the future may need to keep that in mind. According to Waugh, however, the brewing operation will definitely remain.

Big River Grille & Brewing Works

Opened: 1996.

Owner: CraftWorks Restaurants & Breweries Inc.

Brewer: Kent Waugh.

System: 10-barrel Pacific Brewing System Technologies.

Annual production: 900 barrels.

Hours: Sunday through Thursday, 11 a.m. to 11 p.m.; Friday and Saturday, 11 a.m. to midnight.

Tours: On request.

Parking: Free in Boardwalk resort parking lot.

Takeout beer: None.

Special considerations: Handicapped-accessible.

Extras: Outdoor waterfront seating on boardwalk; seasonal release parties.

Cask & Larder Southern Brewery & Kitchen

565 West Fairbanks Avenue, Winter Park, FL 32789
(321) 280-4200 • www.caskandlarder.com

It's said that the key to good beer is good water. Cask & Larder brewmaster Ron Raike believes that strongly, but he's not content with the water readily available in Winter Park. Sure, it might make great-tasting beer, but it would not be authentic to the styles he produces. So through the judicious use of reverse osmosis to filter out unwanted minerals and chemicals and adding others, he tries to precisely re-create the profile and chemistry of the water in the region or brewery in which the style originated. For instance, he'll duplicate Munich's water for his German beers and that of Southern California for his IPAs and pale ales.

The Cask & Larder concept sprang from its nearby sister restaurant, the Ravenous Pig, owned by James and Julie Petrakis, James Beard–nominated chefs. Since its opening in 2007, the gastropub has garnered international recognition for both its seasonal and locally sourced recipes and its list of high-quality beers. When they decided to open a brewpub, the Petrakises hired Raike to help develop the brewery side of the operation, which they later named the Ravenous Brewing Co.

Raike's brewing roots stretch back more than two decades. He was studying engineering at the University of Central Florida and homebrewing when he decided that his passion for making beer gave him the thirst to do it full-time. Shipyard hired him as brewmaster at its newly opened brewpub in Orlando International Airport, a role he held until the airport declined to renew the lease after five years. He then moved into the distribution and marketing side for Shipyard until the Portland, Maine, based brewery opened the Shipyard Brew Pub in Winter Park. He served as head brewer there but eventually was lured over to the same role just down the street at Cask & Larder.

Beers brewed: Lone Palm Golden Ale, Olde Southern Red Wit, Five Points IPA, Broken Ladder Pale Ale, Weissbier, Sour Puss, Happy Camper, American Barleywine, and various specials. Seasonals: Hammertime, a smoked ham beer; All Jacked Up pumpkin beer; Summer Saison; and Shifty, a 10.5 percent ABV Belgian strong ale brewed for the staff's "shift" beer.

The Pick: Five Points IPA, named after the intersection in front of the brewpub, gives the drinker an authentic-tasting West Coast IPA experience with just the right balance of malts to temper the hop bitterness.

According to the pub's website, the building was converted from a failing feed store into a tavern in 1929, in the "waning days of Prohibition," which means, technically, it was at first a speakeasy, surreptitiously serving unlawful hooch to the residents of Winter Park. On the wall is a black-and-white photo from those days, showing customers peeking out from behind curtained booths. "Ring the bell and the server would bring out whatever bottle you wanted," Raike said.

When the Petrakises took over, it was a tavern that had seen better days, with darkly tinted front windows that let little light through. They gutted it on the inside, removed the tint, and built the brewery and restaurant. The new lighting and décor turned the space into a bright and cheery place. "James put a lot of money and effort into the lighting, the aesthetics," Raike said. "At night, it really has a nice, positive feeling to it."

The emphasis on using locally sourced products extends to the brewing. When Raike makes a beer that uses citrus, tropical fruit, or other ingredients that can be bought from local farms, that's where he goes to get it. The most noteworthy food-and-beer-pairing occasions at the Cask & Larder are the whole cookery dinners. A group can reserve a table behind the glass wall that separates the brewhouse from the bar area and feast on signature butchered cuts, such as suckling pig or smoked duck, along with side dishes and desserts, with freshly brewed beer available to wash it down.

Cask & Larder Southern Brewery & Kitchen

Opened: 2012.

Owners: James & Julie Petrakis, chef-owners; Tracy Lindskoog and Dennis Bernard, managing partners.

Brewer: Ron Raike.

System: 5-barrel Premier stainless.

Annual production: To be determined.

Hours: Monday through Saturday, 4 p.m. to midnight; Sunday, 10:30 a.m. to 10 p.m.

Tours: On request, if someone is available.

Parking: Free on site and complimentary valet.

Takeout beer: None.

Special considerations: Handicapped-accessible.

Other area beer sites: Fiddler's Green Irish Pub & Eatery, 544 W. Fairbanks Ave., Winter Park, FL 32789, (407) 645-2050, www.fiddlersgreenorlando.com.

Charlie & Jake's Brewery Grille

6300 North Wickham Road, #137, Melbourne, FL 32940
(321) 752-7675 • www.cjbrewery.com

A visitor walking through the entrance door of Charlie & Jake's is immediately assaulted, but only in a sensory way. Televisions throughout the bar, restaurant area, and outdoor patio broadcast the plethora of sports stations available these days. The mouthwatering smell of slow-smoked meat wafts throughout the brewpub, accompanied on brew days by the sweet scent of boiling wort. Order a flight of the freshly made brew to complete the assault with your palate. So is it a sports bar, a barbecue joint, or a brewery? The answer: yes to all three.

"We do consider ourselves a small brewery," said general manager Andy Pinkerton. People visit Charlie & Jake's from out of state and even across the country for the beer. "We still get quite a few coming through, not only for the beer, but they've heard about our barbecue as well," he said. The sports fans have their place too, especially during football season.

It's the kind of joint where a visitor is greeted with typical southern hospitality, and a regular is greeted with a pint of his favorite brew, poured while he's walking to his usual spot at the bar. Pinkerton estimated that the customer base is about 80 percent local, and the other 20 percent fluctuates with the seasons. "Our busiest time is when the snowbirds are down," he said. "But our business as a whole is not completely predicated on it. There are a lot of great schools in the area, a lot of great communities in the area. We do have enough population in this area to sustain a good business year-round, but when those snowbirds come down, it sure does increase things quite a bit."

It's not far from industries in Brevard County that support the space program. In fact, you might just find yourself rubbing elbows with a rocket scientist at the bar, though with the government phasing out its support of NASA, the chance of that happening is not as great as in the past. "We have been very lucky over the last fifteen years with the space program being right next door," Pinkerton said.

Beers brewed: Anniversary Ale, Brown Bottom Ale, Harbor City Gold, Indian River Red, Wickham Wheat Ale, and one to two seasonals a month.

The Pick: The highly hopped Anniversary Ale goes perfectly with the obligatory plate of North Carolina–style barbecue that you will find necessary to order after being assaulted by the sweet scent of smoking meat.

Charlie & Jake's wants to keep its customers happy, running specials on food or beer most every weeknight. It has promotions typical of other eateries: kids' night on Thursday, when youngsters eat for a discount, and all-you-can-eat catfish on Friday. But Wednesday is special: It's Fill Your Mug night, when patrons can bring in their own beer mugs—any size up to a liter—and get it filled all night for $4.25 (per fill) with any of the house brews. It's also Wing Night, with 45-cent wings, and Pinkerton said the combination of hot wings and cold beer "brings in a pretty good crowd."

Though expansion is never completely off the table, Pinkerton doesn't anticipate Charlie & Jake's growing out of its space in the corner of a strip mall. "We're able to produce enough beer to sustain a healthy flow of different beers here," he said. "If we were to expand, it would probably mean expanding the brewery outside of these four walls. We really love our brewery here and what we do, so maybe we haven't taken as proactive an approach to expand as other places because we're pretty content with what we have here."

Charlie & Jake's Brewery Grille

Opened: 1996.

Owners: Steve McGann and Mike Fischer.

Brewer: Todd Furbeck.

System: 7-barrel New World Brewing Systems.

Annual production: Estimated 550 barrels.

Hours: Monday through Thursday, 11 a.m. to 10 p.m.; Friday and Saturday, 11 a.m. to 11 p.m.; Sunday, noon to 9 p.m.

Tours: On request, Monday through Friday, 11 a.m. to 5 p.m.

Parking: Free on site.

Takeout beer: None.

Special considerations: Handicapped-accessible.

Extras: Outdoor bar and seating.

Cocoa Beach Brewing Company

150 North Atlantic Avenue, Cocoa Beach, FL 32931
(321) 613-2941 • www.cocoabeachbrewingcompany.com

It's very likely that Cocoa Beach Brewing Company is the only brewery to have been featured in *Air & Space/Smithsonian* magazine. "Its tasting room frequently fills with scientists and engineers from nearby launch facilities talking shop about payloads over pints of the brewery's Von Braun Ale," the March 2012 story says. Or, as one of the brewery's bumper stickers says, "Brewing Doesn't Take a Rocket Scientist . . . (but we have them anyway)."

The U.S. space program figures prominently at the brewery, located across the street from the beach. Mission patches and photos signed by astronauts decorate the walls in an eclectic blend with beach and beer paraphernalia. Every time a launch takes place during operating hours, all the customers put down their beers and step outside, the doors are locked, and everyone walks across the street to the beach to watch the spacecraft pierce the heavens.

The place is divided between two small bungalows that originally were built in the 1930s as navy housing for the Banana River Naval Air Station. One bungalow houses the brewery; the other is the taproom. It's not particularly spacious—four or five stools at the bar, a few tables, and some plush brown leather couches in the entry room—but the customers are friendly and welcoming, and the beer is fresh and cold.

Founder, owner, and brewer Chris McCall is proud that his place is the Space Coast's "astronaut bar," and this is reflected not only in the décor and beer names, but also on brew day. "We're one of the most state-of-the-art little breweries you'll ever run into," he said. "One of the benefits of being right next to the Space Center is most of my volunteers are rocket scientists, and that's a good thing and a bad thing. Every time they're here, they basically want to reengineer something, and they're used to working with an unlimited budget, or at least a budget of hundreds

Beers brewed: Cocoa Beach Pale Ale, Cocoa Beach Key Lime Cerveza, Cocoa Beach Dirty Blonde, "Not Just Some" Oatmeal Stout, 888 India Pale Ale, Sofa King Double IPA, Matt's Special Bitter, and Von Braun Ale. Seasonal: Cocoa Beach Oktoberfest Lager.

The Pick: They call the 888 an India pale ale, but even the most avid hophead might categorize this as a double IPA. Brewed with Columbus and Centennial hops, it clocks in at 8 percent ABV. Be careful, because it doesn't taste that strong.

of millions. Twenty-five hundred dollars for a control panel seems like a bargain to them, but it's a big deal to me."

McCall keeps one of the neatest techno-gizmos for brewing in his pocket. He installed and customized a brewery control system, or BCS, designed for homebrewers and small breweries, which connects to a private computer network to control many of the routine aspects of the brewing process. He can call up the interface on his iPhone. "We run the entire brewery off my iPhone," he said. "All the processes are automated. We still have to dump the grain in and still have to throw some valves, but we have it set up by process, like hot liquor tank fill, hot liquor tank heat, mash, refill, sparge, boil. I'll set everything up for brewing the day before, get the hot liquor tank full of water the day before, all the switches set to auto, and then set the timer for twelve hours, say like six o'clock in the morning. It's already starting to make hot water and starting to pump, so when I come in, we're in the mash." But what if a hose pops loose when no one's around? "That's the one thing that we're usually paranoid about," he said. "Want to make sure that you tighten up the clamps."

Cocoa Beach Brewing Company

Opened: 2009.

Owners: Chris and Tracy McCall.

Brewers: Chris McCall and volunteers.

System: 4-barrel custom-built brewhouse.

Annual production: 125 barrels.

Hours: Monday through Thursday, 1 to 9 p.m.; Friday and Saturday, 1 to 11 p.m.; Sunday, noon to 6 p.m.

Tours: On request if someone's available.

Parking: Free on site and on the street.

Takeout beer: Bottles and growlers.

Special considerations: Handicapped-accessible.

Extras: Outdoor seating; great view of rocket launches from Kennedy Space Center.

Other area beer sites: Coasters Pub & Biergarten, 971A E. Eau Gallie Blvd., Melbourne, FL 32937, (321) 779-2739, www.coastersbrewpub.com.

Copp Winery & Brewery

11 Northeast Fourth Avenue, Crystal River, FL 34429
(352) 564-9463 • www.coppbrewery.com

Fran Copp is a self-confessed tinkerer. The proclivity stems from growing up on a Pennsylvania dairy farm, with all its equipment and the maintenance required to keep it running. "We always had to fix everything, so I did all the electrical, the plumbing," Copp told me. His parents grew up during the Depression and had to learn to make do. "You learn to do a lot with a little, so you finagle a lot of things." Copp's father also ran a John Deere business in the 1940s. "I grew up with all these John Deere parts and leftovers, and that's what I made go-carts out of growing up," he said. "So it was always having gears and things to play with and to build because we didn't have much money. If I wanted a new bike, I'd have to weld a new bike up."

After earning a mathematics degree in college in 1985, Copp went into the fitness business, managing gyms and such. He moved to Crystal River to manage a General Nutrition Center store. He also took up kickboxing and competed in and won regional powerlifting and bodybuilding contests—the clean way, with no drugs. In 1999, he entered the American Natural Bodybuilding Conference national championship in the men's masters division. He won. In the meantime, he had started teaching advanced placement calculus at a local high school, which he still does.

In 2006, he and his wife, Donna, opened Copp Winery. Donna, with imported grapes, made and bottled the wine, and Fran made everything else— the bar, bottle racks, and furniture—because his tinkering skills extended to carpentry and woodworking. Then, after years of homebrewing, he decided to bring his beer to the public, and in 2012, he opened the brewery side of the business. Literally. One side of the business is the brewery and taproom. The other, larger side is the winery operation and its tasting room.

Beers brewed: True Grit Pale Ale, Double Black Stout, Center Field Brown Ale, 1821 English IPA, Hoppy Copp IPA, and various specialties and seasonals.

The Pick: True Grit Pale Ale. Brewed with 30 pounds of cooked corn grits in each barrel, this tasty pale ale is especially thirst-quenching, with a clean, crisp taste and just enough sweetness from the grits to leave a pleasant aftertaste on the palate.

Visiting Copp Winery & Brewery feels like visiting someone's home. Sure, the fact that it's in a converted mid-1960s wood frame bungalow contributes to that, but it's also the welcoming atmosphere of the Copps and their regulars. In some ways, Fran merely moved his taps from his "man cave" at home, where he served his homebrews to friends and neighbors for years, to a new spot. Most of those friends and neighbors moved along with him. It's a mainly local crowd of regulars, but it's not uncommon that someone who has heard about it through the grapevine pops in one night, then returns the next weekend and the weekend after that, and before you know it, this person has become a regular too. "We're a place right now that people can come and have a beer, have a glass of wine before they go to dinner," Copp said. "And that's what we want."

But he's never done tinkering. There's always an ongoing project, whether it's a new beer, some custom brewing gizmo he's putting together, or upgrades and maintenance to the building. He's planning to install even larger tanks and add more cold storage, and he's been talking to distributors about sending his product out to other bars. He's been eyeing other property for possible expansion.

The brewery will be what he focuses on after he retires from teaching, he said. "I'm not one to retire and sit. I like to fish and things, but for me, I'd still like someplace where I can talk to people, so to me this is kind of a semiretirement," he said. "If you can call forty-eight hours a week semiretirement."

Copp Winery & Brewery

Opened: Winery in 2007, brewery in 2012.

Owners: Fran and Donna Copp.

Brewer: Fran Copp.

System: 1 barrel custom.

Annual production: 150 barrels.

Hours: Wednesday and Thursday, noon to 9 p.m.; Friday and Saturday, noon to 11 p.m.; Sunday, 1 to 6 p.m.

Tours: On request, if someone's available.

Parking: On site and nearby lots.

Takeout beer: Growlers.

Special considerations: Handicapped-accessible.

Extras: Outdoor deck.

Other area beer sites: Burkes of Ireland, 564 N. Citrus Ave., Crystal River, FL 34428, (352) 795-0956, burkesofireland.com.

Florida Beer Company

200 Imperial Boulevard, Cape Canaveral, FL 32920
(321) 728-4114 • www.floridabeer.com

To say Florida Beer Company was in a state of transition when I visited might be an understatement. After nearly fifteen years of brewing out of a facility in Melbourne, Florida, it was in the process of moving about 25 miles north on Highway A1A to new digs in the town of Cape Canaveral. The tasting room in the Melbourne brewery had been shut down, though brewing was still going on, and the new brewery and tasting room had not yet opened, though brewing had started there.

"We have moved into the Cape Canaveral brewery; we have a 60,000-square-foot facility there," marketing director Eulan Middlebrooks explained. "We're going to have a 5,000-square-foot tasting room with a 90-barrel brewhouse. We just got new bottling lines that are already close to up and running. We're still waiting for the tasting room and still waiting for the bottling line to be fully functional before we move everything up there."

Middlebrooks spoke with me at the old Florida Beer offices building, surrounded by moving boxes, stacks of posters, signs, and other promotional material waiting to be transferred to the new building. No one other than employees and construction workers was allowed to visit the new brewery at the time, so he described to me the future tasting room: "It's circular, and it's windowed out so you'll be able to see all the operations of the brewery," he said. "Unlike our old tasting room, where it was just samples, you'll be able to sit there and enjoy a pint. We can give tours, and we'll have special rooms. Should be a nice, cool, relaxed place to hang out and have a beer. When you walk in there, you will feel like you are in Florida." It will be almost literally a stone's throw from Port Canaveral, with its heavy cruise ship traffic, so the brewery likely will get an influx of customers from across the country and around the world.

Beers brewed: Florida Lager, Swamp Ape DIPA, Gaspar's Porter, Devil's Triangle IPA, Key West Sunset Ale, Key West Southernmost Wheat, and Hurricane Reef Pale Ale. Seasonal: Conchtoberfest.

The Pick: Florida Beer Company released its reformulated Gaspar's Porter in early 2013, using eight different malts—four of them specialty chocolate malts—and the improvement is remarkable. The resulting brew pours smooth and creamy, with rich chocolate tones and just a little spicy kick from the hops.

Florida Beer Company is the Sunshine State's largest craft brewery by volume, but it started small. Originally the Indian River Brewing Company, it first opened in 1997, and then, as was the case with many of the microbreweries in that era, it started struggling financially. Jim Massoni took it over in 2003, and it became a bit of a "Pac-Man" brewery, gobbling up other small operations in Florida: Ybor City Brewing Company out of Tampa and the Key West and Hurricane Reef Breweries in Miami. All were consolidated under the umbrella of the newly named Florida Beer Company.

"We still carry Key West, Ybor, and Hurricane Reef," Middlebrooks said. "We dropped Indian River; we still have the labels around, but they're not out in the market. We also have Kelly's Hard Cider, probably the first brewery in Florida to do hard cider." The brewery started releasing new beers to the market in 2010, the first being Swamp Ape, a double IPA, followed by Florida Lager, the fall seasonal Conchtoberfest, Devil's Triangle IPA, and Gaspar's Porter, which is an old Ybor City Brewing label. The porter itself, though, is a new recipe.

Before long, Florida Beer simply ran out of room, which is why it's moving to the new location, the former Chrysler Corporation Ballistic Missile and Space Activities building. Once everything is in place, the company plans to introduce even more brands and styles. "We'll have more flexibility," Middlebrooks said. "We're going to make an effort to really start coming out with some more challenging beers, using a little more creativity. This facility is going to allow us to do that."

Florida Beer Company

Opened: 1997.
Owner: Jim Massoni.
Brewers: Jack Owen and Jose Ayala.
System: 90-barrel Krones.
Annual production: To be determined.
Hours: Seven days a week, hours to be determined.
Tours: Available.
Parking: Free on site.
Takeout beer: Bottles, kegs, and growlers.
Special considerations: Handicapped-accessible.
Extras: Planned are food truck events, local arts and music, beer dinners, and beer schools.

The Hourglass Brewery

255 South Ronald Reagan Boulevard,
Longwood, FL 32750
(407) 262-0056 • thehourglassbrewery.com

If variety is the spice of life, the Hourglass Brewery is downright fiery. "The whole idea of this place is variety. It will be new and different every time you show up," brewer Sky Conley told me. "The special's different every day, the food truck is different every week, the art is different every month. It's a whole new experience every time you come."

Located in Longwood in Seminole County, on the northern fringes of the Orlando metropolitan area, Hourglass found its customer base thirsty for locally brewed beer, as demonstrated on opening day, August 11, 2012, when more than fifteen hundred people showed up. "We shut down the street and hired cops, food trucks all lined down the street, we had five bands performing," Conley said. "It was a really fun day because there were zero problems—other than almost running out of beer. We had ninety kegs, and went through eight-two kegs, so I was afraid I would have to shut down the second day, but we had just enough beer to stay open the next day. It was fun."

Opening the brewery was a leap of faith for Conley and his business partner, Brett Mason. They had been homebrewing for years, and when the economy went south, they started thinking about taking it to the next level. "So we took the plunge," Conley said. "We had jobs at the time, then took about two to three years of planning just to get it open. We quit our jobs just the day before we opened and crossed our fingers." It seems to have worked. At the time of this writing, the Hourglass Brewery had just celebrated its first anniversary with another overflow crowd.

When looking for a location, they wanted to stay in Seminole County, in part because there was no other brewery there. "Longwood ended up being our stop because we were trying to find a place that already had existing floor drains and that already had the setup that we needed," Conley explained. "We didn't have disposable income to spend on rent and power and electricity, water, and all that for nine months before we even

Beers brewed: Plenty. No regular flagships.

The Pick: Take your pick. The beers on tap are constantly changing. Choose a style you're fond of, and you'll likely be happy with it.

opened. We ended up here because a catering company before had already set it up the way we wanted, and overhead was low. So it got us by. I think we ended up running the place almost a year before we had opening day."

"Here" is a modest wood frame building behind another, larger wood frame building. The tasting room takes up an even more modest space in the front of the building. A perpetually unfinished mural in a style that's sort of a cross between sci-fi fanboy art and R. Crumb alt comics seeks to fill the empty spaces on the wall. Works from the local "artist of the month" hang in the taproom.

Art might be in the building's DNA, as it hosted an artist decades before it was a catering company. "I heard it was a bed-and-breakfast in front of us, and this was the kitchen," Conley said. "Before that, I heard it was an exotic bird store. And before that, it was a painting studio where Bob Ross took classes and ended up teaching how to paint in here." That would be the late Bob Ross, a Central Florida native who gained fame as the host of the PBS series *The Joy of Painting*.

Customers who discover a favorite beer at Hourglass might want to enjoy it while they are there, because it could be a while before that particular beer returns. Conley describes their philosophy as "ADD brewing," saying "We're all about trying new beer after new beer after new beer. It's kind of our quest for new flavor. Every two weeks, the menu's different. We're just constantly making one-offs."

The Hourglass Brewery

Opened: 2012.
Owners: Lance Butterfield, Sky Conley, and Brett Mason.
Brewers: Sky Conley and Brett Mason.
System: 3-barrel Stout Brewing Equipment.
Annual production: Estimated 180 barrels.
Hours: Sunday through Thursday, noon to midnight; Friday and Saturday, noon to 2 a.m.
Tours: Daily at 6 p.m. or on request.
Parking: Free on site.
Takeout beer: Growlers.
Special considerations: Handicapped-accessible.
Extras: Outdoor beer garden; specials every day.

Lagniappe Brewing Company

effinheimer

60 Center Street, Minneola, FL 34715
(352) 243-4149 • effinheimerbeer.com

Lagniappe Brewing Company has taken a different path from other Florida craft breweries on growth tracks that aim to boost the volume of its beer in the market. It's pulled back, going from an 8.5-barrel brewing system to a nano-size 55-gallon system. "We've downsized a little bit just so we can rotate our beers a lot quicker, try some experiments and some new beers," said Ricardo Altman, taproom manager and assistant brewer. "We just brew a little more often. We really never got to capacity with the old system we had, so it was kind of an overkill for what we needed."

The brewery in the small Central Florida town of Minneola was founded in 2009 by Brad Banker, who had gone on hiatus from his electrical engineering career to go pro with his homebrewing hobby, opening Lagniappe, a Cajun French word from his roots in Louisiana that translates to "a little something extra." Banker has since returned to electrical engineering work while letting Altman and other staffers take care of the day-to-day operation of the brewery.

Taking up two units of a strip mall off the main drag of U.S. 27, Lagniappe produces its beer under the Effinheimer brand, using the motto: "Don't Drink Vulgar Beer—Drop an Effinheimer!" One unit houses the brewing equipment, separated from the tasting room by a glass wall so customers can see it without having to leave air-conditioned comfort. The tasting room has a small bar and several tables scattered about. The crowd, Altman told me, is a mix of locals, folks who heard about the brewery through social media and Google searches, and a drop-in crowd lured in by the big "Brewery" sign on the back of the building, highly visible to southbound traffic on the busy highway.

At any time, you can find up to nine or ten Effinheimer beers on tap—none from other breweries—and most of them are full-bodied brews ranging from 5.5 to 10 percent ABV or more. "Sometimes

Beers brewed: Effinheimer Porter, Effinheimer Red Ale, Effinheimer India Pale Ale, and Effinheimer Afterglow Double IPA. Seasonals: Belgian Tripel, Oktoberfest, Winter Ale, Hefeweizen.

The Pick: The Afterglow Double IPA is redolent with grapefruit and piney aromas, and the nearly 8 percent ABV gives the drinker the pleasant afterglow promised by the name.

we do a lighter one, like now we have a cream ale that's made with brewers corn flakes," Altman said. "But most everything we have is 5.5 percent and up."

Customers can purchase six-packs of 12-ounce bottles to go or, if available, kegs for their home tap systems. Kegs are also distributed to some area bars and restaurants. Because of the downsizing, Lagniappe does not participate too often in beer festivals, but those attending local charity fund-raisers and community events often will find a tap or two of Effinheimer available.

For the most part, the best place to taste the brew is in the tasting room, where it's fresher and you can talk about the beer with Altman or Banker, when one of them is there. No food normally is sold at the brewery, though customers are welcome to bring in their own, and there are occasional special events where catered food is available. Local musicians play live on Wednesday nights.

Just because the brewery has cut back its capacity does not mean it is not meeting demand, Altman said. "We still distribute—we supply the beer that we need. If at one point we decide to distribute a lot more than we are now, we'll contract brew or something like that."

Lagniappe Brewing Company

Opened: 2009.

Owner: Brad Banker.

Brewers: Brad Banker and Ricardo Altman.

System: 55-gallon Blichmann.

Annual production: To be determined.

Hours: Monday through Saturday, 11 a.m. to 10 p.m.

Tours: On request.

Parking: Free on site.

Takeout beer: 12-ounce bottles.

Special considerations: Handicapped-accessible.

Extras: Brew Crew mug club.

Other area beer sites: World of Beer–Clermont, 2385 S. Highway 27, Clermont, FL 34711, (352) 241-9797, wobusa.com/Locations/Clermont.aspx.

Mount Dora Brewing and the Rocking Rabbit Brewery

405 South Highland Street, Mount Dora, FL 32757
(352) 406-2924 • www.mountdorabrewing.com

"Everything in here has a story," said Jeff Herbst. But first, perhaps it should be explained that even though Mount Dora Brewing and the Rocking Rabbit Brewery claims it serves "Florida's only mountain-brewed beer," that's technically not correct, seeing as how the small Central Florida town is only 184 feet above sea level. Though fairly lofty for Florida, Mount Dora falls a bit short of being an actual mountain.

Herbst, the brewery's founder, owner, and brewmaster, knows all the stories. For instance, the town and nearby lake were named after Dora Ann Drawdy (1819–85), who hosted federal surveyors in the mid-1800s. They thought so much of the woman that they named the town and lake after her. Herbst hints that Ms. Drawdy and the surveyors may have been more than "just friends," but that's only a rumor. But even he named one of his beers after her: Dora Drawdy Drool, a blend of his blond and red ales.

But the most important story you should probably hear is that of the Rocking Rabbit, an oversize carved wooden rabbit on rockers that sits to the right of the taproom entrance. "I was a woodworker for thirty-two years, and that's what I did in this building. This was my woodworking shop," Herbst told me. "I restored and built furniture. I did hand carving. I was on old-time cabinetmaker, built custom stuff from the ground up. I always wanted to make a big sculptural piece." That would be the rabbit. "That was the last project that I did for myself," he said. After a few years of off-and-on work on the piece, Herbst finally finished it and put it up for sale, but no one would pay what he wanted for it. We'll get back to the rabbit.

Evidence of Herbst's past woodworking career in the space is displayed on the walls, on shelves,

Beers brewed: Beauclaire Blond Ale, Dora Drawdy Drool, Rocking Rabbit Red, Dirty Blond, Rabbit Pellet Porter, and Pistolville Porter.

The Pick: The Rocking Rabbit Red, a filtered Irish Red Ale, borders on the caramel flavor of brown ale, but the addition of orange blossom honey during the brew gives an additional layer of sweetness that is nicely balanced with the roasted malt and light hops presence.

and in the rafters of the 1920s building. He's occupied the building since 1977. Old wooden block planes, antique saws, chisels, and so on are displayed in nooks and crannies. Items brought in by customers have been added: old muskrat traps, an unfortunately bent and painted airplane propeller, more tools. Family photos, some showing relatives enjoying his grandmother's homebrewed beer, and historical photos of the building and the neighborhood hang throughout.

After decades in the building, which now contains several other spaces, including an adjoining restaurant that Herbst recently took over, he was ready to sell the property and retire. But then the Great Recession hit, and property values plummeted. Some trusted friends advised him to run another business in the building until the economy recovered, maybe something that he did as a hobby. "The only real hobby I had was making beer," he said.

So when some brewing equipment that was stored in a warehouse became available, he made a deal for it and got it put together. He traveled over to visit his friend John Cheek at Orlando Brewing to learn a few things about how to brew on a larger scale. He renovated the building, naturally doing all the carpentry himself, including building the bar out of some extra heart pine that he had stored in the rafters, and in early 2010, he opened the doors to the Rocking Rabbit Tap Room. "So now it's turned from a hobby to some kind of job," he said with a laugh.

While over at Orlando Brewing, he spoke with a veteran brewer who advised him to concentrate on making only three beers, and making them right. Herbst found that this made sense, especially since he had only three tanks. But he learned how to blend those beers, meaning there actually are six of his beers on tap. The three base beers are Beauclaire Blond Ale, Rocking Rabbit Red, and Pistolville Porter. The Dora Drawdy Drool is a blend of the blond and the red; the Dirty Blond combines the blond and the Pistolville Porter; and the Rabbit Pellet Porter is a mix of the Pistolville Porter and the red.

The Beauclaire Blond is named after a nearby lake. Dora Drawdy we already talked about. Not surprisingly, Pistolville has a story behind it as well. Herbst said that back in the 1920s, when the building was constructed, this part of town was called Pistolville. "Apparently, people had arguments and they got settled by gunplay, so . . . Pistolville." Here's some related trivia: The writer of the 1959 novel *Alas, Babylon*, Pat Frank (the pen name of Harry Hart Frank), who resided at the time in the nearby community of Tangerine, set the post-nuclear-apocalypse tale in the fictional Central Florida town of Fort Repose, which some folks think was based on Mount Dora. The nearby shantytown in the book went by the name of Pistolville.

Herbst told me that locals love to gather in the tasting room, but some of the customers are from much farther away. "I have a huge crowd of people who come from England," he said. "They're in Orlando and they hear 'brewery,' and they drive thirty minutes up here." Then there are the fans of the house band, the Brewery Boys. Herbst is the lead singer, recruited a few years ago by one of the founders, whose daughter heard Herbst singing around the shop and recognized that he had a good voice. It's a good ol' rock-and-roll band that plays a variety of music from the fifties on. "If the song sounds good and I can sing it, we'll do it," Herbst said.

Oh, and the rabbit. After not being able to find a buyer, Herbst started thinking about other breweries and their mascots, including the Budweiser Clydesdales. He named the brewery operation after his creation and incorporated it into the logo. "Nobody can tell me that I copied anything of theirs, because there's only one of them," he said. "And I made it."

Mount Dora Brewing and the Rocking Rabbit Brewery

Opened: 2010.

Owner: Jeff Herbst.

Brewer: Jeff Herbst.

System: 3-barrel PUB.

Annual production: 100 barrels.

Hours: Brewpub, Friday to Monday, 3 to 11 p.m.; restaurant, seven days a week, 11 a.m. to 3 p.m.

Tours: On request.

Parking: Free on site.

Takeout beer: None.

Special considerations: Handicapped-accessible.

Extras: Outdoor beer garden.

Other area beer sites: Mermaid Juice Naneaux Brewery and Antique Shop, 458 N. Highland St., Mount Dora, FL 32757, (352) 223-3300, www.mermaidjuice.com (not an actual brewery—yet); Maggie's Attic of Florida, 237 W. Fourth Ave., Suite 5, Mount Dora, FL 32757, (352) 383-5451, www.maggiesattic.us.

Orlando Brewing

1301 Atlanta Avenue, Orlando, FL 32806
(407) 872-1117 • orlandobrewing.com

Many of Florida's breweries are found in industrial areas, but some of these areas are more industrial than others. While driving down Atlantic Avenue to Orlando Brewing on the south side of downtown Orlando, you may pass—or be passed by—forklifts carrying pieces of iron, tractor-trailers, and concrete trucks from the mixing plant. Keep a close eye out for the brewery's sign, because the steel building that houses it doesn't have much else to set it apart from its industrial neighbors.

"Sometimes you'll hear people talking about it—'I really had a hard time coming here,'" said brewery president John Cheek, "and I'll say, 'Don't worry, you passed. It's an intelligence test.'" Such candor is typical of Cheek, who fought his way through a lot of setbacks to get the brewery open in 2006—not to mention his appreciation for hand-crafted brew. "I'm from way up north, a little town called Mount Dora, about 30 miles north of here," he said, but he traveled all over the world with his dad, who was in the army, until he returned to Florida for school. "I graduated from high school, I went to college up in Gainesville and basically learned how to drink MD 20/20 and Boone's Farm Apple Wine, and whatever else was handy."

After college, Cheek joined the army himself, and while stationed in Germany, he fell in love with the clean, crisp lagers and pilsners of that country. After about a decade in the service, he was injured "rather severely" and was medically evacuated back to the States, where he eventually was given a military medical retirement. He moved back to Florida, and for about ten years, he sold life insurance and other investments.

During that time, he ran into a client, who was a teacher at Department of Defense schools in Turkey. "He was a very good friend of mine," Cheek said. "He listened to me say, 'Yeah, I've always wanted to learn to brew.' He brought all of his equipment over, taught me how to brew. Two

Beers brewed: Organic Blonde Ale, Organic Red Ale, Organic Pale Ale, Organic O-Town Brown Ale, Organic Olde Pelican English Pale Ale, Organic Poppin' Pilz, Organic Blackwater Dry Porter, Organic Eagle Stout, Organic Eminent Domain Scottish Ale, and Organic I-4 IPA, plus various specials and seasonals brewed with organic ingredients.

The Pick: The full-bodied Organic Blackwater Dry Porter bursts with chocolate and coffee notes while not being overly cloying on the palate.

weeks later, we bottled it and had a party, and all these people were coming up to me, saying, 'Wow, you made this?'" He was hooked.

Then, through a rather convoluted series of events involving brewery openings and closings, Cheek acquired a 5-barrel JV Northwest brewing system and some 10-barrel fermenters. The system eventually landed at the newly opened Orlando Brewery, down the street from its current location. Cheek was a minority partner of that ownership. He gained control of the brewery in October 2004 after it went bankrupt, and he and his partners got the operation back up and running.

But another setback occurred in January 2005, when the Florida Department of Transportation (FDOT) took the property under an eminent domain provision. The state moved the brewery to the building and property where it is currently located; the FDOT said the brewery would be back open within four months. However, "it took fifteen months," Cheek said. "Everybody expected us to kind of go out of business, so we borrowed money, held it together."

Finally, on April 7, 2006, Orlando Brewery reopened its doors to the public. "We've been here ever since," Cheek said. At the time, it was one of the few small breweries in the state and the only one in Orlando. Today it still lays claim to being the only USDA-certified organic brewery in the Southeast. (There are others that use organic ingredients, but they do not have the certification.)

Gaining the organic certification is not easy. "All the ingredients that we use fall into certain criteria," Cheek said. "Their ingredients use no petroleum-based fertilizers, no pesticide, no ionizing radiation, no GMOs (or genetically modified organisms), no sewage sludge. There are practices that are not acceptable to growers from an ingredients standpoint." Thus the brewery has to show the use of organic practices "basically all the way back to where the grain was processed." The certification requires certain action inside the brewery as well. Approved cleaners and sanitizers must be used, and no pesticides, rat poison, bug spray, or other chemical may be used in the brewery. Instead, pest control is achieved through the use of various mechanical and electrical traps.

The tasting room has more than twenty Orlando Brewing beers on tap most of the time, along with three guest taps, including a cider for customers seeking a gluten-free alternative. But because of the stringent requirements, only the beer that it sends out for distribution is officially certified organic by the USDA, though the brewery uses organic ingredients in all its brews. Plus, Cheek said, "when you certify, when you take this logo and put it on a product, you basically pay a tax to the certifying organization for the use of that logo."

Cheek mentioned another point of pride for his brews: "We adhere to the Reinheitsgebot, which is the German purity law, which says only water, yeast, malted barley, and hops are used in the beer." Well, except when the brewers violate the Reinheitsgebot in the aptly named Violator Series, with releases four times a year. The special brews contain locally grown organic ingredients. Those already released include the Grateful Pumpkin Organic Spiced Ale, Uncle Matt's Organic Grapefruit Pale Ale, and Organic Orlando Avenue Orange Wit Bier, brewed with organic oranges and coriander.

Parking can be a little tight during the buzz of the workday, but after quitting time at the local industries, when the workers head home—or to the brewery for a pint—the street belongs to Orlando Brewing. "We have a tasting room, a bar, and we're in an industrial area, so all these guys go home at four o'clock," Cheek said. "So all of a sudden, we have all the parking in the world."

Orlando Brewing

Opened: 2006.

Owners: John Cheek, George Cain, Bill Droste, and Gene Lohri.

Brewer: Graeme Lay.

System: 15-barrel Modern Brewing & Design.

Annual production: 1,700 barrels.

Hours: Monday through Thursday, 3 to 10 p.m.; Friday and Saturday, 1 p.m. to midnight; Sunday, 3 to 9 p.m.

Tours: Free tours Monday through Saturday at 6 p.m.

Parking: Free on site.

Takeout beer: Growlers, bottles, and kegs.

Special considerations: Handicapped-accessible.

Other area beer sites: Orlando may have only one brewery, but it has plenty of great craft beer bars and restaurants in and near downtown. Here are a few: Redlight Redlight Beer Parlour, 2810 Corrine Drive, Orlando, FL 32803, (407) 893-9832, redlightredlightbeerparlour.com; Frank & Steins Eatery & Pub, 150 S. Magnolia Ave., Orlando, FL 32801, (407) 412-9230, www.frankandsteins.com; Tap & Grind, 59 W. Central Blvd., Orlando, FL 32801, (407) 455-1100, tapandgrind.com; Imperial Wine Bar & Beer Garden, 1800 N. Orange Ave., Orlando, FL 32801, (407) 228-4992, www.imperialwinebar.com.

Sailfish Brewing Company

SAILFISH BREWING CO.
27° 26' 20" N 80° 20' 8" W | Ft. Pierce, FL

407 North Second Street, Fort Pierce, FL 34950
(772) 242-8697 • www.sailfishbrewingco.com

The home of Sailfish Brewing Company would fit right in nearly 300 miles south in the historic neighborhoods of Key West. That was a deliberate decision by the founders of this first craft brewery in the region of Florida called the Treasure Coast. "I'm an avid craft beer drinker, and I was kind of tired of beer from everywhere else except the Treasure Coast," said cofounder Nick Bischoff. "So me and my buddy Dave BuShea decided we wanted to start a craft brewery." They started working on it in 2011. "We kind of bounced around the Treasure Coast as far as where we wanted to locate it. We found these two buildings in downtown Fort Pierce and fell in love with them."

The buildings, wood frame cottages built in 1901, now bear a sunshiny yellow paint job on the outside and décor inside that leans heavily toward the local fishing scene. A mounted sailfish greets customers walking into the taproom. Multicolored banners bearing the brewery's logo festoon the outdoor deck. The logo itself gives a nod to seafaring fishermen with the inclusion of the brewery's location in longitude and latitude—27° 26' 20" N 80° 20' 8" W—beneath a sailfish silhouette. And of course, both owners are avid fishermen.

The structure has a noted historical connection. Early in the twentieth century, it was the home of Harry Hill, a local beekeeper and photographer, who was hired by oil and railroad tycoon Henry Flagler to be his official photographer when Flagler was running his railroad line, which eventually stretched to Key West, through the area. Because of Hill, much of Fort Pierce's history was visually documented.

Both BuShea and Bischoff have degrees—and day jobs—in the construction industry, so they could do a lot of the build-out themselves after they negotiated the lease. Much of the lumber they used was salvaged from a 1920s-era house. "The owner of the property and buildings bought them and completely gutted them, did

Beers brewed: Monkfish Abbey Ale, Light Tackle Pale Ale, Harvest Porter, Sailfish IPA, and Grapefruit Pale Ale.

The Pick: The Light Tackle Pale Ale tickles the tongue with its citrusy hops profile, and it goes down great after a day on the water. At 4.5 percent ABV, it's a true session beer. Have more than one.

the exterior, installed new roofs," Bischoff said. "We just kind of fell in love with it."

The brewery is just a few blocks from the sprawling Fort Pierce City Marina, where hundreds of charter, fishing, and pleasure boats dock. The neighborhood has been dubbed Edgartown, its original name when settlers first arrived. Some rezoning was needed to open a brewery there, but it fit right in with the city's effort to turn the historic neighborhood into an entertainment destination.

Some of the Sailfish beers have made it to the taps of local establishments, and plans call for wider distribution, which means bigger tanks that will be installed in the other building on the property. Another improvement will be a raw bar in the taproom, where the current small brewing system stands, to give customers more food options than a limited snack menu. But the main focus of the operation is introducing the Treasure Coast to freshly made, hand-crafted beer.

To that end, when craft beer newbies sit at the bar, whoever's behind it will start them off easy. "You have to introduce them to some sessionable beer, give them the first beer, our pale, which is a real easy drinker," Bischoff said. "Then eventually, once they get hooked on the pale, then have them try the IPA, or try the stout, or try the wheat. They'll slowly progress and become a craft lover like I did. As a group, as a craft beer movement, we all have to be cognizant of the fact that we're competing with tasteless beer. You have to understand that's the audience you're trying to introduce, so it can't be a shock, because they may never come back."

Sailfish Brewing Company

Opened: 2013.

Owners: Nick Bischoff and David BuShea.

Brewers: Kevin Storm and Nick Bischoff.

System: 1.5-barrel Blichman.

Annual production: Estimated 144 barrels.

Hours: Wednesday through Friday, 4 to 11 p.m.; Saturday, noon to 11 p.m.; Sunday, noon to 6 p.m.

Tours: On request.

Parking: On street and in nearby lots.

Takeout beer: Growlers.

Special considerations: Handicapped-accessible.

Extras: Outdoor seating; Wednesday night Introduction to Craft Beer class.

Swamp Head Brewery

3140 Southwest 42nd Way, Gainesville, FL 32608
(352) 505-3035 • swamphead.com

Swamp Head Brewery lies at the end of a winding road off the Archer Road exit of I-75 in Gainesville. Once you arrive at the units in a large warehouse park where the beer is brewed, find a space in the unpaved parking lot across from the entrance. Walk across the road, watching out for forklifts and other traffic, and enter Swamp Head's tasting room, dubbed the Wetlands. You've entered another world.

The space exudes comfort and is an ode to the natural wonders of Florida. Earth tones predominate under the diffused lighting. Cypress knees (those things that stick out of the ground around the trees) support tabletops, and galvanized sheet metal covers the façade of the bar underneath the pecky cypress top covered in a deep coat of resin. Even the sign that hangs over the door outside is crafted from a slab of Florida cypress. "We wanted to relate to all of Florida, since we were looking to be Florida's brewery," said owner and founder Luke Kemper.

Kemper, a Gainesville native, discovered his taste for hand-crafted beer around 2001, when his brother attended college in Fort Collins, Colorado. "Everyone was drinking craft beer out there, and my brother was coming home, he'd be bringing craft beer back home with him," he said. "He'd bring back Sunshine Wheat and Fat Tire from New Belgium. He'd bring back thirty cases or whatever." A few years later, a homebrewing friend, Craig Birkmaier, began sharing his creations with Kemper and other friends. "One thing led to another," Kemper said. "I got a house, and Craig was helping remodel the house, and we kept drinking more of his homebrew. I started thinking, no one here is making beer. At that time—that was back in 2007—it was when other people were just getting ready to get started."

Beers brewed: Wild Night Honey Cream Ale, Cottonmouth Belgian Wheat Bier, Stump Knocker American Pale Ale, Midnight Oil Oatmeal Coffee Stout, and Big Nose American IPA. Seasonals: many, divided into Migrational Series, released annually; Spasmodic Series, released occasionally; and Elusive Reclusive Series, released rarely.

The Pick: The Big Nose American IPA lives up to its name, with an aroma that reflects the massive amounts of aromatic and late flavor hops in the brew, as well as two dry hops additions. The taste is even better.

In 2008, they purchased a 10-barrel, copper-clad Viennese brewing system from a defunct brewpub called Spanish Springs in the nearby retirement community of the Villages, trucked it up to Gainesville, and began installation. Kemper hired Birkmaier as head brewer (he's now their brewing consultant), and Swamp Head was on its way—though not without having to learn a few things along the way. "Everybody pretty much jumped in feetfirst, not having any knowledge of the brewing industry or the beer industry," said Brandon Nappy, who's in charge of Swamp Head's marketing. "It was just a lot of learning. Everything from permitting to how to work with the distributor to Craig brewing at a professional level—everything was a learning experience from day one."

But over the next couple years, things smoothed out. At the time of my visit, Kemper employed fifteen people and spoke of plans for further expansion. "We're hoping to have cans, packaged products, more of our individual barrel-aged beers," he said. "Ultimately our goal is to move to another location. We can't stay here—it's too small. We're kind of on the fence, anything can change. Whether we're going somewhere and restoring an old building, or somewhere that's a little more off the path, more wooded, something that's more in tune with nature . . . who knows; it kind of depends on the city. We'd like to have a large tasting room, in an ideal world, a brewpub attached to that tasting room, and the production facility behind it."

Swamp Head Brewery

Opened: 2009.
Owner: Luke Kemper.
Brewers: Nick Dunn and Dan Wade.
System: 10-barrel DME.
Annual production: 3,700 barrels in 2012.
Hours: Monday through Friday, 4 to 9 p.m.; Saturday and Sunday, 1 to 9 p.m.
Tours: Tuesdays at 5:30 p.m.; sign up on website.
Parking: Free on site.
Takeout beer: Growlers, cans, and special-release 750-milliliter bottles.
Special considerations: Handicapped-accessible.
Extras: Open-air seating in production area.
Other area beer sites: The Brass Tap, 3833 S.W. Archer Rd., Bldg. B, Gainesville, FL 32608, (352) 371-7860, brasstapbeerbar.com.

Beer in Theme Parks

Beer ushered in the modern era of theme parks in Florida. In 1959, Anheuser-Busch opened a new brewery on property north of Tampa that had been part of Henderson Field, a World War II pilot-training base. Open to the public at no charge, the brewery became an attraction in its own right, featuring a self-guided tour and free beer samples. AB planted a garden of tropical plants and flowers on the grounds and offered an exotic bird show to entertain visitors. Those humble Busch Gardens have flowered into today's theme park, but the brewery was demolished in the mid-1990s to make room for more rides.

In early 2009, new owners InBev cut off the free beer samples and put Busch Gardens, along with SeaWorld Orlando, its sister park, and some out-of-state properties, up for sale. Later that year, the parks were acquired by the private equity firm Blackstone Group and now operate under the SeaWorld Entertainment banner.

Here I'll focus on the major parks: Busch Gardens, Disney World, Universal Studios, and SeaWorld. Though they are geared toward family entertainment, there are places on the properties where you can find some great craft beer. I'll offer tips on how to do that and highlight some special beer-focused events.

First, though, if you aren't really sure what a "theme park" is, here's a quick description. The modern theme park is a place with shows, thrill rides, restaurants, games, and other entertainment options geared toward various age groups, usually skewing toward the younger set. Broadly, the park is united by a certain theme but then is further divided into smaller areas grouped around subthemes. For example, Disney's Magic Kingdom could be said to have a theme of Disney characters and shows, but it is divided into different lands: Fantasyland, with a theme of princesses; Tomorrowland, which focuses on futuristic characters; Frontierland, a place for the "Old West" types; and so on. Got it? Now, let's find some beer at them.

Busch Gardens

The beer: As you might guess, the beer at this park's refreshment kiosks and restaurants leans heavily toward Anheuser-Busch InBev products, but the company no longer has an exclusive lock. You can find Yuengling and a few other non–AB InBev brands on tap out in the park, but visit the CC Craft Brews pub on the second floor of the Crown Colony House restaurant for a decent variety of local, regional, and national craft beers on tap or in cans and bottles.

Big beer event: Bands, Brew & BBQ is held on four Sundays beginning in February. The event brings in craft beers normally not available in the park, concerts by national acts, and local and national barbecue joints serving their fare. In the past, attendees have been able to purchase wristbands that allow unlimited sampling of the beer.

Disney World

The beer: The Walt Disney World Resort (its full name) is a big place, covering thirty thousand acres in Central Florida and including four separate theme parks—Magic Kingdom, Epcot, Animal Kingdom, and Hollywood Studios—as well as five golf courses, two water parks, an indoor amusement park, a couple dozen themed resorts, fishing lakes, and restaurants by the score. With the exception of Magic Kingdom, you'll be able to find some sort of alcoholic beverage available nearby wherever you are on the property. But even the exception has an exception: the Be Our Guest restaurant, part of a recent Fantasyland expansion, serves wine and beer, though it's not available to go. Plenty of craft beer is served on Disney property, but it takes some sleuthing to find your favorites. Fortunately, in the "Why Didn't I Think of That?" department, the Beers and Ears website (beersandears.net) and associated smartphone app, developed by a group of fans of both Disney and beer, provide a list of all the beer served at Disney World, maps, a beer finder, and more.

Big beer event: The Epcot International Food & Wine Festival starts each year toward the end of September and runs through mid-November. Though it's not in the title, craft beer has become a bigger part of the festival each year. Booths providing samples of the cuisine of different countries are set up around the park's World Showcase, and beer lovers will find international offerings as well as a booth featuring American craft beer, a Brewer's Collection booth with German styles, and more. Samples and drinks are pay-as-you-go.

Universal Orlando Resort

The beer: This entertainment complex comprises two theme parks—Universal Studios Florida and Universal's Islands of Adventure—along with CityWalk, a dining and nightlife area. In the theme parks, the beer selection runs toward mundane adjunct lagers and mass-distributed imports. You might find one or two of the more popular crafts at some of the restaurants and at the affiliated resort hotels, but the discerning beer geek will want to try the beers brewed exclusively for the parks by Florida Beer Company in Cape Canaveral. At the Hog's Head Pub in the Wizarding World of Harry Potter, the barkeep can pour you a pint of Hog's Head Brew, a Scottish ale. (Note that the Butterbeer served in the Harry Potter area is nonalcoholic.) Over at Universal Studios, in its newest themed area, Springfield USA, an ode to the long-running animated TV show *The Simpsons*, you can quaff a Duff Beer (regular, lite, or dry) at Moe's Tavern or the Duff Brewery.

Big beer event: Universal CityWalk used to host the annual Orlando Beer Festival, but the organizers moved it to downtown Orlando in 2007. However, Jake's Inaugural Beer Festival took place on October 4, 2013, at Jake's American Bar at Loews Royal Pacific Resort, one of the official Universal resorts. As with any inaugural festival, whether it will be an annual event remains to be seen, but its beer list was impressive.

SeaWorld Orlando

The beer: As this is Busch Gardens Tampa's sister park, you might expect the beer selection to be similar. You would be right. Some of the booths and restaurants might have a popular craft on draft, but the beer is mainly mass-produced light lagers and common imports. However, the park has Shamu the killer whale, so that should count for something, right?

Big beer event: As does its sister park, SeaWorld Orlando holds an annual Bands, Brew & BBQ event on Saturdays and Sundays from early February to mid-March. It's a bit more expansive than the Busch Gardens version, with more craft beer choices and concerts on both weekend days.

Tampa Bay Area

First things first: "Tampa Bay" is a body of water. Despite the best efforts of some TV sports announcers and others, there is no city of "Tampa Bay." Instead, it is an inclusive moniker for the counties and municipalities surrounding the body of water (www.visittampabay.com). Depending on whom you ask, the Tampa Bay area comprises up to seven different counties. For the purposes of this book, this section will concentrate on three of the core counties: Pasco, Pinellas, and Hillsborough.

The Tampa Bay area includes the state's oldest microbrewery, Dunedin Brewery, as well as some of its newest, with more coming online in the near future. Because of its history and the number of breweries in the area, it's considered the epicenter of the Florida craft beer scene. Tampa is where you'll find the historic neighborhood of Ybor City (www.ybor.org), where Cuban, Spanish, and Italian immigrants established a thriving cigar industry in the 1880s, giving Tampa its "Cigar City" nickname. On weekends, the district becomes a nightlife hub, with a wide enough variety of bars, clubs, and restaurants to satisfy nearly everyone's taste.

But the region has so much more to offer. Some beautiful **beaches** hug the shores of the Gulf of Mexico, including the relatively unspoiled Honeymoon Island State Park in Dunedin (www.floridastateparks.org/honeymoonisland) and Fort De Soto Park on the southern tip of Pinellas County (www.pinellascounty.org/park/05_ft_desoto.htm) and the more popular and crowded sands of Clearwater Beach (www.clearwaterbeach.com) and Treasure Island (www.treasureislandflorida.org).

East of Tampa is the town of Plant City (www.plantcity.org), famous for its winter strawberry harvest, when roadside stands pop up to sell flats of the juicy red fruit to tourists and residents alike. It's home to the **Florida Strawberry Festival** (www.flstrawberryfestival.com), an old-fashioned fair that takes place over eleven days beginning in late February.

On the other side of the bay in Pinellas County, downtown St. Petersburg (www.stpete.org/downtown.asp) has evolved over the past decade or so from a haven for the retired elderly to a thriving community of artists, musicians, and other creative types, with some fantastic restaurants, pubs, and parks along the bayfront. Farther north in Pinellas County, the funky community of Dunedin (www.visitdunedinfl.com) embraces its Scottish heritage and has become a popular destination and place to live for bicyclists and dog lovers in one of the few "walkable" communities in the state.

Tarpon Springs (www.tarponspringschamber.org) is a bit north of Dunedin, but you might feel as though you're in Greece. That's no surprise, as its population boasts the highest percentage of Americans of Greek heritage of any city in the United States, at nearly 12 percent. An abundance of natural sea sponges were discovered in the waters off Tarpon Springs around 1880, and because Greece had a long history of harvesting sponges, many Greek divers and boat captains immigrated here to take advantage of this newfound mother lode. Though the sponges were decimated by disease for a few decades in the mid-1900s, they have made a comeback, and the industry once again thrives. And the Greek restaurants are some of the best you'll find outside of Athens.

Speaking of restaurants, the craft beer boom has made its way onto the drink menus of so many Tampa Bay–area establishments, from fine dining to beach dives, that there are too many to list in this space. Ask at a local beer bar or brewery for advice; you'll be sure to get some great suggestions. Two world-class restaurants in Tampa, though, deserve mention.

Bern's Steak House (www.bernssteakhouse.com), established in 1956, specializes in aged steaks, vegetables grown in the restaurant's own garden, and wine. Lots of wine. The largest-wine-list-in-the-world type of wine cellar. But Bern's also has a respectable list of local and national craft beers, as well as some fine imports. The exterior might best be described as "mid-twentieth-century warehouse." The interior? Well, imagine Disney's Haunted Mansion crossed with a Roaring Twenties bordello. It must be experienced in person to fully appreciate.

The **Columbia Restaurant** in Ybor City (www.columbiarestaurant .com) opened in 1905. Even if you don't want to eat there, it's worth a visit to study the intricate terra-cotta tile murals depicting events from Spanish history. The tile work continues inside to the various dining rooms, where you can partake of a feast of authentic cuisine from the old country: Spanish bean soup, arroz con pollo, paella, and more. The beer list is not extensive, though it features products from Tampa's Cigar City Brewery. But if you are a fan of sangria, you'll find some of the best here by the glass or pitcher, mixed tableside, and flamenco dancers perform Monday through Saturday nights.

If you're a cultured type, you're in luck. The Tampa Bay area is home to some world-class museums, such as the **Tampa Museum of Art** (tampamuseum.org), **the Dali Museum** (thedali.org), and the **Florida Holocaust Museum** (www.flholocaustmuseum.org), and top-notch concert and play venues, including the **David A. Straz Jr. Center for the Performing Arts** (www.strazcenter.org), **the Lakeland Center** (www.the lakelandcenter.com), and the **MidFlorida Credit Union Amphitheatre** (www.midflorida.com/amphitheatre), as well as dozens of smaller theaters and clubs.

With the exception of the NBA, all the **major sports leagues** are represented in the Tampa Bay area. The Tampa Bay Buccaneers (www.buccaneers.com) of the NFL play at Raymond James Stadium in Tampa, the MLB's Tampa Bay Rays (tampabay.rays.mlb.com) play at Tropicana Field in St. Petersburg, and the Tampa Bay Lightning of the NHL (lightning.nhl.com) has its home ice at the Tampa Bay Times Forum in Tampa. Also, the North American Soccer League's Tampa Bay Rowdies (rowdiessoccer.com) compete at Al Lang Field in St. Petersburg. (Remember, Tampa Bay is not a city!) Major League Baseball spring training games are a huge draw for out-of-state fans, with four big-league teams holding their practice games at stadiums in the Tampa Bay area as part of the Florida Grapefruit League (www.florida grapefruitleague.com). Eleven other teams play spring ball in Central and South Florida.

The **University of South Florida** (www.usf.edu) is the area's largest institution of higher education, with separate campuses in Tampa and St. Petersburg. Its football team, the Bulls, shares Raymond James Stadium with the Buccaneers during the season.

As with all of Florida, outdoor activities abound throughout the region: fishing, boating, cycling, hiking, golfing, and so on. If you're visiting with the family, there are attractions for everyone, such as **Busch Gardens Tampa Bay** (seaworldparks.com/en/buschgardens-tampa) and **Lowry Park Zoo** (www.lowryparkzoo.com), an award-winning zoological park.

Barley Mow Brewing Co.

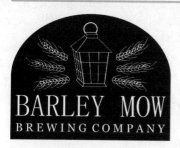

518 West Bay Drive, Largo, FL 33770
(727) 584-7772 • www.barleymowbrewingco.com

Jay Dingman wants to convert his customers, and he trains his staff to help. Any customers who come into Barley Mow Brewing and order one of the popular mass-market fizzy yellow lagers are out of luck. There aren't any. "Before we start to explain to them that we don't carry it because we make our own beer, we're pouring them a sample of something so that as we're telling them that we don't have what they want, we're putting something down in front of them so that they have something to try," Dingman said. "Very rarely do we have people leave."

It's that sort of dedication to customer service and quality crafted beer that has given the nano-brewery the reputation of being an everyman's pub, the kind of place where dedicated craft beer geeks and those just beginning their explorations can gather together. "We do a lot of beer education here, so we like to think that we're almost like a gateway brewery for people," Dingman said.

He remembers the exact day when he and his fiancée, Colleen, now his wife, decided to open their own bar and brewery. "It was the first day of summer in 2010, and we were out walking our dogs and we were complaining about work and talking about brewing," he said. "It was the summer I turned thirty-five and thought, I can't be a bartender for the rest of my life. We need to find something to do. That was, why don't we take a run at this?"

Because they both worked in the restaurant hospitality industry, they crafted a business plan for a small brewery with a bar to serve their creations. After going through about a dozen names, and either not liking them or finding out other breweries had already claimed them, Dingman turned to a fourteenth-century Gaelic drinking song called "The Barley Mow." It's one of those

Beers brewed: Golden Extravaganza! Blonde Ale, Passion Fruit Blonde, Harvest Wind Wheat, Lamp Lighter American Amber, Quackalope American IPA, Imperial Red, Brogue Dry Stout, Nipperkin American Porter, and The Unkindness Hoppy Black Ale. Seasonals: Common Eileen California Common, Grapefruit Pale Ale, BMBC Tinsel Spiced Ale, Lord of the Gourd Pumpkin Porter, Black Rock Rye, and S'mores Stout.

The Pick: A *"nipperkin"* is an old British unit of measurement, believed to be one-eighth of a pint. You'll want a larger glass to enjoy the Nipperkin American Porter, a full-bodied dark brew with a wonderfully aromatic roasted flavor.

songs that add a word—and become harder to sing—each time the refrain comes around. The final verse is "Oh, the company, brewer, bookie [or cooper], slavey, drayer, daughter, landlady, landlord, barrel, half barrel, gallon, half gallon, quart pot, pint pot, half a pint, gill pot, half a gill, quarter gill, nipperkin, and a round bowl. Here's good luck (good luck!), good luck to the barley mow." The words after "landlord" refer to old English units of liquid measurement, and you'll find a nod to them in some of Barley Mow's beers—Nipperkin American Porter, for example.

Just a couple miles from the beach, Barley Mow attracts folks coming by from a day on the sand, residents of the nearby tony beach town of Belleair Bluffs, and locals who walk to the pub. When the weather's nice, the spacious outdoor patio attracts a crowd, especially when there's live music on Fridays. Some patrons have been coming there since its previous incarnation as an Irish pub. Dingman described the old pub as "kind of a dive bar," and conversations with the "old-timers" confirm it.

At the time of my visit, Barley Mow distributed about 10 percent of its beer in kegs to other pubs and restaurants, but now that the Dingmans have worked out most of the kinks in their current operation, they are hatching plans for greater distribution. "We're in the process of building a larger production facility," Jay said. "I feel way more prepared to do this now than I would have if we had tried to do that right out of the gate. Just what we learned in the past few years has been like beer school, plus learning the business side of it, the paperwork and the taxes and all."

Barley Mow Brewing Co.

Opened: 2011.
Owners: Jay and Colleen Dingman.
Brewers: Jay and Colleen Dingman.
System: 2-barrel Stouts.
Annual production: Estimated 200 barrels.
Hours: Monday through Saturday, 3 p.m. to 2 a.m; Sunday, 3 p.m. to midnight.
Tours: "From every bar stool. Just ask your bartender to point things out!"
Parking: Free on site.
Takeout beer: Growlers.
Special considerations: Handicapped-accessible.
Extras: Large outdoor patio.
Other area beer sites: Willard's Tap House, 12500 Starkey Rd., Largo, FL 33773, (727) 581-8600, www.willardstaphouse.com.

Big Storm Brewing Co.

2438 Merchant Ave. #103, Odessa, FL 33556
(727) 807-7998 • www.bigstormbrewery.com

In an area that's threatened half the year by tropical storms, that's in the lightning capital of the Western Hemisphere, and where thunder rumbles and lightning cracks nearly every summer afternoon, you'd think the name Big Storm would be a given. Not so much. At first friends and business partners Mike Bishop and Clay Yarn had an undisclosed name for the brewery they wanted to open. However, Bishop said, "We fell out of love with it after a couple of weeks. We tried the Jimi Hendrix method of just sitting around and drinking and hoping we could come up with something, but we couldn't remember what we did in the morning."

So they came up with ground rules: it had to be easy to say—no tongue twisters; it had to be easy to remember; and it had to be a local identifier of some sort. They held a brainstorming session. "We just started throwing everything out there. How about this? How about that?" Bishop recalled. "I just happened to say, 'How about Big Storm?' It wasn't like a hallelujah moment. We just threw it on the list, and when we were done rattling off about sixty names, we applied the rules to it, and there was only one name left, and that was Big Storm."

Bishop's brewing career had started with a few batches at home, then he volunteered at nearby Dunedin Brewery in early 2009 to learn more about commercial production. He and Yarn had discussed opening a business together. "After a couple of years at Dunedin, he was always barking up my tree about opening up a brewery, and I was like, it's a big pain in the ass," Bishop said. "But slowly he convinced me. Then I left Dunedin April 2011, and we started working on it from there."

They found a space in a warehouse park in Odessa, a small community in the northern Tampa Bay county of Pasco, then had to get it open. "We're the first and only microbrewery in Pasco County," Bishop explained, "and we were very fortunate to have a high-level meeting with the head

Beers brewed: Wavemaker Amber Ale, PalmBender Amber Ale, Arcus IPA, and Firestorm Black IPA, plus various seasonals and one-offs.

The Pick: Though you'll taste diverse notes of coffee, roasted malt, and citrusy hops, the Firestorm Black IPA brings them all together successfully with a fuller flavor than you might expect from a 5.9 percent ABV brew.

of zoning for Pasco," who helped them get zoned for the taproom. "They didn't really have any laws for microbreweries because they didn't have to. . . . For a brewery, you had to be zoned for a few different things in order to operate. So Pasco's been really awesome with us."

The tasting room now operates in front of the brewing area, taking up about half of Big Storm's square footage. At first it was a cramped space in a separate room, and servers had to bring customers' beers from around the back. Business was good, so they started working on expanding the brewery. "We thought through it, saved our pennies, worked on new relationships and on getting more people behind us, and now we're on the verge of expanding just about a year in," Bishop told me.

The partners are aiming high: they want Big Storm to be a major production brewery for the Tampa Bay area. They started with a 3.5-barrel brewing system but have since upgraded to a 15-barrel system and plan to increase that capacity even more. Also on the agenda are canning the beer and getting more of it out into the market to become better known. (At the time of this writing, the brewery's website listed fifteen other area venues that carried its beer.) "People know about us and they're trying to get the feel of us," Bishop said. "We're still waiting to get all over the place."

Big Storm Brewing Co.

Opened: 2012.
Owners: Mike Bishop and Clay Yarn.
Brewer: Mike Bishop.
System: 15-barrel PBST.
Annual production: Estimated 5,500 barrels.
Hours: Thursday through Saturday, noon to 9 p.m.; Sunday and Monday, 3 to 7 p.m.
Tours: Call ahead or on request.
Parking: Free on site.
Takeout beer: Growlers and occasional special-release bottles.
Special considerations: Handicapped-accessible.

Cigar City Brewing

3924 West Spruce Street, Suite A, Tampa, FL 33607
(813) 348-6363, ext. 206
www.cigarcitybrewing.com

Joey Redner never intended Cigar City Brewing to become as big as it is. Then in 2009, the Tampa startup won a gold medal at the Great American Beer Festival (GABF) for its Humidor Series IPA. The accolades continued in 2010, with a gold medal for Hunahpu's Imperial Stout at the U.S. Open Beer Championship and a silver for the Humidor India Pale Ale at the GABF. People took notice, and demand skyrocketed.

"It's definitely exceeded my growth expectations," Redner said. "I figured maybe a couple of thousand barrels a year would be a nice goal to get to. We were not set up to grow fast at all. We had a 15-barrel system and six 15-barrel fermenters, and we literally didn't have a bright tank. We used one of our fermenters as a bright tank. So we had, what, 75 barrels of fermentation capacity? It wasn't a lot."

At the time of this writing, Cigar City had the capacity to brew 16,000 barrels per year—not counting a brewpub about thirty minutes north and another in Tampa International Airport. Since opening, the brewery has taken over all the space in the industrial warehouse building where it started and doubled the size of the tasting room, which sometimes has a standing-room-only crowd even in the middle of the afternoon on a weekday. Its distribution continues to increase, especially after the brewery installed a canning line and started packaging some of its flagship beers in cans for distribution.

It all started because Redner had honed a palate for flavorful beer. For years, he had been an active participant in the local craft beer scene—lending a hand at breweries, running bars, and writing about beer—but he remained puzzled about why there weren't any local options outside of a few brewpubs. "I figured someone would come and do it," he said. "Tampa had a brewpub, but we

Beers brewed: Jai Alai IPA, Maduro Brown Ale, Invasion Pale Ale, Hopped on the High Seas Caribbean IPA, Hotter Than Helles Lager, Florida Cracker White Ale, Tocobaga Red Ale, Cuban-Style Espresso Brown Ale, and Jose Marti American Porter, plus a list of seasonals and one-offs that would likely fill their own book.

The Pick: Of the year-round brews, Tocobaga Red Ale hits the tongue with a blast of citrusy hops bitterness unexpected in a red, but the caramel and malt notes that follow the hops smooth it out to a nicely balanced, full-bodied fermented treat.

didn't have anyone that was packaging craft beer, selling it out, and I really thought that someone would be doing it, and I started investigating what it would take to do that, sort of as an exercise to figure out why it hadn't happened." He decided to be the one to make it happen. Around 2006, he began researching the necessary steps to open a brewery. He incorporated Cigar City Brewing the following year, the next year he started the build-out, and Cigar City brewed its first beer in 2009.

Along the way, Redner hired a brewer. One of the most promising candidates was not comfortable with taking the job, but she recommended he talk to a talented brewer at Foothills Brewery in Winston-Salem, North Carolina, by the name of Wayne Wambles. Redner had met Wambles previously, but they'd had only a brief conversation, and he didn't know too much about the candidate. "I was still interviewing other people at the time, and I had a conversation with Wayne," Redner said. "We talked about beer briefly, but it went very quickly into music and general philosophy of life and things like that. There was a really good comfort level. I think in some ways he thought some of the stuff I wanted to do was a little out there, but he still wasn't flat opposed to it, and to me that was a good sign, so it went from there. I offered him the job, he left Foothills and came down, and it was literally me and him doing pretty much everything for the first year."

Wambles quickly started producing boundary-pushing beer, adding massive amounts of hops, aging brew on top of Spanish cedar and in spirits barrels, and exposing the Tampa Bay area to beer styles that had previously been available only from out-of-state craft breweries. For many customers, even the first flagship beer, Jai Alai IPA, took some getting used to. "A lot of people who had never had IPAs, their first reaction was usually not a positive one," Redner said. "Now it's our best-selling beer—it's 54 percent of our production."

One of the most coveted beers from Cigar City is the gold medal–winning Hunahpu's Imperial Stout. Aged on cacao nibs, Madagascar vanilla beans, ancho and pasilla chilies, and cinnamon, with an 11 percent ABV, it rates a perfect 100 on both of the most popular beer-rating websites, BeerAdvocate (beeradvocate.com) and RateBeer (www.rate beer.com). Hunahpu, in Mayan mythology, was a god who gave cocoa to the Maya, and the beer pours as thick as honey and as dark as used motor oil.

It's released just once a year at a special event the second weekend of March, and thousands of craft beer lovers from around the world descend on the brewery to get the wristband that guarantees them an allotted number of 750-milliliter bottles. The first release day in 2009 drew several hundred people to the tasting room for the release over a four-hour period. In 2013, more than five thousand folks filed through the gates on Hunahpu's Day, which has evolved into an all-day festival featuring live music, food trucks, and dozens of taps set up pouring not only Cigar City products, but many rare and special-release brews from other breweries as well.

From the beginning, it was important to Redner that the brewery and the beers reflect the heritage of his native Tampa, which historically had the nickname of Cigar City because of its Ybor City neighborhood's onetime claim to being the "Cigar Capital of the World." A large population of Cuban immigrants centered in Ybor City once toiled at rolling tobacco into cigars in factories, most of which have since been shuttered, the buildings either leveled or restored.

Many of the beer labels also pay homage to those days: Maduro Brown Ale is named for a particular tobacco leaf; Jose Marti American Porter honors the Cuban political activist who traveled often to Tampa to unify the immigrant community in support of Cuban independence from Spain; Cubano Espresso Brown Ale is brewed with locally roasted espresso beans that are more often used to brew the high-powered coffee drink that remains popular in the area. Other labels were inspired by different aspects of Tampa history, such as Jai Alai, named after the fast-paced pari-mutuel game brought to the United States by immigrants from the Basque region of Spain. Tampa once had a popular jai alai fronton, which shuttered in 1998. Reaching even farther back in time, Tocobaga Red Ale pays tribute to the Native American tribe that lived off the bounty of Tampa Bay hundreds of years before the Spanish conquistadores arrived in the 1500s.

"You've got to name it something, so why don't you name it something that you're passionate about or things that you enjoy or make you smile?" said Redner, a self-proclaimed history buff. "You just can't call it Beer No. 1A—well, you could, that might be funny—but you've got to come up with something, so why not draw from things that intrigue you or are interesting, or that celebrate the culture of the geographic region that you're from and get to share that history with people outside the area, or even people inside the area that are ignorant about some of the history?"

One problem—good or bad, depending on your perspective—is that no matter how many new fermenters, tanks, or other equipment it has added, Cigar City has not been able to meet the demand for its beer, even in Florida. Redner estimates that annual production will be around 55,000 barrels by the spring of 2014, but the brewery will still be trying to supply beer to those who want it. "I want to come up with a way that we can continue to brew into the demand, but I don't want to constantly go into hock to build a new brewery," he explained. "The goal is to try to continue to produce what we can beyond the capacity that we have on-site and find a way that we can grow through cash flow, grow under our own power, not go borrow money so we can build a huge brewery. And that may mean that we stay a little smaller than the market likes."

Cigar City Brewing

Opened: 2009.

Owner: Joey Redner.

Brewer: Wayne Wambles.

System: 45-barrel total brewhouse capacity.

Annual production: Estimated 25,000 to 30,000 barrels.

Hours: Sunday through Thursday, 11 a.m. to 11 p.m., Friday and Saturday, 11 a.m. to 1 a.m.

Tours: Wednesday through Sunday for $5, which includes logo pint glass and one fill of a Cigar City beer. Reservations not required but recommended; register on website.

Parking: Free on site.

Takeout beer: Growlers, bottles, and cans.

Special considerations: Handicapped-accessible.

Other area beer sites: The Pub, 2223 N. West Shore Blvd., Tampa, FL 33607, (813) 443-5642, www.experiencethepub.com/tampa-bay.

Cigar City Brewpub

15491 North Dale Mabry Highway, Tampa, FL 33618
(813) 962-1274 • cigarcitybrewpub.com

Joey Redner wanted to have a brewpub component when he opened the Cigar City Brewing production facility in 2009, but it just wasn't feasible. "It's a lot more expensive to start a brewpub," he explained. "While it's capital-intensive to start a brewery, if you tack a brewpub on to it, you've immediately got all the labor costs, food costs." So he put the idea on the back burner until a few years later, when an opportunity became available on some property about a half-hour drive north of the brewery. "It almost gives you an off-site pilot brewery area," Redner said. "We use a different kind of yeast strain there than any of the ones we use here" at the production brewery.

Redner turned the brewing duties there over to longtime Cigar City brewer Tim Ogden. When he arrived in December 2012, "it was still an empty space," Ogden said. "We were still doing the interior design and doing the planning on the brewery. I worked with our fabricator at the production facility to design what kind of modifications I wanted done with the brewhouse."

The freestanding building most recently was a TGI Friday's restaurant, but there is no reminder left of the casual-dining chain's barberpole color scheme. The brewpub has been transformed into an architectural tribute to the brewing arts. "What Joey told the interior designers was to come up with a design theme that they felt like we would come up with as brewers if we were to take a bunch of materials and a bunch of beer from the brewery and bring it back to our garage and start building things," Ogden said. Those guidelines resulted in a clean and comfortable space using repurposed material commonly found at a brewing operation. Tabletops were made from scrap pallet wood. Barrels in which Cigar City aged beer were disassembled, and the staves, hoops, and barrel heads became chandeliers. Stainless steel from a depalletizer used at the brewery became table legs and trim.

Beers brewed: La Rubia Pernicious Golden Ale, Fountain of Youth Belgian Witbier, Northdale Pale Ale, and Paulina Pedrosa Brown Ale, plus various specials.

The Pick: Some folks might say that the Northdale Pale Ale should be called an IPA. I say it's a damn good beer with a citrusy hops kick and a hint of tropical fruit aroma.

The menu reflects the local Cuban-inspired cuisine, which Redner grew to love while growing up in the city. "We wanted it to be Tampa-centric," Redner said. "We wanted it to focus primarily on the cuisine that was part of Tampa's history—definitely a Tampa-style Cuban," which "kind of evolved separately from Miami and from Cuba. The immigrants came here and the food slowly changed. It got a little more Italian with the Sicilian influence, and so the food here is different. I love Cuban food, and when I travel, I'll get it just to see the differences. The Cuban food in Tampa is very different from the Cuban food in Miami. We also wanted to be playful with some of it, so take that as the starting point—Tampa-style Cuban food—and have fun with it from there."

The brewpub opened not long before my visit, and Ogden was still developing the repertoire of beers that the brewpub would serve regularly, along with brews from the production brewery and guest taps. And Redner now has the brewpub he first wanted in the main brewery's tasting room, in a way. A space was rejiggered to house a small café, offering sandwiches, soups, and snacks for customers to nosh on while they enjoy the beer.

Cigar City Brewpub

Opened: 2013.

Owner: Joey Redner.

Brewer: Tim Ogden.

System: 3-barrel New World Brewing brewhouse.

Annual production: Estimated 150 barrels in 2013.

Hours: Sunday through Thursday, 11 a.m. to 10 p.m.; Friday and Saturday, 11 a.m. to 11 p.m.; bar open later all week.

Tours: On request, if someone is available.

Parking: Free on site.

Takeout beer: Growlers and special-release bottles.

Special considerations: Handicapped-accessible.

Extras: Beer dinners; vintage releases; vertical tastings.

Other area beer sites: World of Beer–Carrollwood, 12904 N. Dale Mabry Hwy., Tampa, FL 33618, (813) 968-7300, wobusa.com/Locations/Carrollwood.aspx.

Cigar City Brewpub, Tampa Airport

Tampa International Airport, Airside C, 4100 George J. Bean Parkway, Tampa, FL 33607
(813) 962-1274

Passengers disembarking at Tampa International Airport's Airside C from Southwest, AirTran, or Frontier airlines, or those who arrive early to catch their flights, don't have to go far to get a taste of local craft beer. In fact, some of it is extremely local, as it's brewed right there at the airport. Because this brewery is at an airside terminal, however, it's available only to those who have passed through the airport security checkpoint, so casual visitors can't go there just to taste the beer.

In late 2011, HMSHost, the company in charge of airport concessions, announced that it was revamping some of its vendor spaces to include more "local flavor," bringing in new eateries with ties to Tampa, including Cigar City Brewing. Joey Redner, Cigar City's founder and owner, wanted to be part of it, but insisted on one thing: "Originally, they just wanted to do a tasting area, where it would just be a restaurant and they would just buy our beer and serve it. I didn't want them to use the word 'brewery' or 'brewing' or anything denoting brewing if we weren't actually going to be brewing on the site."

Initially, HMSHost wasn't too keen on the idea, "but the 'cool factor' that we actually brew the beer there was just too much to pass up," Redner said. "So I pushed really hard. I tried to be very easy as far as what we required from them to actually get it open. The only thing that I really was adamant about was actually brewing some beer there." They came to an agreement that involved Cigar City leasing the brewing equipment to HMSHost and providing the recipes and the brewer, who, at the time of my visit, was Tim Ogden, also the head brewer at the Cigar City Brewpub in North Tampa. Steven Shanks has since taken over brewing duties. Cigar City helped design the food menu, but the HMSHost chef developed it.

The brewpub is housed in a freestanding structure in the terminal, with a red brick façade and a bar that wraps around half of it. About a dozen or

Beers brewed: Tony Jannus Pale Ale, plus occasional seasonals.

The Pick: You'll find some of the beer brewed at the main production brewery on tap, but always go for the brewed-on-premises Tony Jannus Pale Ale, a delicious, lightly hopped brew that will quickly make delays and cancellations a distant bad memory.

so tables in front are reserved for the pub's customers. The Cigar City logo brands it, and customers can purchase T-shirts and other gear. You can even buy six-packs to take on the flight for later enjoyment.

The small brewery system can be spied through glass windows behind the bar, which also serves wine and liquor. There's always at least one beer that's brewed there on tap, usually Tony Jannus Pale Ale, named after the pilot of the first scheduled commercial airline flight in the world, from St. Petersburg to Tampa on January 1, 1914. Other Cigar City beers are available as well.

The Cigar City Brewpub is the second brewery in Florida to make beer in an airport. The first was Portland, Maine, based Shipyard Brewery, which operated a brewpub in Orlando International Airport for about five years in the 1990s. That was before the 9/11 terrorist attacks, though, so Cigar City has to jump through a few more hoops. Everything the brewery brings in has to go through security, "even your grain and your brewer and your buckets," Redner said. But as much as Redner loves beer, he's also a businessman and finds it worth the trouble. "Their beer sales are through the roof. It's probably our number-one beer account in the entire state. They sell a lot of beer."

Cigar City Brewpub, Tampa Airport

Opened: 2012.
Owner: HMSHost.
Brewer: Steven Shanks.
System: 1.5-barrel New World Brewing.
Hours: Seven days a week, 10 a.m. to 9 p.m.
Tours: None.
Takeout beer: Cans.
Special considerations: Handicapped-accessible; available only to those who have passed through the airport security checkpoint.
Extras: Pub food menu.

Cycle Brewing at Peg's Cantina

3038 Beach Boulevard South, Gulfport, FL 33707
(727) 328-2720 • pegscantina.com

If the physical size of a brewery were proportional to the number of accolades and awards it's received, Cycle Brewing at Peg's Cantina would be as big as a hangar for jumbo jets. In reality, it's a 3.5-barrel system and four 7-barrel fermenters without even a building—it all sits shaded from the sun behind Peg's, a restaurant that is so small that most of its customer seating is outside. "We're small and we want to be small," brewer Doug Dozark explained. "Gulfport wants to be small. We're not next to the airport like Cigar City, where they're getting a lot of tourists. We don't get as many tourists as some of the other breweries. Part of it is the factor of marketing. We don't advertise, we don't really work very hard at that angle, and that's a choice."

His system used to be even tinier. For the first six months there, Dozark brewed 5-gallon batches, then upgraded to a 1-barrel system. He did it on weekends while he was working full-time at Cigar City Brewing on the other side of Tampa Bay. In August 2012, he left Cigar City to brew full-time at the Gulfport restaurant, with the brewing side now dubbed Cycle Brewing.

Gulfport sits on the northern shore of Boca Ciega Bay in south Pinellas County. Often described as "Old Florida," the village contains a mixture of early twentieth-century wood frame bungalows, small independent businesses, and artisans' shops on brick-paved streets, many shaded by stands of decades-old live oak trees and palms. The salty breezes coming off the bay make even the balmiest evenings pleasant enough to enjoy dining and drinking on the shaded patio of Peg's Cantina, which takes up what were the front and side yards of a cottage nearly a century old that was converted into the restaurant.

The online forum RateBeer (www.ratebeer.com) ranks Peg's Cantina among the top five brewpubs in Florida, and Dozark's Rare D.O.S., an imperial

Beers brewed: Freewheel Pale Ale, Fixie Session IPA, Ryerish Red, Blind Date American Amber, Bottom of the 9th Brown, and Cream and Sugar Please Sweet Porter. Seasonals: limited-release beers include Rare D.O.S., RareR D.O.S., and other barrel-aged beers.

The pick: More akin to a milk stout than a traditional porter, the Cream and Sugar Please Sweet Porter is creamy, chocolaty, and smooth going down, with a rich coffee flavor from beans freshly roasted at a local Italian market.

stout aged in oak whiskey barrels, has a rank of 96 out of 100 at the BeerAdvocate website (beeradvocate.com), while the rum barrel-aged RareR D.O.S. had a perfect score of 100 as of this writing. Dozark brews a variety of styles, but one in particular has become a favorite. About six months into his career at Cigar City, he found a recipe in the back of a brewing book for a Berliner Weisse, a style that had fallen out of favor over the years, even in Berlin. He sought advice from Wayne Wambles, Cigar City's head brewer, who had brewed pretty much every style, but Wambles told him, "I've never brewed one of those; I can't really help you." Dozark asked other brewers about it, picked up bits and pieces of advice, and brewed it. It turned out pretty well.

Around the same time, other brewers in the state were working on their own versions of the tangy, low-ABV sour wheat beer, infusing it with a variety of local citrus and tropical fruit flavors. The style became so popular that Dozark held the first Berliner Bash on the Bay in Gulfport on May 19, 2012, bringing in Berliners from breweries across the state and the country. It happened again a year later. "The first time, we had more beer than we needed," he said. "It was a nice event, and everyone got everything they wanted. There were almost no lines." But after the fest, interest in the style, which some had started calling Florida Weisse, grew. That second year, "we hit exactly what we expected, or hoped for," said Dozark. "It wasn't too many people, but the lines were there and the place was packed."

At the time of this writing, Cycle Brewing had made big strides toward growing into its reputation by soft-opening a production brewery and tasting room in downtown St. Petersburg at 534 Central Avenue.

Cycle Brewing at Peg's Cantina

Opened: 2009 (brewery).

Owner: Doug Dozark.

Brewer: Doug Dozark.

System: 3.5-barrel Portland Kettle Works.

Annual production: 350 barrels.

Hours: Tuesday through Thursday, noon to 9 p.m.; Friday and Saturday, noon to 10 p.m.; Sunday, noon to 9 p.m.

Tours: On request, if someone's available.

Parking: On street.

Takeout beer: Growlers and occasional special-release bottles.

Special considerations: Handicapped-accessible. Accepts cash, checks, or debit cards only.

Extras: Outdoor beer garden.

Dunedin Brewery

937 Douglas Avenue, Dunedin, FL 34698
(727) 736-0606 • www.dunedinbrewery.com

Dunedin Brewery boasts that it is "Florida's Oldest Craft Brewery." Michael N. Bryant opened the doors to the public in July 1996 in the northern Pinellas County town of Dunedin, which is steeped in Scottish heritage. These days, Bryant has pulled back somewhat from running the brewery and serves as a mentor and advisor to others in the Tampa Bay area. "Right now he's working on helping brewery start-ups get their licensing both for building and for contracting," said his son, Michael L. Bryant, Dunedin Brewery's general manager. "But also with the state and federal licensing, helping people, basically educating them on how to get those things quicker than spinning around in a dark maze. I don't know that they could move as quickly without his help, because we've been around so long and gone through all these things, so it's easy for us to say, 'Don't worry about that; this is what you should worry about.'"

The younger Bryant grew up with the aromas of brewing pretty much a constant in his life, at first in the kitchen of his home, then in the brewery, which started as a smaller operation in a nearby building. "Once I was of age, he would try to give me samples, but I didn't know what to do with it," he said of his father. "I didn't get into beer until later. But growing up around it, he taught me how to make root beer, and we would have root beer on tap for me and my friends. I think I always kind of knew that he built this company for me to eventually come in and start working in it."

From age eighteen to twenty-two, he did indeed work there, cleaning kegs, painting bottles, and doing other such grunt work. He became a bit bored, so he left for the Pacific Northwest for a few years to attend school. When he returned, he had a renewed vision for the direction of the brewery. That included moving away somewhat from the Scottish theme to broaden the scope of what they were trying to do. "The heritage thing has

Beers brewed: Gold Ale, Apricot Peach Ale, Wheat Ale, Red Ale, Pale Ale, Brown Ale, and Nitro Stout. Seasonals: Leonard Croon's Old Mean Stout, Local Honey Ale, Three Copper Coins, Anniversary Bohemian Pilsner, Oktoberfest Lager, Blitzen Ale, and a continuously rotating series called the IPA Chronicle, plus numerous one-off batches of beer throughout the year.

The Pick: Of the year-round offerings, the dark, creamy, and dry Nitro Stout proves a worthy complement to many of the items on Dunedin Brewery's pub fare menu.

not gone to the wayside; we've just morphed in a new way," he explained. "We used to have Piper's Pale Ale and Lowland Wheat. Three years ago, we went away from that. You alienate people who might think they won't like something Scottish. I'd rather someone be like, 'I can enjoy this product because it tastes good' or any other reason, but not just because of nationalism or some specific heritage. I'd rather it be open to anybody."

Though deemphasized, the Scottish angle is not forgotten. The brewery's newest logo is the simple outline of a medieval Claymore broadsword, and Dunedin strongly supports local bagpiping performances and competitions, as well as the annual Highlands game. Bryant himself is a piper, having started after elementary school. "When they first put the tanks in the original brewery, over near the Coke plant, I was the christener with the bagpipes. Of course, it probably wasn't the prettiest sounds you ever heard, but I was one year into it." He joined the local high school band, and then traveled to Scotland as a member of the City of Dunedin Pipe Band to compete in the world championships.

The brewery moved to its current location in 2001. The only building on the property was an old wood frame house that the elder Bryant used as the office for his general contracting business. A new building was constructed, but because it has wide and high overhead glass-paneled doors facing the street, many customers are under the impression that it was converted from a gas station, firehouse, or car dealership. In fact, the doors were built that way to allow large fermenters to be brought into the brewery.

When Bryant returned from his Pacific Northwest sojourn, one of his priorities was to weave more music into the brewery's DNA. "I love to enjoy a beer while experiencing some kind of live entertainment," he said. "Specifically for me, it's live music. If you bring in good talent with musicianship, and you bring in original flavors and original sounds, those two things just vibe together in such a way that people have a great time. We try to put as much effort into it as with our product. And our service. Those are our three main things for Dunedin Brewery." To that end, the brewery frequently hosts local, regional, and national musical acts in a variety of genres, and favorite bands are booked for such events as Oktobeerfest, the Stogies and Stout festival in late February, and the IPA Festival in early June.

In 2012, Bryant added another pillar to the triumvirate of beer, music, and service: exploration. The Dunedin Brewery and Fort George Brewery in Astoria, Oregon, had developed a partnership. Fort George sent some of its staff to brew at Dunedin, and Dunedin was invited to return the favor. After Dunedin Brewery was invited to attend the Oregon Brewers Festival, a road trip plan became a reality. Bryant and some of his staff drove across the country in a caravan that included a refrigerated truck with various kegs of their beer, stopping along the way to visit other craft breweries, and documenting the entire trip—dubbed the "The Great FL-Oregon Trail"—on the brewery's website, Facebook page, and Twitter account. When they arrived, they brewed a Double IPA at Fort George, and a beer developed especially for the festival proved to be a favorite at the event.

The next year, they embarked on the road again, this time towing a mobile 7-barrel brewing system. They used it to brew a collaboration beer with Black Shirt Brewing Co. in Denver. The beer, "Sangre de la Carretera: Blood of the Road" debuted at the Great American Beer Festival in Denver in October 2013.

Dunedin Brewery

Opened: 1996.

Owner: Michael N. Bryant.

Brewers: Norman Dixon, Trace Caley, and Richard Crance

System: 22-barrel JV Northwest.

Annual production: Nearly 2,000 barrels.

Hours: Sunday through Tuesday, 11 a.m. to 11 p.m.; Wednesday through Saturday, 11 a.m. to 1 p.m.

Tours: Thursday through Saturday at 5 p.m.; $5 cost includes a logo glass and beer samples.

Parking: Free on site and in lot across the street.

Takeout beer: Growlers and bottles.

Special considerations: Handicapped-accessible.

Extras: Outdoor seating; a small separate bar called the Nook, which features a rotation of craft beers from other breweries.

Other area beer sites: See 7venth Sun listing on page 129.

Florida Avenue Brewing Company

4101 North Florida Avenue, Tampa, FL 33603
(813) 374-2101 • floridaavenuebrewing.com

Not so many years ago, the neighborhood that Florida Avenue Brewing Company calls home was not one in which you'd want to walk alone at night. But Seminole Heights, just a few miles north of downtown Tampa, has begun to shed that stigma thanks to businesses such as the brewery opening. Now young professionals and families walk from their homes to the tasting room to share pints with friends and chat about their daily lives. "Everybody that lives near here walks in," Sharmi Duncan, the tasting room manager, told me. "I've got people that bring their kids in strollers and all kinds of stuff. People move into the neighborhood, and they discover that, 'Oh my gosh, there's a brewery right here.' It's a really great destination now. It's a good place to be."

Florida Avenue Brewing Company hit the Florida market in the late summer of 2010 under the name Cold Storage Craft Brewery and soon had bottles on store shelves and draft on taps throughout the state with its Florida Avenue line of ales. Brewmaster David Nicholas can take credit for the taps—he brews all the draft beer in the Tampa brewery; bottled beers are brewed and packaged under contract at another brewery. Nicholas has homebrewed—once. "In the very beginning, when I told my wife that I wanted to brew, she bought me a homebrew kit," he said. "And the standard British pale ale failed miserably. Had to pour the whole thing down the drain."

So unlike other brewers who started in their kitchens, he began his career at the once popular microbrewery chain Hops. "I just went in with the attitude of, regardless of what they paid me, it's like going to school," Nicholas said. As the chain began sliding toward bankruptcy, it moved him among stores in an effort to prop up the business. Eventually, he began talking to David Doble at Tampa Bay Brewing Company, who brought him on. He worked there for nearly five years. Nicholas then moved to Yuengling's Tampa brewery for about a year.

Beers brewed: Florida Avenue Ale, Florida Avenue Blueberry, Florida Avenue India Pale Ale, and Betchy Brown Ale, plus rotating seasonals and specialties.

The Pick: Betchy Brown is a full-flavored brown ale, brewed with seven different malts that present a diverse flavor profile to the palate.

"That's a whole other side of the spectrum, working with a 500-barrel system," he said. "I had a lot more appreciation for production, engineering, layout, logistics, and really got more into that side, whereas in the beginning, I laid the foundation working over at Hops, learning technique. Over at Tampa Bay Brewing, I learned a lot about recipe formulation because we just brewed so many beers over there." Then word got out that Florida Avenue was opening and seeking a brewer, and someone at Yuengling suggested Nicholas. He was hired.

Florida Avenue's building once held a neighborhood grocery store, and from the outside, it still maintains that utilitarian appearance. But inside, it has been transformed into a roomy and inviting space, with scattered couches, chairs, and tables; mood lighting; and a stage for performances by local bands and open mic nights. The back part of the building houses the brewing equipment, including the original 20-barrel system that the owners bought from Busch Gardens after the Tampa theme park shuttered a brewery on its property, along with five 40-barrel fermenters.

The flagship brews might best be described as "gateway beers"— nothing too extreme, but solid, clean, and easy drinking. But now that the owners have seen the success of the tasting room, they want to put more experimental beers on tap. "I can only do 40-barrel batches," Nicholas said. "So the thing they're talking about now is bringing in a small pilot system. A 4- to 5-barrel system. We'll set it up maybe in the front window. We'll hire a pilot brewer, and he can just go hog wild."

Florida Avenue Brewing Company

Opened: 2010.

Owners: Andy Delaparte, Brent Berthy, and Bruce Talcott

Brewer: David Nicholas.

System: 20-barrel system, mostly JV Northwest.

Annual production: 3,500 barrels.

Hours: Tuesday, 4 to 10 p.m.; Wednesday, 4 to 8 p.m.; Thursday, 4 to 10 p.m.;
Friday, 2 to 11 p.m.; Saturday, 1 to 11 p.m.

Tours: Open house the third Saturday of the month; $10 cost includes logo glass
to keep and samples. On request other times, if someone's available.

Parking: Free on site.

Takeout beer: Bottles and growlers.

Special considerations: Handicapped-accessible.

Extras: Outdoor seating.

Other area beer sites: The Independent Bar and Cafe, 5016 N. Florida Ave., Tampa,
FL 33603, (813) 341-4883, www.independenttampa.com.

Lagerhaus Brewery & Grill

3438 East Lake Business, Palm
Harbor, FL 34685
(727) 216-9682
lagerhausbrewery.com

Franz Rothschadl Jr. brews his Helms Dunkler Bock using a three-hundred-year-old family recipe. Son of Erna Helm and Franz Rothschadl Sr., the owner and brewer at the Lagerhaus Brewery & Grill boasts an ancestry steeped in the fermentation arts dating to the fifteenth century on his mother's side, when the Helm family began working in the wine business in what was then the kingdom of Bohemia. In 1620, Balthazar Helm von Worlow became the first of the family to enter the beer business, establishing a brewery in a Gothic-style building, which still stands today in the city of Tabor, Czech Republic. During World War I, the family moved to Austria from then-Czechoslovakia. Rothschadl's father was also in the wine business. But you don't need a genealogy lesson to know that Rothschadl knows about making beer. You'll figure that out just a couple minutes into a conversation with him.

The Lagerhaus operates at a strip mall in the community of Palm Harbor. The dark wood trim, exposed beams, and European beer banners, mirrors, and signs herald the authentic German-Bavarian food menu. The beer list leans heavily toward the pilsners, bocks, hefeweizens, and Maerzens one might expect in such a venue, and though Rothschadl is a classically educated brewmaster from the old country, he does not shirk from sometimes bending the Reinheitsgebot, or German Beer Purity Law, and adding local flavor to the classic styles. "I do a lot of varieties—with Florida tangerine, passion fruit—so I always at least adhere to the spirit of the purity law," he said. "I'm not flavoring the beer; I use real fruit."

Rothschadl lets his all of his beer carbonate naturally, rather than injecting carbon dioxide into the finished product to give it the fizz. "I'm one of the very few who does not artificially carbonate their beer," he told me. "My beer ferments in the tank, and then I cut off the pressure valve

Beers brewed: Fischer Hefeweizen, Royal Bohemian Pilsner, Helms Dunkler Bock, Wildberry Lambic, and 44 Magnum, plus many seasonals and special brews.

The Pick: The 44 Magnum is one of those beers you'll be telling people about for years. The sweet, caramel smoothness of the strong scotch ale disguises the 22 percent ABV. Be careful— it's loaded.

and naturally carbonate the beer. We could strictly call even my ales cask-conditioned." The advantages of natural carbonation include a tendency for the beer to take a while to lose its fizz. "You can have a beer which is naturally carbonated sit for an hour," Rothschadl said. "It's warm, but it's still not flat. It's drinkable."

He still speaks with the accent of his youth, animatedly using his arms and hands for emphasis while explaining his brewing philosophy and techniques. After helping revive his family's brewery back in Austria in the late 1980s, he traveled to Paraguay to open a brewery for an Austrian-German company. He moved to Palm Harbor, where his daughter was born, in 1996 and teamed up with the owner of Hoppers Grille & Brewery. "He kind of burned out and sold Hoppers in 2001, just before 9/11," Rothschadl said. "The guy who bought it bought me basically with it. He expanded fast, and it failed in 2005. I bought the equipment from the bankruptcy court, and I got a lease at the original location. It took me almost a couple of years to open. I opened the first month of the Great Recession. The first couple of years were difficult."

The Lagerhaus now bustles with families, young professionals, and beer geeks eager to try some of the more than twenty-five brews in Rothschadl's repertoire, including the extremely powerful and extremely tasty 44 Magnum, which clocks in at 22 percent ABV. Flights are available for those who want to taste several of the styles, and the brewery also offers a large selection of ciders.

Lagerhaus Brewery & Grill

Opened: 2007.
Owner: Franz Rothschadl Jr.
Brewer: Franz Rothschadl Jr.
System: 4.5-barrel prototype made in Slovakia.
Annual production: 200 barrels.
Hours: Monday through Wednesday, 3:30 to 11:30 p.m.; Thursday through Sunday, 3:30 p.m. to midnight.
Tours: On request or by calling or emailing ahead.
Parking: Free on site.
Takeout beer: None.
Special considerations: Handicapped-accessible.
Extras: Outdoor biergarten.
Other area beer sites: Palm Harbor House of Beer, 34970 U.S. 19 N., Palm Harbor, FL 34684, (727) 784-2337, www.palmharborhob.com.

R Bar

245 108th Avenue, Treasure Island, FL 33706
(727) 367-3400 • www.rbarti.com

A dive bar in town differs from a dive bar at the beach. At the former, the regulars don't like outsiders, the beer is warm and bland, and the food is pickled and comes out of a big jar. The latter welcomes all, asking only that because the Health Department requires it, you put on a shirt before you come in. Beers are cold, though generally still bland, and the best beach dive bars serve fresh food cooked to order. But there are elements common to both: neon beer signs. A tattered calendar from one of the macrobrewers. Worn paint. Air-conditioning.

R Bar is a beach dive bar, housed in an old A&W Root Beer stand just a few blocks from the sand of Treasure Island Beach. But behind the bar, above the liquor bottles and taps of macrobrewed and mass-produced imports, hangs a new sign that's an anomaly in the well-worn surroundings: "Try One of Our Fresh Brewed Beers Made Right Here in Our Brew Pub. Ask your server or bartender for a sample today."

Out of three taps isolated from the others, hand-crafted beer flows. The brews are the handiwork of Eric Richardson, a longtime home-brewer who had worked the grill for years at R Bar. But it wasn't his idea to put his beers on tap; it was the new owner's.

Bob Hughes took over the place in February 2012 and set about making improvements, such as fixing the ventilation system and cooking fresh seafood and chicken instead of the frozen stuff his predecessor fed the customers. And he added some local craft beer offerings. During the previous owner's tenure, the burner that Richardson was using for his homebrewing broke, and he got permission to use the burners in the kitchen to boil his wort. After Hughes acquired R Bar, Richardson hesitantly approached him to ask if he could continue to do so. "He said yeah," Richardson told me, and then he became interested and wanted to try the beer. Enamored by the flavorful brew, Hughes set about obtaining the necessary licenses to serve it to customers, installed a modest 10-gallon brewing system, and gave Richardson permission to step away from the grill a couple times a week and do his thing.

Beers brewed: Amarillo IPA, Porter, Pale Ale, and one rotating tap.

The Pick: Who says dark beers don't belong at the beach? The Porter is thick, creamy, and smooth, with a complex layering of roasted malt, coffee, and chocolate flavors.

The regulars at the bar, used to their mass-produced lagers, have had a mixed reaction. "We have the extreme at both ends," Richardson said. "Either they hate it or they love it." But then word got out through a couple articles in local newspapers and on social media. A friend at Willard's Tap House, a craft beer bar up in Largo where Richardson hangs out, started telling folks there about it, and when Richardson came in, they would discuss it with him. "Then the next thing you know, they're in here drinking the beer," he said.

Plenty of people are drinking it, so many that Richardson can't keep up. So he and Hughes have been discussing adding as many as six or seven more taps, upgrading to a 3-barrel system, and possibly adding on to the bar. They've been visiting other area breweries for ideas.

The R Bar is a stop on the St. Pete/Clearwater Craft Beer Trail, created in 2013 by the local convention and visitors bureau, and an R Bar Brewing Facebook page disseminates information about the latest brews. Richardson might need to leave the grill more often as word spreads. "It's pretty good to have a lot of people," he said, "but for me it's more like, 'Oh no, they're drinking all the beer again!' It's a good thing, though." And it's a good thing he feels that way, because the little dive bar at the beach is now a brewpub.

R Bar

Opened: 2013 (brewery).

Owner: Bob Hughes.

Brewer: Eric Richardson.

System: 10-gallon three-tier system.

Annual production: Estimated 50 barrels.

Hours: Seven days a week, 8 a.m. to midnight.

Tours: None.

Parking: Free on site.

Takeout beer: None.

Special considerations: Handicapped-accessible.

Rapp Brewing Company

Rapp Brewing Company
Tampa Bay Florida

10930 Endeavour Way, Suite C, Seminole, FL 33777
(727) 544-1752 • www.rappbrewing.com

Rapp Brewing Company does not have a bar. "It's a serving counter," Greg Rapp said. Don't assume, though, that Rapp is any sort of beer snob. But when you have twenty taps in the brewery you built, all flowing with beer you've created, many in styles that the craft beer newbie likely has never heard of, you can call things whatever you want. Rapp, a genial host and expert brewer, opened his brewery in the Pinellas County town of Seminole on September 1, 2012. Just four months later, the online forum RateBeer (www.ratebeer.com) awarded it the honor of Florida's best new brewer, based on user ratings.

More than thirty years ago, Rapp started making his own wine at home, a hobby he continued for a couple decades until someone gave him a homebrewing kit. Eventually, he founded the Pinellas Urban Brewers Guild homebrewing club, and he began attending local beer festivals and other events with club members to share samples of their brews with the public. People started asking Rapp where they could buy his beer. Then in September 2011, the company he worked for was bought out, and after thirty years in the information technology field, he decided to pursue his dream. "I said, 'Well, at this point in my life, if I'm gonna do it, I should do it.'"

Once he had made up his mind, Rapp started looking for property. He wanted a place close to home, in Pinellas County, but not too close to other breweries. "Something centrally located, easy to get to, affordable, and with a jurisdiction that would allow me to do what I wanted to do," he said. He settled on a space in a small industrial park that is "right in the heart of Pinellas County."

Build-out began immediately. A priority was a space for customers and friends to sample his beer. "I just had to have a tasting room," he explained. "There was no way I was just going to have a brewery. I didn't want a 'bar.' I wanted to re-create that atmosphere that you get when you

Beers available: Maple Wheat Bock, Belgian Golden Strong Ale, Gose, Berliner Weisse, American Pale Ale, Blond, Hefeweizen, and Dunkelweizen, plus many seasonals and specials.

The Pick: Try the Gose. Greg Rapp reached back in time to revive an old German style of wheat beer that is tangy and slightly sour, with a hint of salt and coriander, and is incredible refreshing.

go to a craft-brewing event. When you're a homebrewer and serving your beer, you're able to sit down and interact directly with the people tasting your beer, so a tasting room was a must for me." To that end, he started a crowdfunding campaign on Kickstarter to fund upgrades to the tasting room. He sought $20,000 but fell short by about $4,000. Still, he said, "I was really pleased with that. It shows how much support we had out there for the project, so that was excellent."

He decided to bite the proverbial financial bullet and build the tasting room he had envisioned. It takes up about 650 of the space's total 3,200 square feet. The tasting counter is granite, and a folding overhead glass door opens to provide access to the brewing area and additional seating. Flags from various nations, states, and organizations draped over the exposed metal ceiling rafters add sound buffering, and the air-conditioning flows cold. In back are the brewing and fermenting tanks, the cold room, and a small laboratory.

On the twenty taps, you'll find styles that until recently had been out of vogue in this country, such as Roggenbier, Gose, Lichtenhainer, or Berliner Weisse. "My whole philosophy is to explore beer styles, and then explore the older styles and have a venue where people can try different things that you can't find anywhere else," he said. Rapp Brewing is a bit of a family affair, with Greg Rapp's daughter, Candice, often behind the bar and his wife, Dawn, filling the role of office/tasting room manager. "I'm living the dream. I've arrived," he said with a grin.

Rapp Brewing Company

Opened: 2012.

Owner: Greg Rapp.

Brewer: Greg Rapp.

System: 2-barrel custom-engineered system.

Annual production: 325 barrels.

Hours: Monday through Thursday, 3 to 10 p.m.; Friday, 3 to midnight; Saturday, 2 to midnight; Sunday, 3 to 8 p.m.

Tours: On request.

Parking: Free on site.

Takeout beer: Growlers and occasional limited-release bottles.

Special considerations: Handicapped-accessible.

Extras: Seating in brewery area; classes on beer styles and brewing for all levels.

Other area beer sites: Cajun Cafe on the Bayou, 8101 Park Blvd., Pinellas Park, FL 33781, (727) 546-6732, cajuncafeonthebayou.com.

Saint Somewhere Brewing Company

1441 Savannah Avenue, Unit E, Tarpon Springs, FL 34689

(813) 503-6181 • www.saintsomewherebrewing.com

Bob Sylvester lays claim to being one of the pioneers of the Tampa Bay–area craft beer scene, at least the second wave, which began in the middle of the first decade of the twenty-first century. When he started, the newest brewery in the area was Dunedin Brewery, which had been open for about a decade. But his attitude harks back to the early days of the modern craft beer movement, when Fritz Maytag, Jack McAuliffe, and Ken Grossman used their ingenuity and drive to jump-start an industry that had been stifled by mass production and corporate consolidation.

Saint Somewhere Brewing Company is a one-man operation, except for a platoon of eager volunteers that help out on bottling days. The brewing equipment was repurposed from dairy equipment. Production is a modest 450 barrels a year. And Sylvester's farmhouse ale and saison styles are the most widely distributed beers out of the Sunshine State, shipped to forty-two states, Montreal, and Denmark. How does this lone brewer manage that? "I don't," he replied with a laugh. "I'm so deep over my head in purchase orders, there's no way out."

A few years back, the quality of Sylvester's ales, brewed in an open fermenter with a good dose of local wild yeast, caught the attention of Shelton Brothers, the worldwide beer, wine, and spirits distributor, and Saint Somewhere became one of the few U.S. breweries in its portfolio. "They're very choosy," Sylvester said. "They've picked up a few American brands that fit into their philosophy. The first American beer they picked up was Jolly Pumpkin. We were the second."

As with many small brewery owners, Sylvester started as a homebrewer, going through various styles for about ten years until he discovered he had a knack for the Belgian farmhouse style. "You kind of run through the same evolution. You start something like a Sierra Nevada Pale Ale, and it

Beers brewed: Saison Athene, Pays du Soleil, and Lectio Divina.

The Pick: Lectio Divina, a Belgian strong pale ale, assaults the nose with a blend of sour, funky, and sweet aromas, but once it hits the tongue, they blend together in a wonderfully satisfying, refreshing, and complex drink with a non-oppressive fruity tartness.

opens your eyes: This has flavor! What is that?" he explained. "Then you end up over your head in hops, you go with the imperial pale ales, double IPAs, you can't get enough hops. Then you move into stouts and porters, and you can't get enough roast, you can't get enough big beer. Eventually, everyone ends up at some point in time with Belgians. I got there at a certain point in my homebrew career and stuck with it."

He eventually decided to take the plunge and open his own brewery. "I worked in retail for thirty-some-odd years and really couldn't do that any longer, and came to a crossroads in my career where I could go in a couple of directions." He decided he didn't want to go either way. "I didn't see myself doing either thing a minute longer. And even though it was only 2006, that was still on the cusp of the whole craft beer explosion. I somehow was able to sell the idea to the wife to open just a real niche brewery. From the onset, we were going to be just saison, farmhouse ales, maybe a Belgian dubbel. But we were kind of geared never to venture out of that."

The name of the brewery comes from a line in the Jimmy Buffett song "Boat Drinks": "Lately, newspaper mentioned cheap air fare, I got to fly to Saint Somewhere." The logo and beer labels are reproductions of a series of drawings from pamphlets distributed by the state during the land boom of the 1920s, when unscrupulous developers would sell lots unseen to northerners that often were not quite as advertised. The pictures portrayed angelic figures floating above lush flowered gardens and bountiful fruit groves with pristine creeks flowing through, but the buyers would often travel down to their new lots and find that they were in swamps or undeveloped tracts in the middle of nowhere.

Saint Somewhere is in a couple units of an industrial warehouse park, a stone's throw from the Gulf of Mexico, which you can smell but not see from the parking lot. A GPS will be your best friend the first time you visit, because it's a little off the beaten track. Once you arrive, if you do it at the right time, you'll find Sylvester and a gang of enthusiastic volunteers either furiously hand-bottling ales or standing around enjoying the product with fans of his line of beers.

Until December 2011, the only way you could ensure seeing the small-batch brewery in action was to be on an email list of local beer geeks who gladly troop out to Saint Somewhere to volunteer on bottling days, in exchange for a handful of freshly filled 750-milliliter bottles and some pizza. But then Sylvester decided to give "brewery tours" for the general public. For ten bucks, you get an engraved Saint Somewhere glass and three 10-ounce pours of whatever is on tap. The tour consists of Sylvester standing atop a platform next to the open fermenting tank and pointing at the various pieces of equipment in the

1,250-square-foot space. "The brewery tour takes six to ten seconds," Sylvester said with a chuckle. In reality, it's more like ten to fifteen minutes, but it can make for an unstructured evening. Sometimes those attending bring along bottles from their cellars to share. Sometimes it goes on a wee past the official ending time.

Back in the fall of 2011, when the Occupy Wall Street movement captivated the nation's attention, something spontaneous happened. Sylvester had plans to be out of town during one of the regularly scheduled tour nights, and he turned the responsibility over to a couple of his volunteers. They dubbed it "Occupy Saint Somewhere" and set up a Facebook page for it, jokingly indicating that Sylvester might find the brewery in shambles on his return. Those attending were invited to bring along rare or vintage beers to share. It packed the place and became a phenomenon. Other "Occupy" nights have since taken place on an irregular schedule.

But even if it's not an official tour night, a beer pilgrim visiting the area should feel free to call. Sylvester might be working in the brewery, or he might come down to open it up for the visitor. Often folks are astonished at the compactness. "We get a lot of people from out of state that are pretty excited to be at Saint Somewhere," he said. "They'll come from Philadelphia or Chicago or even San Francisco, and they're expecting to see a big brewery. They walk into here and say, 'Is this your pilot brewery or do you have the whole building?' and I'm, 'No, no, no. Everything comes out of here.'"

Saint Somewhere Brewing Company

Opened: 2006.

Owners: Bob and Anne Sylvester.

Brewer: Bob Sylvester.

System: 7-barrel converted dairy system.

Annual production: 450 barrels.

Hours: Thursday and Friday, 6 to 8 p.m.

Tours: Thursday and Friday, 6 to 8 p.m.

Parking: Free on site.

Takeout beer: None.

Special considerations: Handicapped-accessible.

Extras: Occasional Occupy Saint Somewhere bottle shares.

Other area beer sites: Tarpon Tavern, 21 N. Safford Ave., Tarpon Springs, FL 34689, (727) 945-1000, tarpontavern.com; 701 Taphouse, 701 N. Pinellas Ave., Tarpon Springs, FL 34689, (727) 940-5257, www.tarpontaphouse.com.

Sea Dog Brewing Co.

26200 U.S. Highway 19 North, Clearwater, FL 33761
(727) 466-4916 • www.seadogbrewing.com

Sea Dog Brewing Co. in Portland, Maine, wanted to provide a place for locals on vacation to find a taste of their hometown brew. So it opened a brewpub in Florida. "Beginning in October and through March, we get a lot of that New England crowd that comes in and sits down," said Bobby Baker, the brewer at Sea Dog's brewpub in Clearwater. "They come down and they recognize the name, so it's a slice of home for them."

The interior is modeled after a New England pub, though it's infused with a postindustrial veneer. Rustic wood panels and trim mix with burnished steel underneath exposed steel girders and ductwork, painted flat black. Industrial light fixtures interspersed with lights made from clear glass bottles provide illumination. Enormous pictures, images, and Sea Dog branding on the walls dwarf the spacious, open dining area. Sitting at the bar, you can see out onto the expansive outdoor covered deck, where a high concrete wall capped with about a foot of decorative wrought iron buffers the noise of the nonstop traffic on busy U.S. 19.

The New England influence extends to the menu, which leans heavily toward local seafood and, of course, flown-in-fresh Maine lobster. Most of the beer taps flow with brew shipped down from the Maine brewery and Sea Dog's sister brewery, Shipyard Brewing Company. A nano-size brewing system on the premises usually supplies one of the taps. Baker makes that beer.

It was a chance encounter in a Lakeland wine and beer shop that led Baker to the job. He was working there when Sea Dog owner Fred Forsley walked in, and not knowing who he was, Baker, then a homebrewer, struck up a conversation with Forsley in which he revealed his desire to work as commercial brewer. One thing led to another, and Baker was off to Maine to train up there for the job in the planned Clearwater brewpub.

In a way, Baker said, the system in Clearwater provides a research-and-development opportunity for Sea Dog to tailor brewing toward its fans in the Sunshine State. "They've got a pilot system up

Beers brewed: Sea Dog and Shipyard beers brewed in Maine dominate the taps, but at least one tap is always devoted to the latest in-house brew.

The Pick: The style of the in-house beer changes with each brew, but it's the one to try because it's the only place you'll find it.

there as well, but since we're in a different market than Maine, it's just learning how people react in a whole different region. That's the idea behind it right now." He has mostly free rein on his recipes now, though he will consult with his trainer and other folks in Maine. Among the styles he's produced so far are a barrel-aged English IPA, a black IPA, a hazelnut porter, and an Oreo cream stout.

Customers have generally been positive about the brews. "Not all of them have been a home run, but the majority have gone over real well," Baker said. He eagerly accepts feedback on those that fall short of his goal, both in person and from the brewpub's social media channels. "With the help of the public, we get to make those tweaks and make the next batch even better."

In 2013, Sea Dog opened another Florida pub, near Disney World in Orlando. As of this writing, brewing had not started on those premises, but Baker was helping the company turn the pub into something similar to the Clearwater location. In addition, the Clearwater pub had started construction on a 20-barrel production brewery to make Sea Dog and Shipyard beers as well as special brews for the pub, with Baker as brewmaster.

Sea Dog Brewing Co.

Opened: 2013.

Owner: Fred Forsley.

Brewer: Bobby Baker.

System: 1-barrel SABCO v350; 20-barrel system being installed.

Annual production: Estimated 100 barrels, plus an additional 40,000 barrels with the new system.

Hours: Monday through Thursday, 4 p.m. to midnight; Friday and Saturday, 11 a.m. to 1 a.m.; Sunday, 11 a.m. to midnight.

Tours: None.

Parking: Free on site.

Takeout beer: Bottles, cans, and kegs.

Special considerations: Handicapped-accessible.

Extras: Large, covered outdoor seating area; beer and how-to-brew classes; personalized beer for parties, weddings, and other events; mug club.

Other area beer sites: Lueken's Big Town Liquors, 23025 U.S. 19 N., Clearwater, FL 33759, (727) 412-8924, www.luekensliquors.com.

7venth Sun Brewery

7venth Sun®

BREWERY

1012 Broadway, Dunedin, FL 34698
(727) 733-3013 • www.7venthsun.com

When 7venth Sun Brewery opened its doors to the public on January 7, 2012, an overflow crowd packed the tiny tasting room in the corner of an older concrete-block strip center and spilled out into the roped-off parking lot. At 2 p.m., the first beer, Donut Porter, was split between three glasses for the trio of gentlemen who paid $202.50 for the pleasure. They had scored this opportunity by submitting the winning bid in an eBay auction. The money went to a local organization to help the homeless. The taps flowed steadily the rest of the day, revealing the eagerness of the Tampa Bay–area craft beer community to show its support for Dunedin's second craft brewery.

When it opened, 7venth Sun brought something new to many beer lovers in the area at the time. Brewer and cofounder Justin Stange specializes in saisons, tart Berliner Weisses, and sour Belgian styles aged in oak and spirit barrels. He also brews IPAs, porters, stouts, and other styles, but he really enjoys working with the citrus and tropical fruits of Florida to tart up his beers. He experiments a lot, producing one-offs that sometimes are so popular that he'll put them in rotation. "Seems like every time we put something new on, that's our bestseller that week," he said. "Clearly people like the variety that we offer here. As far as the beers that we do all the time, it's kind of a tie between the Berliner Weisse and Graffiti Orange. Midnight Moonlight was kind of a surprise. We didn't know if Berliner Weisse would be received that well."

Stange met his partner, Devon Kreps, when they both worked at Atlanta's SweetWater Brewing Company, Kreps as production manager, Stange as a brewer. Kreps had arrived at SweetWater after she graduated from Oregon State University with a degree in fermentation science and did a stint brewing with Anheuser-Busch. After leaving SweetWater, Stange brewed with Cigar City Brewing in Tampa.

Beers brewed: Graffiti Orange, Intergalactic Pale Ale (IPA), Midnight Moonlight Berliner Weisse, Belge d'Or, and Saison in Paradise.

The Pick: Did you like Creamsicles growing up? Try the Graffiti Orange, a wheat beer with an infusion of citrus that will bring back those lazy days of summer break when you and your pals would chase after the ice cream truck waving the bills you earned mowing lawns.

But it was while at the Atlanta brewery that they began scheming to open their own. However, "7venth Sun wasn't exactly what we had envisioned," Stange said. "We wanted a bigger brewery to go for more production. That's what we were familiar with at the time. Two and a half years later, after trying everything we could, taking out a loan on the house and maxing out a bunch of credit cards . . . now we have a brewery."

Even though they started smaller than they'd hoped, they've already begun to grow, first by leasing the unit next to them and moving their equipment to that side, then by distributing kegs to pubs and restaurants through the area. They're doing more barrel-aged beers, and the customer base in the tight-knit Dunedin community keeps the tasting room busy. All of the bartenders are cicerone-certified beer servers who will gladly offer on-the-spot beer schooling and tours, if the place is not too packed.

And their relationship with the town's other brewery remains strong. "Michael Bryant, owner of the Dunedin Brewery, was general contractor for this project," Stange said. "He did everything that he could do to make sure we were open, outside of writing us a check." "We spoke with him before we opened the business," Kreps added. "We didn't want to step on anyone's toes, and we said, 'What would you think if we opened a brewery here?' and he said that it would be fantastic to make Dunedin a beer destination, and we're like, 'That's the vision we have too. That's fantastic.'"

7venth Sun Brewery

Opened: 2012.

Owners: Devon Kreps and Justin Stange.

Brewer: Justin Stange.

System: 4.5-barrel Stouts.

Annual production: Estimated 1,000 barrels in 2013 (post-expansion).

Hours: Tuesday through Thursday, 2 p.m. to midnight; Friday and Saturday, noon to midnight; Sunday, noon to 10 p.m.

Tours: On request if someone's available.

Parking: Free on site.

Takeout beer: Growlers and special releases in 750-milliliter bottles.

Special considerations: Handicapped-accessible.

Extras: Outdoor seating.

Other area beer sites: Dunedin House of Beer, 927 Broadway, Dunedin, FL 34698, (727) 216-6318, www.dunedinhob.com.

Southern Brewing & Winemaking

4500 North Nebraska Avenue, Tampa, FL 33603
(813) 238-7800 • www.southernbrewingwinemaking.com

If Southern Brewing & Winemaking were a human, you'd describe him as a Renaissance man, one who has wide-ranging interests and expertise in a variety of areas. There's the homebrewing area, shipping supplies all over the world and selling out of the storefront. Winemaking, the same thing. Teaching, helping beginners, experts, and in-betweeners learn how to make their own beer and wine or improve their techniques. And then there's the brewery, serving the beer crafted on its nano-size system to folks who drop in to buy supplies or just sit at the bar to drink and chat.

The well-rounded business near downtown Tampa is the brainchild of Brian and Kelly Fenstermacher, a husband-and-wife team who met in 1996 during a Belgian beer festival at Atlanta Brewing Company, where Brian was the brewmaster. In 2001, the couple moved to Tampa, where Brian took the job of head brewer at Ybor City Brewing, which closed in 2003, though the label lives on with Florida Beer Company in Cape Canaveral.

He left Ybor City to start his own brewery, planning to work with Shipyard Brewing Company out of Portland, Maine, but after the contracts were written, a financial partner backed out, and Brian had to abandon those plans. But he noticed the burgeoning growth of craft breweries in the southeastern United States, so he decided to start supplying their ingredients. "At that time, I developed a relationship with Crisp Malting through Shipyard. As a part of the business, I was going to distribute Crisp Malts throughout Florida," he said. "So I just kind of ran with the distribution side after the brewery fell apart and did that for ten years." Then, after Tampa's only homebrew supply shop closed in 2008, the Fenstermachers opened a retail component and began selling ingredients and supplies to local brewers from their warehouse in North Tampa.

In 2010, they sold the successful wholesale operation and moved to their new address, and

Beers brewed: Black Veil IPA, Saison Le Chiffre, Moonraker Imperial Stout, Atonement Rye, Hopburst Ale, Westside IPA, and Fragmented Porter, plus various seasonals and one-offs.

The Pick: The Moonraker Stout pours dark and creamy, and that's how it tastes, too, with sweet chocolate and coffee notes that leave a pleasant roasted malt aftertaste on the tongue.

that, said Brian, "put me back on the path to build the business I always wanted to have, which was a straight homebrew shop with a small brewery, so that's kind of where we are." They moved to the Seminole Heights neighborhood for a variety of reasons. "It was mostly the space, the proximity to our house, and it turned out this neighborhood was absolutely fantastic for craft beer lovers," Brian said. "It's really an eclectic neighborhood, young people live right in this area, so a lot of our customers turned out to be here. And this whole southeast Seminole Heights is really turning into a real nice craft beer destination. It's really an ideal spot for us."

When I visited, Southern Brewing & Winemaking was serving from twenty-two taps, but the Fenstermachers planned to increase that to as many as thirty-five to allow for the cider, mead, and wine that the shop recently began making, along with more house-brewed beer and guest taps. Outside, a quiet beer garden area allows customers to enjoy their drinks of choice when the weather is pleasant. Inside, the tasting bar sits against one wall across from shelves and stacks of homebrewing equipment. The in-house brewers and homebrewers trade recipes and tips, helping both improve in their craft.

The Fenstermachers aim at improving the existing storefront, with no plans for aggressive expansion. "We're not in a rush to build the business or build the beer side," Brian said. "We're more just trying to have fun while we do it, so this will be something that will be around for thirty years as we move into retirement."

Southern Brewing & Winemaking

Opened: 2011 at current address.

Owners: Brian and Kelly Fenstermacher.

Brewers: Brian Fenstermacher, Rick Etshman, and Tyler Singletary

System: 1-barrel custom.

Annual production: Estimated 150 barrels.

Hours: Sunday through Wednesday, 11 a.m. to 7 p.m.; Thursday and Friday, 11 a.m. to 11 p.m.; Saturday, 10 a.m. to 7 p.m.

Tours: On request, if someone's available.

Parking: Free on site.

Takeout beer: Growlers.

Special considerations: Handicapped-accessible.

Extras: Outdoor beer garden; homebrewing supplies.

Other area beer sites: Mermaid Tavern, 6719 N. Nebraska Ave., Tampa, FL 33604, (813) 238-5618, www.mermaidtaverntampa.com.

Tampa Bay Brewing Company

RESTAURANT & BREWERY

1600 East Eighth Avenue, Tampa, FL 33605
(813) 247-1422 • www.tampabaybrewingcompany.com

The Tampa Bay Brewing Company story is a family story. And like many family stories, part of it is tragic. Travel back to 1996, when John G. Doble III started a brewpub in Tampa's historic Ybor City district, roping into the project his brother David and their parents, John Jr. and Vicki. John III and David had entered into various entrepreneurial projects before: selling water filters door to door, running a landscaping business, and breeding birds for pet shops. Yes, birds. "That was a real low point," David Doble told me with a laugh.

The brewpub, housed in former horse stables, and a homebrew supply shop were his brother's idea, but David eagerly jumped into the project. "I was just assumed to be free help, which is great," he said. "At least we were going to get to brew and drink now. That worked out." After the brewpub had been running for nearly two years, David decided it was time to get out from under someone else's wings and spread his own. He went to school and then got a job flying commercial regional jets based at Chicago's O'Hare airport. But then tragedy entered the story.

John III died in a house fire in 2003. It shook the family and their business. "The pub just started to go its own way, and it wasn't good," David Doble said. "The quality of the beers on tap was going downhill, and my mom was starting to lose control of the staff because her heart wasn't really here. So I quit my job and came back to the pub." He started back officially on January 1, 2004, but the brewpub continued to struggle.

When the lease ended, the family decided to take a chance and reopen in Centro Ybor, a shopping, dining, and entertainment complex built in and around the former El Centro Espanol club in the midst of the historic district. Tampa Bay Brewing Company opened in its new location in 2006. It proved to be a wise business decision. According

Beers brewed: Old Elephant Foot IPA, One Night Stand Pale Ale, Redeye Amber Ale, Iron Rat Imperial Stout, Jack the Quaffer London Porter, Wild Warthog Weizen, True Blonde Ale, and Moosekiller Barley-Wine Style Ale. Also two rotating seasonal taps and one rotating cask hand pull (cask tapped weekly on Thursdays at 4 p.m.).

The Pick: Old Elephant Foot IPA is always a tasty treat, with its bountiful amounts of Northern Brewer, Cascade, and Centennial hops, and at 80 IBUs, it should make any hophead except the most extreme happy.

to Doble, "Our first year open here, our sales were just a hair over 100 percent over the first year" at the old pub. "Today, comparatively, we're about 300 percent over sales from the original pub. We just got a chance to solve a lot of issues that our model had at the first place."

Good things happened. Celebrity chef Guy Fieri visited the brewpub for an episode of his Food Network Show *Diners, Drive-Ins, and Dives*. Customers flocked there after it aired in October 2011. Then, after years of back and forth with state regulators, the brewpub obtained permission to sell its beer off the premises. The beer was first sold in growlers and kegs, but soon after, a small canning line was shoehorned into the brewery, and four-packs of 16-ounce cans of the flagship Old Elephant Foot IPA started going out the door and onto store shelves. And the craft beer craze started booming. "It all hit at once," Doble said. "We had already built the rocket ship. All we needed was fuel."

The tragedy of his brother's death still remains with the family, but they have honored him by establishing the John G. Doble III Memorial Scholarship, which is awarded to a Florida brewer each year through the Florida Brewers Guild at its annual Beerfest. The scholarship covers tuition and travel expenses for the World Brewing Academy Concise Course in Brewing Technology, held each fall at the Siebel Institute in Chicago.

One of the things that drew Fieri's attention to Tampa Bay Brewing was the food. Many of the dishes use the house brews as ingredients, including beer cheese soup made with True Blonde Ale, a gumbo that includes Old Elephant Foot IPA, and the Moosekiller Meatloaf with Wild Mushroom Demi, cooked with the Moosekiller Barley-Wine Style Ale.

The family-friendly restaurant is usually packed on weekends, with customers lined up outside waiting for tables. The outside patio bar is a great place to order a beer on a Friday or Saturday night and watch the people, some more colorful than others, who walk by as part of Ybor's bustling nightlife scene.

Doble is the brewmaster and his mother, Vicki, serves as general manager, but at the time of my visit, they employed a staff of more than sixty. "The past few years is the first time we made enough to employ a proper management team, so it's not just me and my mom running around with our heads cut off trying to keep all this glued together," Doble said. "We finally employed enough staff to get everything in place, to get it all to work, and we really have our eyes set on the future now."

Part of this future is to spread the Tampa Bay Brewing Company brand even farther. A former assistant brewer, Norm Lehman, partnered with the Doble family to open the Tampa Bay Brewing Co. Coral

Springs Tap House at 1221 North University Drive in February 2013. Doble didn't want to be too specific about some of his other plans, but he outlined them in general terms. "We believe our brand has really grown to the point where it's a decent footprint in Tampa Bay, and we believe in going beyond that," he said. "So I would love to expand, but I really don't want to expand outside of the state because I believe craft beer is all about local beer. If you can cover a state, I think that's great. That's fun. I think these people now that are just trying to expand from coast to coast, it's really neat, it's great, and there's room for a few of those brands, but beyond that, the fun part about craft beer is about the actual journey to obtain the beer. And that's a blast."

Tampa Bay Brewing Company

Opened: 1996.

Owners: Vicki Doble, John Doble, David Doble, and Stuart Mills (equity partner).

Brewer: David Doble.

System: 10-barrel 1996 Criveller brewhouse.

Annual production: 2,100 barrels.

Hours: Monday through Thursday, 11 a.m. to 11 p.m.; Friday and Saturday, 11 a.m. to midnight; Sunday, noon to 11 p.m.

Tours: Currently on request; scheduled tours coming soon.

Parking: Some free street parking nearby, valet service, and nearby pay-to-park garages.

Takeout beer: Growlers, cans, and kegs.

Special considerations: Handicapped-accessible.

Extras: Covered outdoor patio with full bar and restaurant service.

Other area beer sites: New World Brewery (bar), 1313 Eighth Ave., Tampa, FL 33605, (813) 248-4969, newworldbrewery.net.

Three Palms Brewing

1509 Hobbs Street, Tampa, FL 33619
(813) 685-6151 • threepalmsbrewing.com

It's the old story: man drinks beer, man likes beer, man makes beer, man's friends tell him he should open a brewery. Randy Reaver listened. "After a while, I started to take it seriously and consider it," he said. "That's really how it came about." That was the start of Three Palms Brewery, which moved into a space in an East Tampa warehouse park in April 2012 and brewed its first batch on July 4.

"Palms" is an obvious choice for a Florida brewery name, but why three of them? Reaver chuckled. "What I had in my mind was three partners getting into the brewery," he explained. The plan with the other two partners did not come to fruition, so it ended up being just one "palm." But Reaver liked the name, so he ran with it.

When I visited the brewery, Reaver had just received clearance from the county and opened a tasting room, which had been a main goal all along, so he can use capital from on-premises sales to fund future expansion. "Not that I'm necessarily looking to grow quickly," he said. With the new tasting room in place, Reaver can concentrate more on distribution. He's already sent kegged beer to area venues, a limited number of 22-ounce bottles have landed on store shelves, and now he can move growlers and more kegs out the door. He said he also hopes to begin canning some beer, and "who knows, from there? If it really goes well, possibly expanding."

Reaver likes to tinker with his recipes, but the beers he serves are based on the styles he likes—and he likes many styles. "Of course, you want everybody to like your beers, that's important, but you have to like what you're making as well," he told me. "Initially, I was really into IPAs, years back. I was a real hophead, went through my whole IPA phase, and then transitioned more into Belgian-style beers. I like them all, really; it's hard to say. I

Beers brewed: Queen of Wheat Hefeweizen, Ruby Pogo Hoppy Red Ale, Burley American Barleywine Ale, choCCa Belgian Imperial Stout, Enjoy the Ride Imperial IPA, Black Durgeon Imperial Stout, Pindo IPA, Sir Albert's Reserve American Imperial Chocolate Stout, Brew Baby Milk Stout, Mystieke Zon Saison, and 1509 English Style Mild Brown Ale, plus various specialties and seasonals.

The Pick: The malty Ruby Pogo boasts a whopping 7.5 percent ABV, on the high end for a red ale, but a citrusy hops presence gives it a nice balance on the tongue.

like imperial stouts; I like barleywines. It's really hard to decide on the next beer I'm going to put out. But I guess that's the best part of being a craft brewer—being independent and being on your own, you can do whatever you want. It's not dictated by anybody except yourself."

Before the tasting room opened, Reaver introduced his beers and his brewery to the public on Wednesday nights, when he would open the doors, charge folks $10 for a logo glass, pour samples, and answer questions. Now people can come by five days a week during regularly scheduled hours and sit down to leisurely enjoy Reaver's product. He's been working on new recipes, now that he has a place to try them out before committing to them. "Our goal is just to keep creating new beers, new tasty beers, and put them out there," he said, "serving our customers and trying to get a following like other bars or breweries."

Three Palms Brewing

Opened: 2012.

Owner: Randy Reaver

Brewer: Randy Reaver.

System: 4-barrel custom.

Annual production: 300 barrels.

Hours: Wednesday and Thursday, 5 to 9 p.m.; Friday, 5 to 10 p.m.; Saturday, noon to 10 p.m.; Sunday, 2 to 8 p.m.

Tours: On request.

Parking: Free on site.

Takeout beer: Growlers

Special considerations: Handicapped-accessible.

Other area beer sites: Booth's Brewing & Bar Supply, 333 Falkenburg Rd. N. D-405, Tampa, FL 33619, (813) 685-1909 or (877) 685-1909, boothsbrewing.com (homebrewing supplies); The Brass Tap, 775 Brandon Town Center, Brandon, FL 33511, (813) 654-4712, brasstapbeerbar.com.

Other Beer Producers

The brewery chapters in this book focus on those that make beer on their premises. But the Florida brewery scene also includes beer producers of other types, and it would be remiss to not include them in this book. Some you can visit; others are business entities based in the state.

Contract Brewing

When a brewery or brewpub farms out production to another brewery, that's known as *contract brewing*. The contract-brewing model allows startups to get their products out to consumers without the expense of opening their own breweries. Sometimes a brewery uses the funds generated to help open an on-premises brewery; others continue with the contract model. In some cases, a brewer will lease equipment in breweries to produce a specialty or one-off label.

Some folks in the beer world think contract brewing means an inferior product, but some of the most notable craft beer in the nation started as contract brews. Jim Koch, founder of Boston Beer Co., the producer of Samuel Adams beer, started by contract brewing to save the expense of opening a brick-and-mortar operation, thereby having more funds to invest in growth.

The Native Brewing Company (www.nativebrewingco.com). Opened by Adam Fine in 1999 in Fort Lauderdale, Native produces four beers. One, Native Lager, is made at Florida Beer Company in Cape Canaveral. Two others are brewed at Shipyard Brewing Company in Portland, Maine, and one is made at Thomas Creek Brewing in Greenville, South Carolina.

The Abbey Brewing Co. (abbeybrewinginc.com), 1115 16th St., Miami Beach, FL 33139, (305) 538-8110. This brewpub, first opened in 1995, serves four house beers that are brewed at Florida Beer Company in Cape Canaveral.

Inlet Brewing Co. (www.inletbrewing.com). Based in Jupiter, this company produces two beers—Monk in the Trunk Belgian Style Organic Amber Ale and Monk IPA Belgian Style IPA—brewed by Thomas Creek Brewing in Greenville, South Carolina.

Uncle Ernie's Bayfront Grill & Brew House (uncleerniesbayfront grill.com), 1151 Bayview Ave., Panama City, FL 32401, (850) 763-8427. This brewpub offers three house beers, all brewed by SweetWater Brewing Company in Atlanta.

In Transition

At the time of this writing, a pair of breweries that have contracted their beer are in the process of opening brewing operations in Florida.

Orange Blossom Brewing Company (www.facebook.com/obpbeer). Tom Moench started marketing his flagship honey beer in 1999, brewing Orange Blossom Pilsner under contract at Thomas Creek Brewery in South Carolina, along with Orange Blossom Pilsner Squared and Toasted Coconut Porter. At the time of this writing, Moench was in negotiations to open a tasting room with a 3.5-barrel system in Orlando, but in the meantime, he had started brewing experimental and one-off batches of new brands in Spring Hill, Florida, at a small brewery that had not been used for a few years.

Grayton Beer Company (www.facebook.com/graytonbeer). This Santa Rosa–based company has supplied its Pale Ale and India Pale Ale to the local market since 2009 by brewing it under contract with Florida Beer Company, but at the time of this writing, Grayton expected to have a 30-barrel brewhouse in South Walton County in Florida's Panhandle online by early 2014.

Partial Brewing

Two brewpubs in Florida offer house-brewed beer but do not have complete brewing systems, opting instead to ship in malt product and finish the brewing in fermentation tanks on the premises.

Karibrew Brewpub & Grub (cafekaribo.com/post/8), 37 N. Third St., Fernandina Beach, FL 32034, (904) 277-5269. This brewpub on Amelia Island serves four year-round house beers and one seasonal.

Marco Island Brewery (marcoislandbrewery.com), 1089 N. Collier Blvd., Marco Island, FL 34145, (239) 970-0461. Four or five of its house brews are on tap at this Southwest Florida brewpub.

Hard to Classify

A handful of beer operations in the Sunshine State do not easily fit into any of the above categories, so I'm listing them here.

Fantasy Brewmasters (www.fantasybrewmasters.com). Florida native Chris Guerra, a longtime fan of fantasy fiction and gaming, created Burdisson's Dwarven Ale, which is available in bottles throughout the state and at a small storefront in Naples. His description: "Robust and flavorful, this beer proudly boasts a boldness that most elves fail to appreciate, and a subtle complexity only the most seasoned of men can comprehend." It's brewed by Butternuts Beer and Ale in upstate New York.

Brewers' Tasting Room (www.brewerstastingroom.com), 11270 Fourth St. N., St. Petersburg, FL 33716, (727) 873-3900. This operation has an unusual business model, at least in the Sunshine State. It has a 1-barrel brewing system but no brewer. Instead, local homebrewers are invited to use the system to produce their beer and put it on tap. Brewers' Tasting Room supplies the ingredients, the system, and assistance. The final product is hooked up to one of the self-service taps, and using wristbands with computer chips, customers can purchase samples or pints of the beer and offer feedback. Bonus: Sometimes local commercial brewers use the system to brew up a batch of special beer, and if it's during business hours, you can sit at the bar next to the brewhouse and chat them up. Twenty taps behind the bar pour other craft beer, most of it from Florida breweries.

Gwar Beer (chalmersbrewingcompany.com). Tampa Bay area homebrewer Rob Chalmers teamed up with the band Gwar, described in its Wikipedia entry as a "satirical heavy metal band formed in Richmond, Virginia, in 1984," to produce Gwar Beer. If you're not familiar with the band, Google its name, because that description does not do it justice. Regardless, Chalmers sought permission to use the band's official imagery on the label, and Gwar agreed. He brewed the beer in collaboration with Tampa's Cigar City Brewery and served it at the band's annual GWAR-B-Q festival in Richmond in 2013.

Rock Brothers Brewing (www.highroadale.com). Rock Brothers' first beer was also a band-themed collaboration with Cigar City, High Road Ale, a pale ale brewed for local band Have Gun, Will Travel. It won top honors in the Pale Ale category of the U.S. Beer Tasting Championship's Summer 2013 competition. Rock Brothers recently announced that it had signed with another local group to produce JJ Grey's Nare Sugar Brown Ale.

Brew Bus Brewing (www.tampabaybrewbus.com), (813) 990-7310. This outfit offers brewery tours, private parties, and trips to local sporting events and beer festivals aboard an air-conditioned bus. Such tours would not be complete without something for passengers to drink en route, so Cigar City stepped in to provide Brew Bus branded beers: Are Wheat There Yet?, a wheat ale; Rollin Dirty Red Ale; Last Stop IPA; and You're My Boy, Blue, a blueberry wheat ale. The brews are also available on local store shelves.

South Florida

In an ideal beer world, this section would be split in twain: Southwest Florida
and Southeast Florida. Unfortunately, neither of those regions alone
has enough breweries yet, but looking into my crystal beer ball, I forecast that if a second edition of this book were printed in a year or two,
the separation would exist. The tropical wetlands of the Everglades
take up a huge hunk of real estate in between, with the vast majority of
the population living in communities that hug the two coasts.

Because of retirees, the population skews older than in the rest of
the country. In Sarasota County, for example, more than 30 percent of
the population is sixty-five or older, and the median age is fifty-two,
according to U.S. Census data. In comparison, the overall median age
in the United States is thirty-nine, with 13 percent of the country's population being sixty-five or older.

The South Florida population increases dramatically during "Snowbird Season," which roughly runs from just after Thanksgiving to shortly after Easter. Snowbirds are those folks, often retired, who live in the
northern states but go to Florida each winter to avoid the harsh weather. Local businesses welcome them because they spend money. If
you're visiting the area during this "season," expect some of the finest
weather Florida has to offer, along with heavier traffic, long lines at
restaurants, and a preponderance of vehicles driving miles and miles
down the highways with their left turn signals blinking.

Southwest Florida

From Bradenton in the north to Marco Island in the south, the stretch
of South Florida that hugs the Gulf of Mexico has some of the world's
most beautiful beaches, a thriving cultural scene, and a history linked
to famous personalities such as the Ringling Brothers, Thomas Edison,

and Henry Ford. Circus magnate and showman John Ringling settled in Sarasota in 1927, bringing with him the winter headquarters of the traveling Ringling Brothers and Barnum & Bailey Circus, and his legacy permeates the community. Other well-known circus families and performers moved to the area after Ringling and his brother, Charles, settled there. The **John and Mable Ringling Museum of Art** (www.ringling.org) is a world-class facility featuring the huge collection of Baroque art amassed by the couple, as well as dozens of other collections and traveling exhibits. For more information on all that Sarasota has to offer, see www.visitsarasota.org.

Farther down the coast in Fort Myers, you'll find the **Edison & Ford Winter Estates** (www.edisonfordwinterestates.org), once the winter homes of close friends Thomas Edison and Henry Ford. Today it's a historical museum and 17-acre botanical garden with hundreds of inventions and artifacts, exhibits, restored laboratories and homes, and educational programs. The area also boasts some beautiful beaches (www.fortmyers-sanibel.com/), including those of Sanibel Island (www.sanibelisland.com), renowned for huge accumulations of seashells and the **J.N. "Ding Darling" National Wildlife Refuge & Bird Sanctuary** (www.fws.gov/dingdarling/visitorinformation.html).

Continuing south, the city of Naples (www.naples-florida.com) boasts that it is the "Golf Capital of the World," with the second most golf holes per capita in the country. The area has more than ninety courses, and as you might expect, the city tends to attract the wealthy, with a median annual household income of more than $77,000, about $30,000 more than the state as a whole.

Lest you think a traveling beer geek of modest means might find Southwest Florida too pricey, fear not. Plenty of reasonably priced accommodations and eateries are available throughout the region, though the snowbird effect boosts those prices during season.

Of course, if staying overnight in the budget chains makes your skin crawl, there are always the Ritz-Carltons: 1111 Ritz-Carlton Drive, Sarasota, FL 34236, (941) 309-2000, www.ritzcarlton.com/en/Properties/Sarasota/Default.htm, and 280 Vanderbilt Beach Rd., Naples, FL 34108, (239) 598-3300, www.ritzcarlton.com/en/Properties/Naples/Default.htm; or the five-star South Seas Island Resort near Fort Myers, 5400 Plantation Road, Captiva Island, FL 33924, www.southseas.com.

Southeast Florida

This region is what most folks think of as South Florida. You might picture the old *Miami Vice* television series, with its stylish threads, Art Deco architecture, and cocaine cowboys ensconced in palatial waterfront mansions purchased by ill-gotten means. Or perhaps you envision European beauties sunbathing topless on the beaches during the day, while at night bling-dripping hip-hop artists and their entourages bypass the velvet ropes of exclusive nightclubs for an evening of champagne and cigars in a private booth. Those might seem like clichés, but they do exist. Yet Southeast Florida, which stretches from Tequesta south to Key West, is more.

Beach lovers from around the world flock to the sands along the Atlantic Ocean, and the names of many locations here are familiar from literature, film, and TV, such as Palm Beach, Boca Raton, Fort Lauderdale, and Miami Beach. The population ranges from the very poor to the very rich. The median annual household income for ritzy Palm Beach is around $110,000; in rural Florida City, it's $25,000. Visitors fluent in Spanish may hold an advantage in parts of this region: 64 percent of Miami-Dade County residents speak Spanish at home, while 28 percent speak only English. But blending so many cultures produces a vibrant rainbow of music, art, food, and language that keeps Southeast Florida hopping.

Heading south from Florida City, there's only one place to go: the Florida Keys, a series of laidback communities that culminates in Key West, "the Southernmost City in the Continental U.S.," which is a mere 90 miles from Cuba. The city of Key West, a.k.a. "The Conch Republic" from a tongue-in-cheek secessionist movement in 1982, is a funky, historic community with more than its share of unique personalities and businesses. Though some might say that it's become "Disney-fied" in the past couple decades, with chain businesses, bars, and restaurants, it retains enough of its old-time flavor that Jimmy Buffett's "Margaritaville" remains a fairly accurate telling of the lifestyle. You should plan to spend at least one full day there to shop, sunbathe, and explore historic sites such as the *Ernest Hemingway Home & Museum* (www. hemingwayhome.com), the *Harry S. Truman Little White House* (www.trumanlittlewhitehouse.com), *Audubon House & Tropical Gardens* (www.audubonhouse.com), and *Fort Zachary Taylor Historic State Park* (www.floridastateparks.org/forttaylor). Finish your day by joining "Conchs" and visitors alike at the nightly *Sunset Celebration at Mallory Square Dock* (www.sunsetcelebration.org). And if you're up to it, you should experience a night of bar-hopping along Duval Street (duvalstreet.net), preferably with a cold beer or tropical cocktail in hand. There are far too many options for hotels to list; for suggestions on places to stay, visit www.fla-keys.com/keywest.

Big Bear Brewing Company

1800 North University Drive, Coral Springs, FL 33071

(954) 341-5545 • www.bigbearbrewingco.com

Walking into Big Bear Brewing Company, you might think at first that you've stepped through a time portal to an era when the Rat Pack ruled Vegas. The lighting is low, jazzy instrumental music plays softly in the background, and the plush, darkly upholstered booths are accented by shiny brass metal railings. Retro neon signs complete the scene. Sure, you can order a made-to-order martini to continue the illusion, but why would you do that when there are nine taps of fresh beer that were brewed just a few feet away?

The place takes the "bear" in the name seriously. Black-and-white prints of various species of the critter hang on the red brick–faced walls, interspersed with beer-themed prints and photos of the area. The menu does not have bear steaks, stews, or ribs on it, however. What you'll find instead is standard pub food that leans toward the gourmet end of the scale: Kobe burgers, seared rare ahi tuna, roasted free-range chicken, lobster mac and cheese, and fresh, locally caught seafood. And though bear is not on the menu, the kitchen loves to use beer as an ingredient. "The chef and I work together," said brewmaster Matt Cox, "and when new beers come out, we'll go through tastings and see how to put that beer into new dishes on the menu. He just made a blackberry porter cheesecake that was unbelievably good. The chef here is really into craft beer."

Cox started brewing 5 gallons at time in his garage, as did so many current commercial brewers. He brewed at the Brewzzi brewpub in Boca Raton and at the now-closed Bootleggers Brewing Company in the Southwest Florida town of Englewood. In 2001, Big Bear hired him, and he's been there since.

Big Bear has the trappings of a fine-dining restaurant, and visitors sometimes are not aware of the brewing side until they walk through the doors and see the brewery behind the windows

Beers brewed: Polar Light, Hibernation India Pale Ale, Grizzly Red Ale, Brown Bear Ale, Kodiac Belgian Dubbel, and Black Bear Stout, plus various seasonals and specials.

The Pick: The Hibernation India Pale Ale delivers the crispness of the style with the expected hops punch. Not incredibly complex but very well balanced.

that separate it from the bar area. "People are surprised to come into a small place in Coral Springs and find a brewery, and then they're also surprised to find a brewery that does fairly big, aggressive beers on a regular basis," Cox said. "Some people are amazed to find a little brewpub that does more than two or three beers. Our repeat business is very strong."

In terms of strength, the standard beers range from Polar Light at 4.9 percent ABV to the Kodiac Belgian Dubbel at 7.5 percent, but Cox has brewed special releases and seasonals stronger than 12 percent. Big Bear does not as yet sell growlers or other beer to go; its liquor license makes gaining the necessary permits and licenses a difficult proposition. It's something the owner is looking into, but there are no plans as yet to grow beyond current capacity. According to Cox, in-house production is close to just covering the in-house sales, so trying to send kegs to a distributor is not an option at this point.

In deference to the growing interest in craft beer and food pairings, there's been discussion about holding beer dinners and matching up Cox's brews with special dishes from the kitchen. "We have a couple of months in the summer where we can slow down and do smaller things like that," Cox said, "Put maybe thirty or forty people out on the patio and do a beer dinner, but the one thing that restricts us from doing something like that most of the year is, we're too busy."

Big Bear Brewing Company

Opened: 1997.
Owner: Greg Wentworth
Brewer: Matt Cox.
System: 10-barrel DME.
Annual production: 500 barrels.
Hours: Monday through Thursday, 11:30 a.m. to 10:30 p.m.; Friday and Saturday, 11:30 a.m. to 11:30 p.m.; Sunday, 11 a.m. to 10 p.m.
Tours: By appointment.
Parking: Free on site.
Takeout beer: None.
Special considerations: Handicapped-accessible.

Brewzzi Boca Raton

2222 Glades Road, Boca Raton, FL 33431
(561) 392-2739 • www.brewzzi.com

Matt Manthe's young face belies his experience in the brewing industry. Soon after starting to talk with him, you realize this affable, intelligent man is more conversant in all things beer than many of his colleagues. The brewmaster at Brewzzi Boca Raton earned a degree in microbiology at Clemson University but then decided to get into brewing, figuring it would be a career that would be fun and also satisfy his inclination toward things scientific. Manthe worked for three years at Thomas Creek Brewery in Greenville, South Carolina, starting as assistant brewer and working his way up to head brewer. He then earned his brewmaster degree at the VLB Berlin brewing school in Germany and stepped into the head brewer job at Brewzzi in 2012.

To call Brewzzi a chain might be an overstatement—it has only two locations. The Boca Raton store was the first, and another in West Palm Beach opened in 2003. Standard beers are served at both, but each brewer has enough free rein to create his own styles for the taps. "I try to keep a good selection on tap," Manthe said. "Obviously, it's too hard to hit all the styles with the taps available, but I try to have a good variety as far as something that's full-bodied, something that's a little sweet and malty, and something that's hoppy, more like an IPA." Manthe first discovered good beer in Belgium, where he went to high school—his dad worked for NATO—and the Belgian styles remain his favorites. "I've always really liked Belgian-style beers, and I try to have at least a couple of Belgian styles on."

He likes to surprise the palates of his customers, many of whom are older and haven't experienced some of the styles he brews. "I like the challenge of changing people's outlook on beer," he told me. "When I made a sour beer, there were a lot of people here who had never had a sour beer before and didn't really know what to expect. A lot of them found that they really liked

Beers brewed: Boca Blonde, City Fest, and Black Duke, plus specials and seasonals.

The Pick: Pick up a pint of the Black Duke, a traditional German schwarzbier, a dark, full-bodied pilsner with notes of caramel, coffee, and chocolate. It's a great accompaniment to the stick-to-your-ribs comfort food served at the brewpub.

it." Most of the beers are sessionable, but Manthe likes to push the envelope on occasion, such as with a French oak–aged Belgian quadrupel that clocked in at 11.1 percent ABV. "That's actually been a really good seller for us, which I was frankly surprised by, because typically when I'm going out to a restaurant or a bar, I'm not looking for an 11 percent beer," he said. "I like a strong beer, but not until at the end of the night when I'm at home."

The dining side of the operation has been a big draw for the local and tourist crowd, but Manthe said he's seeing more folks coming in for the beer. "We have typically more of an older crowd here that mostly comes in for the restaurant," he said. "But we get a lot of people, especially in the past six months, who are more interested in different types of beer." And Manthe wants to make sure they leave satisfied. "My goal is that anyone who comes in here will find a beer they like," he said. "It may not have the style they're familiar with, it may not be a style they can find anywhere else, but my goal is that people who come in here are able to find beer that they like regardless of what they normally like to drink."

Brewzzi Boca Raton

Opened: 1997.
Owner: Morris Stoltz.
Brewer: Matt Manthe.
System: 15-barrel DME.
Annual production: 600 barrels.
Hours: Monday through Thursday, 7 a.m. to 10:30 p.m.; Friday, 7 a.m. to 11:30 p.m.; Saturday, 8 a.m. to 11:30 p.m.; Sunday, 8 a.m. to 10 p.m.
Tours: Call ahead, or on request if someone's available.
Parking: Free on site.
Takeout beer: None.
Special considerations: Handicapped-accessible.
Extras: Outdoor seating; occasional beer dinners.
Other area beer sites: The Sybarite Pig, 20642 State Road 7, No. 2, Boca Raton, FL 33498, (561) 883-3200, www.sybaritepig.com.

Brewzzi CityPlace

700 South Rosemary Avenue, Suite 212, West Palm Beach, FL 33401
(561) 366-9753 • www.brewzzi.com

CityPlace in downtown West Palm Beach offers dining, shopping, entertainment, and nightlife—and fortunately for the traveling beer geek, the sprawling complex also houses a brewpub. Brewzzi CityPlace can be a place for the weary shopper to knock back a pint or two and grab a bite to eat before, during, or after a day of visiting trendy stores. It also serves as a way station where the spouse (usually a husband) can escape for a few minutes from a significant other's buying binge. "I've had guys come in and say, 'I've only got a few minutes. My wife's downstairs,'" head brewer Reinhard "Reiny" Knieriemen told me with a laugh.

The brewpub opened in 2003 as an extension of the original Brewzzi in Boca Raton and features the same classic lineup of traditional German lagers, though ales occasionally make their way onto a tap. Knieriemen told me that although he was trained in brewing those styles, the longer fermentation time required sometimes becomes an issue for the most popular brews. "We do lagers and most people don't," he said. "Lagers take four weeks [whereas most ales take two]. I've had a 10-barrel batch sell out in fourteen days, so the challenge is to make sure to keep up with everything."

As you might deduce from his name, Knieriemen is of German ancestry, but though brewing might be in his genes, he moved into his career methodically. Originally from Upper New York State, he studied education at Arizona State University before moving to South Florida to teach high school biology. He also homebrewed, and in 2008, he approached Brewzzi's brewer and offered to volunteer during summers and other school breaks. "I did it all for free just for the experience," he explained. After a couple years, Knieriemen was hired as assistant brewer, and two years later he became the head brewer.

The restaurant occupies a prime piece of real estate in CityPlace, being just outside the entrance

Beers brewed: Boca Blonde, City Fest, and Black Duke, plus specials and seasonals.

The Pick: Classics never go out of style. City Fest is a traditional Vienna lager with a medium body and a crisp finish. It won a silver medal at the 2011 Great American Beer Festival competition.

from the complex's parking garage. A covered outdoor bar and patio provide a top-notch spot to people-watch while enjoying a beer and noshing on something from the menu, which says that it is "based on Old World Italian and traditional American comfort food." Inside, the brewing equipment is displayed behind big glass windows, and the food is prepared in an open kitchen. The clientele is a mix of tourists and locals, though the balance shifts toward out-of-staters during the winter months. "In the summertime, we get locals and businesspeople," Knieriemen said. "Once the season kicks in, we get a lot of tourists."

His background as a biology teacher may have given him a leg up in understanding the microbiological aspects of brewing, but the only teaching Knieriemen does these days is educating the restaurant staff about the beers he makes at a job he loves. "You can't beat being able to brew here—and live—in sunny Florida," he said.

Brewzzi CityPlace

Opened: 2003.

Owner: Morris Stoltz.

Brewer: Reinhard "Reiny" Knieriemen.

System: 10-barrel DME.

Annual production: 600 barrels.

Hours: Monday through Thursday, 11 a.m. to 1 a.m.; Friday and Saturday, 11:30 a.m. to 2 a.m.; Sunday, 11:30 a.m. to 1 a.m.

Tours: On request.

Parking: Metered street parking and attached pay-to-park garage.

Takeout beer: None.

Special considerations: Handicapped-accessible.

Extras: Outdoor seating; occasional beer dinners.

Other area beer sites: The Brass Tap, 550 S. Rosemary Ave. #158, West Palm Beach, FL 33401, (561) 366-9226, brasstapbeerbar.com; Bx Beer Depot (homebrew supply), 2964 Second Ave. N., Palm Springs, FL 33461, (561) 965-9494, bxbeerdepot.com.

Darwin Brewing Company

ANDEAN INFLUENCED BEER 1525 Fourth Street, Sarasota, FL 34236
(941) 343-2165 • darwinson4th.com

Beer geeks in Sarasota in January 2011 celebrated the news that the city's second brewpub, Mad Crow Brewery & Grill, was finally open. Less than a year later, it closed. The brewery didn't collect dust long. Darwin Santa Maria, a well-respected and award-winning chef and restaurateur in Sarasota known for cuisine from his native Peru, teamed with business partner Bill Cornelius. The chef was eager to open a new restaurant, but what was he to do with all that brewing equipment?

The seemingly obvious answer was to hire a brewer for the restaurant, dubbed Darwin's on 4th. So he lured Jared Barnes from his job at Southern Tier Brewing Company in Lakewood, New York, to become Darwin's first brewmaster. Barnes had studied brewing at the Siebel Institute in Chicago and Munich's Doemens Academy, earning degrees in brewing technology and biochemistry. It was a tip from Siebel that alerted him to the position. "I didn't know there was another brewery besides Sarasota Brewing Company in Sarasota," Barnes said. "My grandfather lives close by in Venice, so I just happened to come down here and visit him anyway."

While there, he came by to talk to Santa Maria and Cornelius about the brewmaster position. Shortly after, they called to offer him the job, and he accepted. A little more than a year later, he won thirteen medals at the 2013 Florida Beer Championships and third-place Best of Show for his Summadayze IPA, cementing Darwin's as a brewpub that deserved respect.

Barnes has since left for a position at another brewery, but Santa Maria did not take long to bring in a new brewmaster with an impressive résumé of his own. Jorge Rosabal also earned his brewing degree at the Doemens Academy and had shepherded the development and brewing of the Holsten brand in the Honduran market. Rosabal uses some of Barnes's recipes and has developed new ones since starting in the summer of 2013,

Beers brewed: Marron Ale, Ayawasca Belgian Dubbel, Summadayze IPA, and Evolution American Wheat Ale, plus various seasonals and specials.

The Pick: Summadayze IPA is an amazing example of the style, bursting with citrusy hops and tasting much bigger than you would expect from an India pale ale with a 5.8 percent ABV.

often working in conjunction with the kitchen to pair beers with menu items and plan the monthly beer dinners.

The building that Darwin's occupies dates to 1926, when it was the Sarasota headquarters of the Citrus Exchange, formed to unite growers and wholesalers in the burgeoning citrus industry. Intricate iron- and brickwork adorns the outside, and the interior décor evokes the essence of a southern European public plaza. The owners improved on that look, with seats reupholstered and tabletops clad in copper. They installed glass shelving, as well as a new draft line system. Patrons in the bar area can study the brewery, which is behind windows. A separate dining area caters to the lunch and dinner crowd, whose primary motivation is the cuisine, which Santa Maria dubs "authentic urban street foods from the cuisine capitals of the world," focusing on Latin American fare.

Shortly before this writing, Darwin's announced that the business had obtained property in the city of Bradenton, about thirty minutes or so north, for a production brewery. Plans call for the new operation, Darwin Brewing Company, to make its beers more widely available through distribution. They plan to package them in cans and have released images of half a dozen of them. At least one of the beers will play off the scientific theory from the other Darwin: Evolution Wheat Ale, with the tagline "Only the Strongest Beers Survive." The new brewery is expected to be online by early 2014.

Darwin Brewing Company

Opened: 2012.
Owners: Darwin Santa Maria and Bill Cornelius.
Brewer: Jorge Rosabal.
System: 7-barrel PUB brewhouse.
Annual production: 500 barrels.
Hours: Sunday through Tuesday, 5 p.m. to 10 p.m.; Wednesday and Thursday, 5 p.m. to 11 p.m.; Friday and Saturday, 5 p.m. to 1 a.m.
Tours: On request, if someone's available.
Parking: Free on site, with valet service on weekends.
Takeout beer: None.
Special considerations: Handicapped-accessible.
Extras: Beer dinners.
Other area beer sites: Growler's Pub, 2831 N. Tamiami Trail, Sarasota, FL 34234, (941) 487-7373, www.growlersonline.com; Shamrock Pub, 2257 Ringling Blvd., Sarasota, FL 34237, (941) 952-1730, www.shamrocksarasota.com.

Due South Brewing Co.

2900 High Ridge Road #3, Boynton Beach, FL 33426

(561) 463-2337 • www.duesouthbrewing.com

If Mike Halker's wife, Jodi, had liked beer all along, Due South Brewing Co. might not exist today. Halker had already run a few successful businesses—a couple of motorcycle shops in Tennessee and a bar and grill in the Charlotte, North Carolina, area—when he walked into a homebrew store and told the clerk that he wanted to learn to make wine because his wife had discovered she was allergic to the sulfites common in commercial varieties. The clerk told him that wine took too long to make, and he should instead brew beer. But Halker didn't much like beer at the time—he was a bourbon guy, and the only brews he was familiar with were the mass-produced fizzy, yellow lagers. "So we started drinking beer, and the next thing you know, I said, 'Yeah, I can do this,'" he told me.

That started Halker on the homebrewing route. "I started really getting into the hops and the IPAs and all that. But my wife still didn't have anything to drink. She couldn't drink wine, and she didn't like beer either." Then he brewed the first version of the Caramel Cream Ale. She still didn't like it, but it was closer to something she might enjoy. So after more than a year, and more than a hundred batches later, he finally made a version that she enjoyed drinking.

It became a flagship brew. "They're going crazy over it," Halker said. "Right now, we produce about 4,000 gallons a month, just of that. And we're only here in South Florida." And that's not counting another handful of year-round brews and a long list of seasonal and special releases.

Due South opened its doors on May 12, 2012, after a few years of seeking a municipality in South Florida willing to be its host. Zoning and city ordinances kept getting in the way. But then the city of Boynton Beach ended up adjusting its codes to allow Halker to open in a warehouse park.

Beers brewed: Category 3 IPA, Caramel Cream Ale, Roasted Cocoa Stout, and Honey Vanilla Wheat. Seasonals and specialties: Raspberry Blonde, Category 4 IPA, Category 5 IPA, Mariana Trench Imperial Stout, Florida Blonde, Southbound Brown, Northern Exposure Caramel Maple Cream Ale, Red Reef, and Isle of MaGourdo Pumpkin Ale.

The Pick: The flagship Caramel Cream Ale delivers what its name promises, a smooth, creamy ale with a hint of caramel flavor along with a touch of vanilla. There's a sweetness to it, but it's not overpowering.

Walking into the 15,000-square-foot brewery, you realize that the space was chosen to allow for growth. Much of the floor is empty. The brewing tanks are in one corner, and about a third of the open space is the tasting area, roped off from the rest of the brewery. Ceiling fans that hang over the bar and scattered tables keep the air moving, but it can still be sultry, especially during the summer. But for those who can't stand the heat, there's an air-conditioned oasis behind a door in the back, with another bar and more tables where customers can enjoy the fruit of the brewers' labors without breaking a sweat.

Though a fair number of tourists walk through the doors, it's the locals who keep it running. "The locals . . . are very supportive, not only as far as coming in here and hanging out with us and getting jazzed up about new releases and that kind of thing, but going out in the market and buying up our beer," he said. "We'll do 3,500 to 4,000 barrels this year, and 90 percent of that will be sold in this county."

And according to Halker, there will be much more to buy in the new future. He plans to install a 30-barrel brewhouse while keeping the current 15-barrel system running. Due South beers are currently available on many taps in the area, and there are a few in other parts of the state, but he anticipates canning his beers to make them available at retail stores.

Due South Brewing Co.

Opened: 2012.

Owners: Michael and Jodi Halker.

Brewer: Michael Halker.

System: 15-barrel Premier stainless brewhouse.

Annual production: 3,000 barrels.

Hours: Tuesday through Thursday, noon to 10 p.m.; Friday and Saturday, noon to 11 p.m.; Sunday, noon to 6 p.m.

Tours: Free tours Saturday and Sunday at 1 and 3 p.m.; no reservations needed. VIP tour Saturday and Sunday at 2 p.m. for $10, which includes a logo glass and samples; reservations suggested.

Parking: Free on site.

Takeout beer: Growlers and limited bottle releases.

Special considerations: Handicapped-accessible.

Other area beer sites: The Backyard Boynton Beach, 511 N.E. Fourth St., Boynton Beach, FL 33435, (561) 740-0399, thebackyardboyntonbeach.com; Sweetwater Bar & Grill, 1507 S. Federal Hwy., Boynton Beach, FL 33435, (561) 509-9277, www.facebook.com/sw1933.

Fort Myers Brewing Co.

12811 Commerce Lakes Drive, Suite 27–28,
Fort Myers, FL 33913
(239) 313-6576 • www.facebook.com/FMBrew

At the time of this writing, the banner on the Facebook page for Fort Myers Brewing Co. proclaimed, "Hobby Gone Wild." Owners Rob Whyte and Jennifer Gratz had no idea just how wild it would go after they moved from California to Florida to open a brewery. On opening day, March 2, 2013, thirsty residents packed the modest tasting room to try the beers from Lee County's first craft brewery.

"We estimated something between fifteen hundred and two thousand here," Whyte said. "It was shoulder to shoulder in here, shoulder to shoulder back there" in the brewery area, "and the line went out to the parking lot, down to the corner, and around to the side of the building. We went through 10 barrels of beer that day—twenty kegs." Even though the tasting room is open only two days a week—both owners have day jobs—Whyte's been struggling to keep up with demand ever since.

Whyte started homebrewing back in the early 1990s, and though it was "pretty awful beer," he said, it was strong. He gave it up for a while, then started brewing again in 2004 and volunteered at Oceanside Ale Works in San Diego. Later they were living in Sacramento, and Whyte, a software writer, lost his job. He found another one pretty quickly, but the company wanted him to transfer to the East Coast. "That's what brought us to Florida," he said. "We moved into the Gateway area here and quickly discovered that there were no microbreweries around. We had toyed with the idea of opening a brewery when we were in Sacramento." So they found a space in an industrial park on the west side of Fort Myers, obtained the necessary licensing and permits, and opened Fort Myers Brewing.

Beers brewed: Gateway Gold Honey Blonde Ale, City of Palms Pale Ale, Cypress Strong American Ale, and Tamiami Tan Brown Ale, which alternates on tap with Red Tape American Amber/Red Ale. Seasonals: Black IPA, IPA, Double IPA, Smoked Vanilla Porter, Belgian Tripel, Caloosahatchee Kolsch, Blueberry Wheat, Oatmeal Stout, Belgian Golden Strong, Russian Imperial Stout, and Hefeweizen.

The Pick: The Kolsch style from Germany has grown in popularity here in the States, and the Caloosahatchee Kolsch proves to be an excellent version, with a taste that nicely balances sweet grains and pilsner malt, with just a hint of slightly bitter hops. It's a real thirst-quencher on a hot South Florida day.

Ten tap handles, for now, are installed behind the bar. Some of Whyte's homebrewing medals hang on the wall. Customers come mostly from the surrounding homes, but when I visited the brewery, it had been open only a few months, and the owners were relying on Facebook and word of mouth to spread the news that it was open. Not that it has had any problem attracting customers. "Our business plan had certain parameters laid out that we thought we might exceed, but we didn't want to be too optimistic," Whyte said. "We have completely and totally blown our business plan out of the water." The owners plan on more growth, once they catch up. Fort Myers beers were on tap in a couple area pubs. Whyte had already bought bigger fermenting tanks, and he forecast wider distribution.

As far as the beer, he said he would like to start brewing Belgian-style sour beers, and he's done some 12-gallon batches of specialty beers that might eventually get made on the bigger system. He would really like to brew the hops-forward IPAs that he enjoyed back in California. "I can't get the hops right now to make mine," he said. "Well, I can, but I'll go broke doing it. Until I can get my hands on the hops I need, it's really going to be tough for me to do the big West Coast super-hoppy stuff. But I will. I'll get there eventually, once I can catch up on production."

Fort Myers Brewing Co.

Opened: 2013.

Owners: Rob Whyte and Jennifer Gratz.

Brewer: Rob Whyte.

System: 7-barrel customized from refurbished dairy tanks.

Annual production: To be determined.

Hours: Thursday, 4 to 9 p.m.; Friday, 3 to 9 p.m.; Saturday, noon to 9 p.m.; Sunday, noon to 7 p.m.

Tours: On request during tasting room hours.

Parking: Free on site.

Takeout beer: Growlers.

Special considerations: Handicapped-accessible.

Extras: Local food trucks; patio seating.

Other area beer sites: Stillwater Grille, 13451 McGregor Blvd., Fort Myers, FL 33919, (239) 791-8554, stillwatergrille.com; World of Beer–Fort Myers, 13499 S. Cleveland Ave., Suite 111, Fort Myers, FL 33907, (239) 437-2411, wobusa.com/Locations/FortMyers.aspx.

Funky Buddha Brewery

1201 Northeast 38th Street, Oakland Park, FL 33334
(954) 440-0046 • funkybuddhabrewery.com

The original Funky Buddha Lounge & Brewery in Boca Raton (see page 158) is a cozy, dark, and quiet place. The Funky Buddha Brewery, its big brother in Oakland Park, is spacious, bright, and noisy. But such growth is inevitable when beer geeks around the world are clamoring for a taste of the brewery's beer.

Going from the 1.5-barrel system at the original site to a 30-barrel brewhouse here does not come without its share of headaches and stress, and co-owner and head brewer Ryan Sentz didn't hesitate to seek advice from colleagues who had already been down this road, including Joey Redner of Tampa's Cigar City Brewing. "We definitely did it with the intent to grow," Sentz explained. "I was going to start with a 15-barrel system, and Joey said, 'If you do that, you will outgrow it before you open.' And to a certain extent, he was right. We're having a hard time right now making enough beer and we just opened. We haven't opened up a lot of accounts."

On opening day, June 1, 2013, the owners expected about a thousand people to show up. The estimate was about three thousand short. Instead of the tours and casual, informative conversations that Sentz had anticipated, it was all hands on deck for employees as they frantically took orders, filled pints, and changed kegs to keep the chaos down to a manageable level. They nearly ran out of beer. "It's a good problem. I am not crying," Sentz said. "But it was definitely nerve-racking."

The original location in Boca Raton still brews in-house, but it's become something of a test kitchen for experimental beers. The new brewery includes a 3.5-barrel system for pilot brews as well, which allows tasting-room customers the opportunity to sample beers that may never make it beyond the walls. He's shooting for a total of about thirty taps in the tasting room, most pouring

Beers brewed: Cabana Boy Wheat Ale, Doc Brown Ale, Floridian Hefeweizen, Hop Gun IPA, Missionary Blonde Ale, OP Porter, and Red Dawn Red Ale, plus many seasonals, special releases, and brewery exclusives.

The Pick: Hop Gun IPA almost overwhelms the palate with a multitude of hops flavors: citrus, tropical fruit, and pine. The caramel malt backbone cuts the hops edge just enough to make it delight the taste buds as it goes down.

Funky Buddha beer and the others guest taps of brews produced in Florida. When I visited the brewery, there were around fourteen taps with brewed-on-premises beer, topped with "Standing Buddha" handles, and half a dozen or so guest taps.

In the tasting room, the 70-foot-long bar curves around one wall, behind which large windows offer a look at the brewing equipment. A long, wooden table at bar height invites communal interaction, while the other tables and chairs scattered throughout provide places for more intimate conversations. Glass overhead doors open onto what used to be a railroad loading dock, now set up for outdoor seating. The railroad line is still active, by the way, so you might see one or two roar by while you're sipping a brew.

Funky Buddha already supplies kegs of its beer to some local venues, and either canning or bottling for distribution lies in the future. Sentz hasn't decided which way to go yet. He favors cans for the same reasons many other craft breweries are turning to them—less expensive, more easily recyclable, better for the beer because it's protected from light—but he's concerned that those new to microbrews may still feel that cans are for inferior beer. "It depends on the day you ask me," he said. "Right now, I'm leaning toward cans."

Funky Buddha Brewery

Opened: 2013.

Owners: Ryan Sentz, K. C. Sentz, and Giani Rocha.

Brewers: Ryan Sentz and Alex Postelnek.

System: 30-barrel brewhouse and 3.5-barrel pilot system.

Annual production: Estimated 2,500 barrels.

Hours: Seven days a week, noon to midnight.

Tours: Saturday and Sunday at 1, 2, and 3 p.m. Reservations recommended for 1 and 2 p.m. tours; the 3 p.m. tour is for walk-ins only. Cost of $5 includes logo glass to keep and free samples. Private and group tours can be arranged at other times.

Parking: Free on site and across the street in city lot.

Takeout beer: Growlers.

Special considerations: Handicapped-accessible.

Extras: Outdoor seating; separate game area with bocce ball court, cornhole, giant Jenga, and foosball.

The Funky Buddha Lounge & Brewery

~FUNKY BUDDHA LOUNGE~
&
BREWERY

2621 North Federal Highway, Boca Raton, FL 33431
(561) 368-4643 • www.thefunkybuddha.com

"Buddha" implies peace, as in a placid environment. The "funky" aspect may be found not only in the occasional Belgian sour beer, but also throughout the Funky Buddha Lounge & Brewery, with its low lighting, eclectically unmatched furniture, plush couches and chairs, and tables grouped for maximum conversation. A simple wooden stage sits against one wall.

Art, most locally created, hangs on the walls, and hookahs line a shelf behind the bar, along with various tobacco blends in capped jars. And Buddha statues and figurines peek out from corners expected and unexpected. "We try to have a relaxed environment with music, with couches, stuff like that," said brewer Morgan Pierce. "People say when they come in here that they can't believe this is open in Florida. This seems like it should be in San Francisco or Austin or somewhere like that." The exterior is all modern Florida, though, part of a nondescript strip mall on street of strip malls.

The Funky Buddha started as a hookah bar and coffee shop in a smaller space at the other end of the strip mall. Ryan Sentz bought the business in 2007. "When I bought the place, it was called R&R Tea Bar & the Funky Buddha Lounge," Sentz said. "So we came in, dropped the R&R Tea Bar, and we brought in craft beer. We were there for about two or three years, and we started looking for a bigger spot, primarily because we had just outgrown that one and we wanted to have bigger music acts."

Once moved into the larger space, Sentz installed a 1.5-barrel brewing system and obtained the necessary licensing to serve the beers. "I had no delusions about opening up a brewery; it wasn't part of the plan," he said. "We brewed beers not exactly to style, just kind of what we liked. We weren't really in it to win awards." But then they brewed the Maple Bacon Coffee Porter, a delicious dark beer that perfectly melded all of the ingredients in its name, and sold a limited amount in

Beers brewed: Floridian Hefeweisen, Red Dawn Red Ale, Piiti Porter, and Hop Gun IPA, plus many seasonals and specialties.

The Pick: The Floridian Hefeweisen bursts with the banana, clove, and citrus flavors that this style of wheat beer should ideally have. It's a delicious treat.

bottles. It quickly became the top-rated porter on the BeerAdvocate website (beeradvocate.com), and around the same time, the brewery was rated as number twenty-seven on the list of top breweries in the world on RateBeer (www.ratebeer.com). And the world took note.

"We would get phone calls from all over the country asking where they could get our beer, if we bottled it," Pierce said. "People would sell it on the Internet for obscene amounts of money. To have one of the number-one beers in the world coming out of Boca Raton, Florida, was amazing. It was cool, and it was nice, all the support we got from people around here and how excited everyone was that they had a brewery get national attention down here." The growing popularity of the beer sparked Sentz to expand the operation, and in June 2013, he opened a new production brewery and tasting room, known simply as Funky Buddha Brewery (see page 156), in the nearby town of Oakland Park.

The lauded porter exemplified the experimental styles coming out of the tiny brewery, which also included Ginger Lemongrass Wheat Ale, Blueberry Cobbler Ale, and No Crusts, a peanut butter and jelly sandwich–flavored beer. Those are special releases that may or may not be on tap during a visit. The year-round brews hew more closely to traditional styles. "We like to make normal styles, but the ones that people know us for are the crazy ones," Pierce said. "We did a sweet potato casserole beer, and we just had the Rice Krispies Treat Ale. We like just trying to produce things like that and try to wow people."

The Funky Buddha Lounge & Brewery

Opened: Brewery in 2010.

Owner: Ryan Sentz.

Brewer: Morgan Pierce.

System: 1.5-barrel custom.

Annual production: 150 barrels.

Hours: Monday through Friday, 5 p.m. to 2 a.m.; Saturday and Sunday, 6 p.m. to 2 a.m.

Tours: On request.

Parking: Free on site.

Takeout beer: None.

Special considerations: Handicapped-accessible.

Extras: Homebrew supply shop next door. Hookahs and exotic coffees and teas available.

Other area beer sites: Yard House, 201 Plaza Real, Boca Raton, FL 33432, (561) 417-6124, www.yardhouse.com/FL/boca-raton-restaurant.

Kelly's Caribbean Bar, Grill & Brewery

key west

301 Whitehead Street, Key West, FL 33040
(305) 293-8484 • www.kellyskeywest.com

People who have never been to Key West generally harbor some preconceptions about it, but a place for craft beer usually isn't one of them. Kelly's Caribbean Bar, Grill & Brewery started brewing there in 1992, however, and anyone who wanders in while barhopping will find that out pretty quickly.

The building in which Kelly's operates once served as the original headquarters of Pan American Airways in the United States, and that quickly becomes obvious as well. The servers and staff all wear shirts with the original Pan Am logo on the sleeves, historic pictures and posters of that era hang on the walls, and a pair of ceiling fans are fashioned like airplane motors with propellers—part of an illusion that a Sikorsky seaplane has plunged in the roof of the aptly named Crash Bar. The bar top is fabricated like an airplane wing out of riveted aluminum, and even the legs of the barstools are carved to look like propeller blades.

Jim Brady brews the beer for Kelly's, coming in a few times a month to make sure the serving tanks remain stocked. He honed his love for quality beer when he served in the military and was stationed in Germany for seven years. "When I got back, I was left wanting for a better beer," he said. After leaving the military, he landed a job in the pari-mutuel industry at a greyhound track in New Hampshire. The owner bought a track in Key West and sent Brady down to run it. As so often happens with people who move to the Conch Republic, he ended up staying for the long term.

With Key West "being at the 'end of the earth,' there was very little distribution of craft beer at the time," he said. "Homebrewing was the next option. I've been doing that down here for about twenty years." Brady founded the local homebrew club, the Conch Republic B.U.B.B.A.'s (Brewers

Beers brewed: Southern Clipper Wheat Beer, Havana Red Ale, and Key West Golden Ale.

The Pick: After a long drive through the Florida Keys and having to walk several blocks in midsummer from where I parked, I found the Key West Golden Ale to be an outstanding thirst quencher, with a mild malty backbone and citrusy hops taste. It's advertised as an IPA, but it's more of the British style than American.

United Brewing Better Ale), and is now considered a "go-to" brewing expert in Key West, often hosting and teaching seminars and classes at various events. "Kelly's was built at the time when I was getting into homebrewing, so consequently I was always over there involved in something," he said. "I either knew the brewer, or I recommended the brewer, or I was trying to train the brewer."

Kelly's flew in a brewer from the South Florida mainland for a while, but then had to stop. Brady offered his services after that, and they worked out a deal. Though Brady was in the process of opening his own brewery at the time of this writing, he said he'd be willing to stay with the part-time gig for as long as Kelly's wanted him there.

Certain features define the Key West style, and Kelly's, which calls itself the "southernmost brewery" in the United States, incorporates them all: Caribbean-style cuisine rich in freshly caught seafood, tropical cocktails, and architecture that takes advantage of the climate. The Crash Bar occupies a space with shutters, doors, and windows that can be thrown open to let the sea breezes waft through or closed during the pounding thunderstorms of summer. The bar overlooks an outdoor garden patio with tables shaded by flowering tropical plants, palm trees, and towering oaks. That and another rooftop garden patio have served as the backdrops for many weddings, receptions, and other catered events over the years.

In addition to the beer brewed on the premises, Kelly's carry several taps of other craft beer, a promising sign that the southernmost city in the United States has jumped on the good beer bandwagon.

Kelly's Caribbean Bar, Grill & Brewery

Opened: 1992.

Owner: Fred Tillman.

Brewer: Jim Brady.

System: 7-barrel custom-built.

Annual production: 300 barrels.

Hours: Seven days a week, 9 a.m. to 10 p.m.

Tours: None.

Parking: Paid street and lot parking.

Takeout beer: None.

Special considerations: Handicapped-accessible.

Extras: Outdoor seating.

Other area beer sites: The Porch, 429 Caroline St., Key West, FL 33040, (305) 517-6358, www.theporchkw.com; World of Beer–Key West, 511 Greene St., Unit 101, Key West, FL 33041, (305) 517-6260, wobusa.com/Locations/KeyWest.aspx.

The Mack House

9118 West State Road 84, Fort Lauderdale, FL 33324
(954) 474-5040 • flales.com

The Mack House came about through a series of events that started in 1993. That's when Fort Lauderdale native Bobby Gordash started homebrewing. Three years later, he entered his old English ale recipe into the Samuel Adams Longshot American Homebrew Contest and ended up being one of the winners. The brew was produced and distributed by the Boston Beer Company in special six-packs containing the three winners' beers.

Ten years later, Gordash started Holy Mackerel Beers, based in Florida, with its products contract-brewed at Thomas Creek Brewery in Greenville, South Carolina, and Florida Beer Company, then in Melbourne, Florida. So, though most folks considered it a Florida beer, there wasn't a physical Holy Mackerel brewery in the state. Then in 2011, Gordash sold the brand to Larry Hatfield, agreeing to stay on for a year to help in the transition. Part of that transition involved Hatfield's opening a nanobrewery and pub to brew and serve experimental batches that might become new labels for Holy Mackerel. On October 12, 2012, the Mack House opened in a Fort Lauderdale shopping plaza, and Holy Mackerel was finally making beer for sale in its own South Florida brewery. Gordash has since left on good terms. It's all Hatfield's baby now.

Holy Mackerel is brewing only 1.5 barrels at a time, however. "Being a contract brewer," Hatfield said, "our biggest challenge is that we can't quite get enough beer, because we're sold out a lot at our distributors. Looking at this and looking at the market and the potential penetration of craft beer in South Florida, which is still kind of in its infancy, if you will, I thought that it would be a good idea for Holy Mackerel to have a footprint here, even on a small scale."

The Mack House took over the space that had housed Stage 84, an intimate music café, and it still retains some of that vibe. Tables and a plush couch and loveseat occupy a raised platform behind the front window. Across from that, visible

Beers brewed: Beers are brewed on the house system on a rotating basis; other taps carry beers from parent company Holy Mackerel and other Florida breweries.

The Pick: Try any of the on-premises brewed offerings—you will find at least one or two. If they don't float your boat, order a Holy Mackerel Panic Attack, an unfiltered Belgian-style ale with a hint of spice that clocks in at 10 percent ABV.

through the other window, is the nano-size brewing system. A spinet piano along a side wall is owned by a local piano teacher, who still occasionally holds recitals in the taproom. Talented and likely not-so-talented customers have been known to sit at the keyboard and tickle the ivories during business hours.

A large, lighted "Brewery" sign with bright red letters alerts folks of the taproom's existence, and Hatfield said he's looking at a variety of promotions to draw more customers. "Business is getting better on a month-to-month basis," he said. "More people are finding out about it. We're getting a fan base, and it's helping our commercial beers in the local market. People hear about us, they come in and try something, and they head down to Total Wine or Publix and buy some bottles. So it's a win-win situation from that perspective."

Miles often uses local ingredients to spice up the beer—sometimes literally, with hot peppers in some of the brews. Coffee beans from Miami's Café Don Pablo Gourmet Coffee go into the Panic con Pablo, a 10 percent ABV beer that's a treatment of the Holy Mackerel Panic Attack recipe. The taproom recently started holding beer dinners, with local restaurants providing the courses, and brewer Justin Miles keeps the beer flowing on the taps, along with the commercial Holy Mackerel brews and American craft beers from Florida and other states. Occasional live music acts perform at the Mack House, but that's not a priority for Hatfield. "We're trying to focus on the beer," he said.

The Mack House

Opened: 2012.

Owner: Larry Hatfield.

Brewer: Justin Miles.

System: 1.5-barrel Brickman.

Annual production: 50 barrels.

Hours: Tuesday through Thursday, 4 to 11 p.m.; Friday and Saturday, 4 p.m. to 2 a.m.; Sunday, noon to 8 p.m.

Tours: None.

Parking: Free on site.

Takeout beer: None.

Special considerations: Handicapped-accessible.

Other area beer sites: Tap 42 Bar & Kitchen, 1411 S. Andrews Ave., Fort Lauderdale, FL 33316, (954) 463-4900, www.tap42.com.

Miami Brewing Co.

30205 Southwest 217th Avenue, Homestead, FL 33030
(305) 242-1224 • www.schneblywinery.com/brewery

Miami Brewing Co.'s home is inside Schnebly Redland's Winery, which Peter and Denisse Schnebly opened in 2006. The drive to the operation runs through some agricultural property, but instead of corn and wheat, it's groves of citrus, mango, papaya, and other tropical fruits. When you pull into the parking lot, you'll first see a stately columned building framed with towering palm trees, not unlike a structure from the wine country of California's Sonoma Valley. This impression continues inside, where you'll find a large, free-standing tasting bar in the center of the open space, racks and shelves holding bottles of the wine produced there, and a separate bar to the right where the beer is poured.

But step out the back door and you're transported into a Caribbean paradise, complete with waterfalls and tiki hut structures roofed with thatched palm leaves, surrounded by flowering tropical plants. The owners consider this to be their beer's *terroir*, to borrow a winemaking term referring to a grape's growing environment, which gives a wine its distinctive characteristics. When the Schneblys opened their winery, they had the goal of using as much local tropical produce as possible, and they have applied the same *terroir* concept to their beer. Local brewery consultant Matthew Weintraub explained that the Schneblys "use whatever they can use locally. They always strive for some kind of local flavor into the beer." The brews likely will never be made with all local ingredients, as South Florida's climate does not lend itself to growing hops or barley, but coconut, mango, guava, and other tropical fruits flavor many of the beers.

A few years after opening the winery, Peter began planning for a brewery as well. This required changes in both state and local statutes, but eventually, the Schneblys managed to clear the paperwork hurdles. The winery crew custom-built the fermenters and some bright tanks, and initially the winemakers brewed the beer. At first

Beers brewed: Big Rod Coconut Ale, Shark Bait Wheat Ale, Gator Tail Brown Ale, and Vice IPA, plus specials and seasonals.

The Pick: In my travels across Florida, I've become quite fond of mango as an ingredient in beer, and Shark Bait Wheat Ale makes good use of the tropical fruit to give the brew a smooth, slightly sweet finish.

it was exclusively on tap at Schnebly Redland's, then kegs were distributed to some local accounts.

In mid-2013, Andrew Guthrie, a lauded local homebrewer, came on board as head brewer. Weintraub, who helps run the brewing sciences program at nearby Florida International University, was hired as a consultant at about the same time. At the time of this writing, an expansion of the brewing operation was under way, with some new fermenters and bright tanks having been added. But the biggest development was the arrival of a canning line, expected to be operational in late 2013, with distribution of cans to store shelves anticipated shortly after. "We're developing quality control right now to make sure the cans are perfect," Weintraub told me. "We want to make sure that's ready before we start releasing cans to the market."

Having the beer out in the world should help spread the Miami Brewing Co. name. The winery and brewery lies off the beaten path in Homestead. Other than agricultural operations, there's little else in the area, and sometimes that makes it difficult for visitors to find. "But once you're there, it's really nice," Weintraub said. "You can sit there and relax. People are enjoying the beers that we put on tap."

Miami Brewing Co.

Opened: 2012.

Owners: Peter and Denisse Schnebly.

Brewer: Andrew Guthrie.

System: 15-barrel custom-built.

Annual production: To be determined.

Hours: Monday through Thursday, 10 a.m. to 5 p.m.; Friday and Saturday, 10 a.m. to 11 p.m.; Sunday, noon to 5 p.m.

Tours: Saturday and Sunday at 2 and 4 p.m. for $7.

Parking: Free on site.

Takeout beer: Growlers.

Special considerations: Handicapped-accessible; cover charge for music events Friday and Saturday starting at 6 p.m.

Extras: Patrons can purchase a logo pint glass for $10, which includes a beer sampler and one full pour.

Naples Beach Brewery

4110 Enterprise Avenue, Suite 217, Naples, FL 34104
(239) 304-8795 • www.naplesbeachbrewery.com

Will Lawson was expecting a shipment of sixty new kegs, but that still wasn't enough to satisfy the demand from his accounts. He needed another forty of the 7.75-gallon "slims," a.k.a. quarter barrels, and was expecting them by the end of the summer. "That will be the point at which I own two hundred slims and a handful of half barrels, and we'll rock on all the way through next season and run at full capacity," he said. "That will give us an idea of how much bigger we want to go from here." It's likely that the growth of Naples Beach Brewery will continue for a while, since it was the only brewing game in town at the time of this writing.

Naples sits on the southern Gulf Coast of Florida, just a few miles west of the point where I-75 cuts to the east and becomes the Everglades Parkway, more commonly known as Alligator Alley, which bisects the Everglades. There's not much below the town on the coast, other than swamp.

Lawson originally moved to Naples in 2003, and the lack of craft beer on the local store shelves inspired him to start brewing his own. "I started homebrewing as a hobby and eventually moved back up north to do brewing school in Chicago and work at a brewery in my native Michigan for the experience that I needed to open my own brewery," he told me. "Then, when it was time to choose a spot, not only did my wife really miss the beach, but she hates winters now. We figured because there was nothing really going on like this here in Naples, it would be a good place to start."

Naples Beach Brewery opened in 2011. It's going well, except that Lawson must keep the brewery distribution-only because of the time and expense that would be involved in rezoning the industrial park in which it is located. That doesn't mean folks can't come by to try out his products and see the brewery. The law allows Lawson to hold tours a couple days a week, when visitors

Beers brewed: Naples Beach Weizen, Special Red, Pale Ale, Black IPA, and Imperial Pub Ale. Seasonals: Mango Ginger Belgian Tripel, and Stout.

The Pick: The Pale Ale has a blend of hops that brings out a citrusy, piney taste and aroma, with tropical fruit notes thrown in for good measure. It's a very drinkable, tasty unfiltered version of this style.

can purchase a logo glass for a nominal charge and sample the beer. "I invite people to come into the brewery," he said. "I sell you a tour, I bring you back into the production area, and I talk about the brewing process. I show you the equipment. I'll basically take you through what my duties are to get beer from a bag of grain all the way to being packaged in a keg."

The brewery is a one-man operation, with Lawson putting in anywhere from fifty-five to seventy hours per week. His beer styles are mostly basic, but he finds the time to brew special ones too, such as Mango Ginger Belgian Tripel, which he was hoping to put into regular production. When he brewed it the first time, the ABV came in at a toe-curling 10.4 percent. The most recent version is 7.75 percent. "The beer tastes exactly the same," he said. "The popularity is probably the same or even greater now, because people can have more than one or two of them and not be on their backside."

That fits right in with his brewing philosophy and personal taste. "Most beers I do around here aren't high-alcohol beers, because my turnover has to be relatively quick," he explained. "I'm as excited as the next guy about these big, bold, creative, high-alcohol big-flavor beers, but at the end of the day, I like to be able to drink a couple of beers at a sitting." Lawson hopes that perhaps sometime in 2014, he'll have the resources to open in a larger space where he can build a tasting room.

Naples Beach Brewery

Opened: 2011.
Owner: Will Lawson.
Brewer: Will Lawson.
System: 55-gallon custom-built.
Annual production: 200 barrels.
Hours: Friday, 4 to 8 p.m.; Saturday, 3 to 7 p.m.
Tours: Tours and tastings during hours given above. Private group tours available by reservation on Thursday evenings. Cost of $15 includes a logo glass, samples of all six beers on tap, and two full pours.
Parking: Free on site.
Takeout beer: None.
Special considerations: Handicapped-accessible.
Other area beer sites: South Street Grill, 1410 Pine Ridge Rd., Suite 4, Naples, FL 34108, (239) 435-9333, www.southstreetnaples.com.

Organic Brewery

290 North Broadwalk, Hollywood, FL 33019
(305) 414-4757 • organicbreweryhollywood.com

Florida has nearly 2,000 miles of coastline, but there's only one brewery—so far—where you can step out the front entrance and onto beach sand. Well, technically, there's a sidewalk to cross, but let's not nitpick. Organic Brewery on Hollywood Beach offers a stunning view of the Atlantic Ocean from its front dining deck, a perfect place to enjoy one of its European-style lagers or ales while watching beachgoers do their thing and people stroll by on the Broadwalk.

According to general manager Johnny Quinones, the owner, Sergey Novov, operates a couple breweries in Europe and wanted to open one in South Florida. "Hollywood Beach was a good location. It's on the boardwalk. It's on the beach. You can't beat that location."

Inside, the air-conditioned brewpub's décor has a European theme, with a giant mural of what looks like a German village street on one wall and beer stein sculptures embedded in another. Customers can view the shiny tanks of the brewing system through plate glass windows that stretch from floor to ceiling. A handful of TVs are tuned into U.S. sporting events or European soccer games. "We have soccer on TV all the time because many customers here are Eastern Europeans, plus for all the locals that love the game," Quinones explained.

Indeed, tourists from all over the world flock to the beaches of South Florida, and many like to frequent restaurants and pubs that make them feel at home. "The European tourists that come here love the beach," Quinones said. "That's why the location is perfect for that. You have a beer and you're at the ocean." The food menu also offers fare inspired by British, German, and Eastern European cuisine, as evidenced by the sausage and schnitzel dishes and fish and chips, along with steaks, salads, and typical American pub fare. More than a few craft beer fans have made their way to Organic Brewery since it opened, Quinones said. "We have a lot of tourists or people that are in town for business,

Beers brewed: Belgian Ale, German Pilsner, British IPA, Wheat Beer, and Russian Knight (stout).

The Pick: The British IPA is a refreshing beer to enjoy while sitting on the front deck and taking in the view of the Atlantic Ocean over the white sand of Hollywood Beach.

they Google 'breweries,' we pop up, and they drive a half hour or even an hour just to come by here and try the beer."

One of the most striking sights in the place is a line of jars with spigots lining a shelf behind the bar, looking remarkably like medical specimens in a biology lab. They contain homemade schnapps, some with traditional flavors such as cherry or lemon, but others with cucumber, chili pepper, or horseradish as the base.

The beers at Organic Brewery are brewed with all organic ingredients, Quinones said, though they are not officially USDA certified yet. The brewpub is working on it. In the meantime, it has obtained the necessary licensing to sell its beer outside the brewpub through a distributor, supplying some local venues with kegs and hoping to expand even further. "We're providing hand-crafted beers that are delicious. Hopefully it catches on and we can open a brewery and start distributing more so more people can be able to have our beer," he said.

Organic Brewery

Opened: 2011.
Owner: Sergey Novov.
Brewer: Sergey Myshenko.
System: 4.2-barrel ZIP Technologies.
Annual production: 696 barrels.
Hours: Open daily, 11:30 a.m. to midnight.
Tours: Any time the brewery is open.
Parking: Paid street parking that can be hard to find.
Takeout beer: Growlers.
Special considerations: Handicapped-accessible.
Extras: Outdoor covered deck—on the beach!

Sarasota Brewing Company

6607 Gateway Avenue, Sarasota, FL 34231
(941) 925-2337 • www.sarasotabrewing.com

The evolution of the Sarasota Brewing Company began in the 1980s, when it was a local hotspot called the Gingerbread Man and had a beer selection unusual for that time. "It was a specialty beer bar," said brewmaster Vincent Pelosi. "A place where you could actually go and get European varieties that you wouldn't find in most other places at that time. People tell me it was a hopping bar." But that was before his time. Pelosi did not walk through the doors for a few more years, not until after the Gingerbread Man was no more, having evolved into the Sarasota Brewing Company.

Pelosi and his family left New York to come to Florida in the early 1990s after their children were born. He had begun homebrewing a few years before, and after he worked at a few unfulfilling jobs, he sought a position in the brewing industry, but not many existed outside of the major breweries in Tampa and Jacksonville. Then he landed a gig at Sarasota Brewing. "It was a short-lived assistant's job," he said. "I kept applying any place I could. Eventually Ybor City Brewing opened up in 1994, and I got hired as the primary assistant brewer. I worked for them for four and half years as the lead brewer—not the brewmaster, but the lead brewer. And when the opportunity came for an opening here, I applied for it and got it." That was in 1999, and he's been here since.

The décor of Sarasota Brewing calls to mind an old European brewery cellar, with openings between the various rooms framed by archways of stone and dark wood. The bar is topped in copper, and green fabric covers the padded seats and barstools. Its storefront sits among the other restaurants, shops, pubs, and businesses of Sarasota's Gulf Gate district, a popular but aging destination for residents and tourists alike.

From the start, Sarasota Brewing sold itself as not only a brewpub, but also a sports bar. A cluster of TVs hangs behind the bar, and other screens

Beers brewed: Sarasota Gold, Sequoia Amber Lager, India Pale Ale, and Midnight Pass Porter, plus rotating seasonals and one-offs.

The Pick: Because Sarasota Brewing is as much a sports bar as a brewpub, go for the Sequoia Amber, a smooth-drinking lager with a hint of caramel. With an ABV of 5.5 percent, you can have a few while watching the game and not worry about having to crawl home.

are tucked into nooks and crannies throughout the space. But watching athletes compete doesn't do much for Pelosi: "I'm not a sports guy," he said. "I try to get out of here when there are sports events going on." He'd rather be plying his craft back in the brewery, ensuring that the standard beers remain on tap while toying with new recipes to introduce to his customers, all the while sticking to the basics. He's not one to follow the latest trends in craft brewing, such as adding fruit or other adjuncts. "I don't use anything other than barley, hops, water, and yeast," he said. "I'm—and I hate to say it—a stodgy old-school brewer."

When he's not at the brewery or with his family, Pelosi lends his mandolin-playing skills to a local band he's part of that plays "acoustic, old-school rock and roll—a lot of Johnny Cash, Tom Petty, that kind of Americana rock and roll." He started teaching himself to play the mandolin in the mid-1990s, choosing the instrument because so many others picked up guitars: "I have a different job than most other people; I play a different instrument than most other people."

Sarasota Brewing Company

Opened: 1989.
Owner: Anthony Fricano.
Brewer: Vincent Pelosi.
System: 7-barrel JV Northwest.
Annual production: 350 barrels.
Hours: Monday through Thursday, 11 a.m. to midnight; Friday and Saturday, 11 a.m. to 2 a.m.; Sunday, noon to midnight.
Tours: By request if brewer is available. Generally Monday through Friday between 11 a.m. and 5 p.m., unless previously arranged.
Parking: Free on site.
Takeout beer: None.
Special considerations: Handicapped-accessible.
Extras: Occasional beer dinners.
Other area beer sites: Mr. Beery's, 2645 Mall Dr., Sarasota, FL 34231, (941) 343-2854, mrbeeryssrq.com; Cock & Bull, 975 Cattlemen Rd., Sarasota, FL 34232, (941) 363-1262, www.facebook.com/CnBpub; The Beer Box, 5767 Beneva Rd., Sarasota, FL 34233, (941) 923-1002, www.facebook.com/FloridaCraft.

Tampa Bay Brewing Company
Coral Springs Tap House

1221 North University Drive, Coral Springs, FL 33071
(954) 227-2337
www.facebook.com/TampaBayBrewingCo
CoralSpringsTapHouse

Norm Lehman hung around for several years at the Tampa Bay Brewing Company in Tampa's Ybor City district, but he did not just sit at the bar—he was helping head brewer David Doble make the beer for the popular brewpub, first as a volunteer and later as a bona fide assistant brewer.

Then the company he worked for offered voluntary separation packages. He refused the first two times, but as the offers became increasingly generous, he readied himself to accept in the next round. Lehman told me he then approached the Dobles with a proposition: "I said, 'I'm going to take the third one. Would you be interested in opening up a Tampa Bay Brewing Company in Coral Springs?' And they said, 'Absolutely; we would be delighted to do that.' That is how this was born." Lehman emphasized that he does not operate a franchise: "It's a private relationship between two families—the Doble family, owners of Tampa Bay Brewing Ybor, and Tampa Bay Brewing Coral Springs Tap House and the Lehman family here."

The tap house operates in the corner unit of a shopping plaza on one of the main drags in Coral Springs. The décor mimics that of the Ybor City brewpub, with a copper-top bar, brickwork, dark wood, and the signature red, purple, and green highlights drawn from the logo. Lehman built the bar from repurposed wood from the brewing equipment's shipping crates. A small stage features live music on weekends, and an outdoor patio provides extra seating for customers. The menu bears a similar look to Tampa's, but it's much thinner because the tap house does not serve food, though folks are welcome to order in or bring their own. The bar has twenty-four taps plus a hand-pull beer engine for casks. Two of the taps are for root beer and cream soda, with another pair reserved for cider and mead.

Beers brewed: Still being determined; a mix of beer brewed on premises and shipped from the Tampa brewery, plus guest taps.

The Pick: Order the newest on-premises brewed beer and you should be satisfied.

At the time of this writing, the Coral Springs tap house was still a work in progress. The brewing system was set up, but Lehman and Doble were still fine-tuning it and determining which beers would be brewed on-site and which would be shipped down from Tampa. A large overhead exhaust unit with a fire-suppression system determined the layout of the brewery, because it would have been far too costly to move it. Lehman wanted a 7-barrel brewhouse, but it needed to sit under the exhaust unit, so a single tank would have been too large to fit. Instead, he opted for a tandem system of two 3.5-barrel tanks. The rest of the brewpub was built to fit around that.

After the brewing regimen stabilizes, Lehman hopes to expand into more creative offerings. "It's our desire here to fool around with a lot of oak-aged or bourbon oak-aged beers in the double IPA range or porter range, and some experimental barleywine in small batches," he said. And looking down the road, Lehman thought a physical expansion of the tap house might occur: "We will probably expand into the suite right behind here, and that will allow us to do canning and expand brewing operations a little bit."

Tampa Bay Brewing Company Coral Springs Tap House

Opened: 2013.

Owner: Norm Lehman.

Brewer: Norm Lehman.

System: 3.5-barrel tandem system (7 barrels total) Stout Tanks and Kettles.

Annual production: Estimated 1,200 barrels.

Hours: Monday through Thursday, 4 to 11 p.m.; Friday, 2 p.m. to 2 a.m.; Saturday, 11 a.m. to 2 a.m.; Sunday, 11 a.m. to 11 p.m.

Tours: On request, if someone's available.

Parking: Free on site.

Takeout beer: Growlers, cans from Tampa brewery.

Special considerations: Handicapped-accessible.

Extras: Outdoor seating; live music; dog-friendly Tail Waggin' Tuesday first Tuesday of each month.

Tequesta Brewing Co.

287 South U.S. Highway 1, Tequesta, FL 33469
(561) 745-5000
www.facebook.com/pages/Tequesta-Brewing-Co/
111644658847904

Tequesta Brewing Co. occupies a space in a strip mall next to the Corner Café, where co-founder and co-owner Matt Webster started brewing for a paying audience. It's a long and narrow space, with the brewery in back and the tasting area up front. The regular customers filter in and out throughout the day, having a pint or two and filling their growlers.

Once your eyes adjust to the interior lighting after walking in on a sunny afternoon, the first thing you'll likely notice is the bar, an intricately carved wooden piece with original glass on the backbar. It looks as if it belongs in a hundred-year-old watering hole, which is exactly where it would be if it were still in its original home. The grandfather of Webster's partner, Fran Andrewlevich, bought the bar in 1944. "We have the document over there that my grandmother and grandfather signed," Andrewlevich said. "It was in a small coal town in Central Pennsylvania. The coal went away, so the town just kind of shut down. This was left behind." The antique had been set up in his grandparents' basement, and Andrewlevich and his siblings played there when they were children. Eventually his mother put it up for sale, and Andrewlevich bought it for $4,000.

He hired an antiques expert to disassemble it and moved it down to Florida in the early 1990s—and wound up moving it several times to different storages. "It ended up in my garage, and it took up my whole garage," he said. Matt saw it in the garage, "and he said, 'We've got to put this thing up,' and I said, 'Absolutely.' It's one of those things like, it was meant to be here. It was supposed to be in the beer bar business somehow, someway."

Andrewlevich attended culinary school and then worked in the kitchen at the former Irish Times Pub & Brewery in West Palm Beach. He

Beers brewed: Terminally Ale American Brown Ale, Gnarly Barley American Pale Ale, and Der Chancellor, a classic German Kolsch. Seasonals: Pumpkin Ale and Coffee Porter (Thanksgiving).

The Pick: Terminally Ale is a top-notch example of the American brown ale style, with rich caramel and chocolate notes perfectly balanced with citrusy hops. And it's only 4.3 percent ABV, so you might want to take a growler or two of this ale home, where you can drink as much of it as you want.

started helping out with brewing operations, and after the pub closed, Kelly's Caribbean Bar, Grill & Brewery in Key West approached him about being its head brewer. He got the job, and for four years, he flew between Fort Lauderdale and Key West monthly to brew there. After that, he worked as a brewer at the two Brewzzi brewpub locations in South Florida.

Meanwhile, Webster left his job in the mortgage industry and—in between deep-sea fishing trips and golf, his other two passions—started brewing on a 55-gallon system at the Corner Café. He and Andrewlevich became friends and discussed opening their own brewery. In 2011, they opened Tequesta Brewing next door to the Corner Café, which still serves their hand-crafted beer.

"We just make real drinkable beers, full of flavor," Andrewlevich told me. "Not particularly a style; in between styles is just fine. Whatever we end up liking. We'll travel somewhere and try a black walnut porter, and go, 'Hey, talk to the brewer, then we'll do that.'" The partners have plans to open another brewery in the area, with up to triple the capacity of the current operation, but they will still focus on the local market. "We want to do local beer," said Andrewlevich, "and if it all stays in Palm Beach County, so be it."

Tequesta Brewing Co.

Opened: 2011.
Owners: Fran Andrewlevich and Matt Webster.
Brewers: Fran Andrewlevich and Matt Webster.
System: 15-barrel DME.
Annual production: 2,500 barrels.
Hours: Tuesday through Sunday, noon to 11 p.m.
Tours: On request, if someone's available.
Parking: Free on site.
Takeout beer: Growlers, special-release bottles, and kegs.
Special considerations: Handicapped-accessible.
Extras: Cask night Wednesdays.

Titanic Brewing Company

5813 Ponce de Leon Boulevard, Coral Gables, FL 33146
(305) 668-1742 • www.titanicbrewery.com

The Titanic Brewing Company embraces the tale of the doomed ocean liner that sank in 1912 after striking an iceberg in the North Atlantic Ocean on its maiden voyage. The theme dominates the space, from the photos, posters, and memorabilia on the walls to the framed front page of the *St. Louis Post-Dispatch* reporting the disaster. It is also the basis for the names of the beers and food items. Seeing as how the brewpub lies in fairly close proximity to the world's busiest cruise port in Miami, it might seem counterintuitive to have a motif that trumpets the most infamous cruise line disaster in history, but founder Kevin Rusk explained that the modern cruise industry inspired it.

Fresh out of college in 1982, Rusk and a business partner bought Tobacco Road, the oldest still-operating bar in Miami. The establishment had a colorful history, but at the time of the purchase, it was in a rough part of town, with clientele to match. Today it's a successful blues club in a revitalized neighborhood, but the sense of being on the edge remained with Rusk.

In the mid-1990s, Rusk got the itch to open a brewpub. At first it was going to be in Coconut Grove, he explained, and one of the potential shareholders worked in the cruise industry. "When I was developing the concept and writing the business plan, he came to me and said, 'Listen. If you could somehow try to tie this in with the cruise industry, I can bring buses of people every weekend from the Port of Miami,'" Rusk recalled.

The first idea that popped into his mind was to call it the Love Boat Brewing Company, he said, but he opted to go with Titanic. Like Tobacco Road, the name of the doomed ocean liner evoked an off-kilter vibe. "The term *Titanic* still had a bit of an edge to it," Rusk explained, before the 1997 James Cameron romantic-disaster film dulled some of that. The *Titanic* "was a marvel of its time," he said, "though it was very tragic. The fact

Beers brewed: Triple Screw Light Ale, Boiler Room Nut Brown Ale, Brittanic Best Bitter, Captain Smith's Rye Ale, White Star India Pale Ale, and Shipbuilder's Oatmeal Stout, plus many seasonals and specials.

The Pick: Drinking the Brittanic Best Bitter, I could close my eyes and imagine that I was bending elbows in the local pub with the Titanic's shipbuilders. The imported British hops and malt make this an authentic extra special bitter, with a bit of a dry finish.

that over a hundred years ago, they could build a ship that could hold that many people, it's just unbelievable."

The Titanic Brewing Company borders the University of Miami campus, but that's not where most of its clientele originate. "People always assume that we're a college bar, and that's not the case at all," Rusk said. "The actual students only make up about 10 percent of our sales. We have a fairly high-end menu. We kind of fancy ourselves as a gastropub. I have really qualified cooks in the kitchen. We're very food conscious."

The menu, which features a mix of traditional and gourmet pub fare, is a big part of why Rusk believes the brewpub survived the shakeout of the late nineties, after a wave of microbreweries and brewpubs opened but relatively few survived. "These guys would open a brewpub or a small brewery, and they thought, 'Well, I'll just make great beer and that will be enough.' That just doesn't work," he explained. "You have great beer, that's going to make it that much greater of a restaurant. But first and foremost, you have to be a good restaurant or you'll never succeed."

Titanic Brewing Company

Opened: 1999.

Owner: Kevin Rusk.

Brewer: Steve Copeland.

System: 5-barrel DME system.

Annual production: 500 barrels.

Hours: Sunday through Thursday, 11:30 a.m. to 1 a.m.; Friday and Saturday, 11:30 a.m. to 2 a.m.

Tours: Call ahead to schedule.

Parking: Free on site and on street.

Takeout beer: None.

Special considerations: Handicapped-accessible.

Extras: Live music.

Beerfests, Beer Weeks, and Beerwebs

Beerfests

Along with the growth of craft breweries and craft beer knowledge in Florida has come a rise in the number of beer festivals. These days, it seems that nearly every weekend brings at least one fest. Some return year after year; others are onetime affairs.

Most of the festivals featuring multiple breweries require one admission price for unlimited sampling, usually 2-ounce pours. Consequently, a few have the reputation of being "drunkfests" in which a certain segment of the festival goers attend merely to get hammered. Fortunately, most attract folks who love tasting different styles of beer and having a good time with those of like minds.

Following is a sampling of some of the best beerfests in the state. It is not a complete list by any means, but these are festivals that—in most cases—have been held for a few years and feature multiple craft breweries, many of them local, where the tasting booths are often staffed with the brewers and brewery representatives in addition to volunteers. Local homebrewing clubs are often represented, and it's not unusual to find your favorite festival beers at those booths. Dates vary each year; check the festival website for up-to-date details.

Jupiter Craft Brewers Festival, January in Jupiter, jupitercraftbrewersfestival.com

Space Coast Craft Beer Festival, February in Palm Bay, www.spacecoastcraftbeer festival.com

Florida Brewers Guild Fest, March in Tampa, floridabrewersguild.org

Cajun Café Spring Craft Beer Festival, April or May in Pinellas Park, cajuncafeonthe bayou.com

Berliner Bash on the Bay, during the spring in Gulfport, www.pegscantina.com

Jacksonville Craft and Import Beer Festival, May in Jacksonville, www.beerfestjax.com

Hogtown Craft Beer Festival, May in Gainesville, www.hogtownbeerfest.com

WaZoo, August in Tampa, www.lowryparkzoo.com/wazoo

Key West BrewFest, Labor Day weekend in Key West, www.keywestbrewfest.com

Emerald Coast Beer Festival, September in Pensacola, emeraldcoastbeerfest.com

Baytowne Wharf Beer Fest, October in Sandestin, www.baytownewharfbeerfestival.com

Grovetoberfest, October in Coconut Grove, www.grovetoberfest.com

Cajun Café Fall Craft Beer Festival, November in Pinellas Park, cajuncafeonthe bayou.com

Sunshine Challenge Beer Competition and Festival, November in Orlando, www.cfhb. org/sunshine-challenge

Treasure Coast Beer Fest, November in Port Saint Lucie, www.treasurecoastbeerfest.com

Beer Weeks

In 2010, the phenomenon of the regional craft beer week, which highlights a community's craft beer and breweries for several days, did not exist in Florida. But four were held in 2011, and more are in the pipeline.

South Florida Beer Week, January in Southeast Florida, southfloridabeerweek. blogspot.com

DeLand Craft Beer Week, late January or early February in DeLand, www.delandcraft beerfestival.com

Tampa Bay Beer Week, early March in the Tampa Bay area, tampabaybeerweek.com

Jax Beer Week, early April in Jacksonville, beerweekjax.com

Beerwebs

Hundreds of craft beer lovers across the country have taken to writing down their thoughts about the subject, some in traditional print publications, but others online. Zephyr Adventures, the company that sponsors annual Beer Blogger Conferences in North America and Europe, lists almost twelve hundred North American "citizen" beer bloggers on the conference site (beerbloggersconference.org/blogs), most of them still active, in addition to almost 600 international bloggers.

These are blogs not affiliated with breweries, distributors, or others in the industry. Following are valuable online resources for those who wish to learn more about craft beer and its community.

Florida

Beer in Florida (beerinflorida.com). I'll start off with a shameless self-promotion of my blog, which chronicles the burgeoning craft beer community in the Sunshine State. Here you'll find the latest about new breweries and other developments, as well as a complete-as-possible map and list of all the on-premises breweries in the state.

Pensacola Beer (pensacolabeer.com). Brothers and Pensacola natives Gary and Terry Ryan write about craft beer happenings and news in the Florida Panhandle, from Pensacola east to Tallahassee, occasionally crossing the state line into Alabama with their coverage.

Jax Brew Bitch (www.jaxbrewbitch.com). Regina Heffington makes me a bit jealous sometimes. Her endless energy and knowledge of the Jacksonville craft beer community have resulted in a blog that covers a subject about as well as it can be done. It's the go-to site for Northeast Florida.

Orlando Beer Guide (www.orlandobeerguide.com). For logical and non-nefarious reasons, the author of this blog requests that he remain anonymous. That's a shame, because he deserves a lot of credit for doing a bang-up job of keeping visitors and residents of Central Florida aware of craft beer happenings.

Beer for the Daddy (beerforthedaddy.com). Sean Nordquist writes mostly about craft beer in the greater Tampa Bay area not only on his blog, but also in local print publications. His industry connections and his communications skills make this an excellent resource for the region's craft beer news and events. If you ever get a chance to meet Sean, be sure to ask him where he got the name of the blog; it's a great story.

Beer Geek (www.ticketsarasota.com/category/blog/beer-geek). Alan Shaw's official position is assistant metro editor at the *Sarasota Herald-Tribune*, but he still finds the time to embrace his Beer Geek alter ego and supply a steady stream of Southwest Florida craft beer news on his blog and in a weekly print column, also available on the newspaper's website.

Daily Beer Review (www.dailybeerreview.com). A South Florida craft beer aficionado who goes by the alias Beer Drinker Rob writes this blog, which mostly covers Southeast Florida events and news, with a large dose of sarcasm. As the name implies, he's also penned a good number of beer reviews.

Party Through the Parks (www.partythroughtheparks.com). Run by a "graphic designer wife & creative writer/photographer husband," this blog embraces a neat concept: adult drinks in Florida's major theme parks. It previews events and offers lists of beer, wine, and cocktails at various venues in the parks, among other features. It's a must-read for grown-ups seeking a liquid respite from the thrill rides, screaming kids, and costumed characters.

National

CraftBeer.com (www.craftbeer.com). A publication of the Brewers Association, the nonprofit trade association dedicated to small and independent brewers and their fans, the site contains a cornucopia of resources and information for both commercial brewers and the public.

Brookston Beer Bulletin (brookstonbeerbulletin.com). Jay R. Brooks, a veteran chronicler of the craft beer renaissance, provides nuggets and in-depth perspectives on issues in the industry. His commentary ranges from whimsical to scathing, especially the latter when he deconstructs poorly researched news stories and studies about beer and other adult beverages.

BeerPulse (beerpulse.com). This website created by Adam Nason is the clearinghouse for breaking news from the craft beer industry. Anyone who's interested in new beer labels, new breweries in planning, or comings and goings in the industry should make this required reading.

BeerAdvocate (beeradvocate.com). Beer consumers power this site with reviews, discussion forums, and event listings. Its founders, Jason and Todd Alström, and their staff publish a monthly print magazine and sponsor several beer festivals throughout the year.

Breweries to Come

More than forty breweries are on their way to coming online in Florida, but at the time of this writing, none had started serving beer brewed on the premises. Some are closer than others to their goal. Here is a list of the ones I know about, with physical addresses, phone numbers, and websites, if available.

Angry Chair Brewing, 6401 N. Florida Ave., Tampa, FL 33604, (813) 892-1651, www.angrychairbrewing.com

Barrel of Monks Brewing, 1141 S. Rogers Circle, Boca Raton, FL 33487, (561) 771-9807, barrelofmonks.com

Big Top Brewing Company, 6111B Porter Way, Sarasota, FL 34232, (800) 590-2448, www.bigtopbrewing.com

Bone Island Brewing, 1111 Eaton St., Key West, FL 33040, (305) 304-3472, www.facebook.com/BoneIslandBrewing

Brew Hub Lakeland, 4100 S. Frontage Rd., Building 700, Lakeland, FL 33815, (636) 532-2700, www.thebrewhub.com (St. Louis headquarters)

Bugnutty Brewing Company, 715 N. Courtenay Parkway, Merritt Island, FL 32593, (321) 452-4460, www.bugnutty.com

Bury Me Brewing Company, 10045 Gulf Center Dr., E110, Fort Myers, FL 33913, (239) 332-6800, www.burymebrewing.com

Coppertail Brewing Co., 2601 E. Second Ave., Tampa, FL 33605, (813) 247-1500, coppertailbrewing.com

Cycle Brewing (production brewery), 534 Central Ave., St. Petersburg, FL 33701, (727) 328-2720

Dead Lizard Brewing Company, Alden Road, Orlando, FL 32803, (407) 710-8949, deadlizardbrewingcompany.com

ESB Brewing, 333 N. Falkenburg Road N. D-407, Tampa, FL 33619, (813) 990-0700, www.esbbrewing.com/wordpress-esb

Fat Point Brewing, 611 Charlotte St., Punta Gorda, FL 33950

Florida Keys Brewing Co., Key Largo, FL, (305) 509-7477, www.facebook.com/FloridaKeysBrewingCo

GrassLands Brewing Co., Tallahassee, FL, grasslandsbrewery.com

Gravity Brew Lab, Wynwood, FL, (786) 536-7085, gravitybrewlab.com

Green Bench Brewing, 1134 First Ave. N., St. Petersburg, FL 33705, (727) 214-4863, greenbenchbrewing.com

Idyll Hounds Brewing Company, 845 Serenoa Road, Santa Rosa Beach, FL 32459, www.idyllhoundsbrewingcompany.com

Infinite Ale Works, 204 S. Magnolia Ave., Ocala, FL 34471, infinitealeworks.com.

Intracoastal Brewing Company, 652 W. Eau Gallie Blvd., Melbourne, FL 32935, (321) 872-7395, www.facebook.com/intracoastalbrewingcompany

J. Wakefield Brewing, 120 NW 24th St., Miami, FL 33127, www.facebook.com/pages/ J-Wakefield-Brewing/420903834614051

JDub's Brewing Company, 1215 Mango Ave., Sarasota, FL 34237, (941) 955-2739, www.jdubsbrewing.com

Lagerhead Brewing Company, Palm Beach County, FL, (561) 320-1522, www.lagerheadbrewing.com

Lakeland Brewing Company, 640 E. Main St., Lakeland, FL 33801, www.facebook.com/lakelandbrewingcompany

LauderAle, 3305 SE 14th Ave, Dania Beach, FL 33316, (954) 214-5334, www.facebook.com/lauderale.

The Little Giant Brewery, 301 Seventh St. E., Bradenton, FL 34208, www.littlegiantbrewery.blogspot.com

M.I.A. Brewing Co., 10400 N.W. 33rd St., Suite 150, Miami, FL 33172, (305) 567-5550, www.miabrewing.com

Mad Beach Brewing, 12945 Village Blvd., Madeira Beach, FL 33708, (727) 362-0008.

Motorworks Brewing, 1014 Ninth St. W., Bradenton, FL 34205, (813) 230-1008, www.motorworksbrewing.com

Nature Coast Brewing Co., 564 N. Citrus Ave., Crystal River, FL 34428, (352) 795-0956

New Smyrna Beach Brewing Company, 112 Sams Ave., New Smyrna Beach, FL 32168, (386) 957-3802, www.facebook.com/pages/New-Smyrna-Beach-Brewing-Company/ 631667833527440

Ormond Brewing Company, 301 Division Ave., #13, Ormond Beach, FL 32117, (386) 795-2739, www.ormondbrewingcompany.com

Pair O' Dice Brewing Company, 400 118th Ave. N, Suite 208, Clearwater, FL 33762, www.pairodicebrewing.com

Point Ybel Brewing Company, 16120 San Carlos Blvd, Fort Myers, FL 33908, (239) 980-2764, www.pointybelbrew.com

Saltwater Brewery, 1701 W. Atlantic Ave., Delray Beach, FL 33444, (561) 450-9519, www.saltwaterbrewery.com

Six Ten Brewing, 7052 Benjamin Road, Tampa, FL 33634, (813) 886-0610, www.sixtenbrewing.com

St. Pete Brew, 544 First Ave. North, St. Petersburg, FL 33701, www.stpetebrew.com

3 Daughters Brewing, 222 22nd St. South, St. Petersburg, FL 33712, (727) 495-6002, 3daughtersbrewing.com

Tomoka Brewery, 188 E. Granada Blvd., Ormond Beach, FL 32174, (352) 875-6609, www.tomokabrewery.com

Two Henrys Brewing Company, 5210 W. Thonotosassa Road, Plant City, FL 33565, (813) 752-3892, www.facebook.com/twohenrysbrew Twohenrysbrewing.com.

Ulele, 1810 N. Highland Ave., Tampa, FL 33602, www.uleletampa.com.

The Waterfront Brewery, 201 William St., Key West, FL 33040, www.facebook.com/thewaterfrontbrewery

The Wild Rover Brewery, 8740 N. Mobley Rd., Keystone, FL 33556, (813) 475-5995, www.thewildroverbrewery.com.

Wynwood Brewing Company, 565 N.W. 24th St., Miami, FL 33127, wynwoodbrewing.com

Zeke's Brewing, 333 N. Falkenburg Rd., Suite D-408, Tampa, FL 33619, (813) 410-5438, www.zekesbrew.com

Glossary

ABV. Alcohol by volume, the standard measure in the United States to show how much of an alcoholic beverage's total volume is ethanol, the scientific name for the component that gives you a buzz. It's important to be aware of this because some craft beers can have stratospheric ABVs compared with mass-produced adjunct lagers. For example, Cigar City Brewing's Marshal Zhukov's Imperial Stout clocks in with an 11 percent ABV, while Budweiser has an ABV of 5 percent. That means a 6-ounce snifter of Zhukov's packs more of an alcoholic wallop than a 12-ounce can of Bud.

ABW. Alcohol by weight, another way of measuring alcohol content, used more often by foreign brewers. ABV and ABW are not equivalent; ABW is comparatively a lower number. To convert ABW to ABV, multiply by 1.25. For example, a beer with a 5 percent ABW would be equal in strength to one with a 6.25 percent ABV

Adjunct. Anything used in addition to or in place of malted barley in the beer-brewing process. Malted barley is used for its fermentable sugars, which, with the aid of yeast, become alcohol. Rye, wheat, pure sugars, and other adjuncts are popular with some craft brewers. Rice and corn have traditionally been used by macrobrewers to save money and to lighten the taste of their beers. This draws the scorn of beer geeks, who say those detract from, rather than enhance, the flavors. Those adjuncts, though, are beginning to find a place in some craft brewers' recipe books despite the stigma.

Ale. The older of the two main types of beer, the other being lager. The characteristics of the yeast used in brewing determine whether a beer is an ale or a lager. Ales are made with top-fermenting yeast, which does its work at the top of the fermenting tank. Ale yeasts thrive at temperatures warmer than lager yeasts and ferment more quickly. In general, ales have more flavor, bitterness, and complexity. They include such styles as India pale ales (IPAs), porters, stouts, and barleywines.

ATTTB or TTB. The Alcohol and Tobacco Tax and Trade Bureau, also known as the Tax and Trade Bureau. Once a part of the old Bureau of Alcohol, Tobacco and Firearms, this is the federal agency in charge of approving, licensing, and inspecting breweries. A new brewery cannot open without its blessings, and the ATTTB can shut down existing breweries for violations. Hence, you will find few brewers openly critical of the agency.

Barley. The grain most used in brewing beer. Enzymes in the barley convert its starch into sugar and other fermentables during the brewing process, and yeast converts the fermentables into alcohol. Barley must be malted before entering the brewing process, which means the maltster germinates the grain kernels, then heats them up to stop the germination and thereby achieve the highest starch content.

Barleywine. Very strong, flavorful, and full-bodied ale with a higher ABV, often 12 percent or more. American barleywines tend to be more highly hopped than British versions.

Barrel. A unit of measurement for beer equal to 31 U.S. gallons. This is the unit used in this book for brewhouse sizes and annual production figures.

Beer. Why you are reading this book. Beer is a fermented alcoholic beverage of varying strengths and styles mostly brewed with malted barley, hops, yeast, and water, though many other ingredients can be used in the process. The two basic types of beer are ales and lagers, and you'll find a rainbow of styles within each of those categories.

Beer blogger. Someone who shares his or her thoughts about beer mainly through online media, specifically blogs. Sometimes these blogs go dark as the folks writing them start working in the industry or get too busy with other things. Many great and not-so-great beer blogs remain active. (See "A word about . . . Beerfests, Beer Weeks, and Beerwebs" on page 178.)

Beer geek. Loosely, someone who has a greater interest in beer, especially craft beer, than the general populace. Some folks used to feel this moniker was a bit insulting, but now most embrace the title, especially because it helps differentiate them from the beer snobs. I proudly admit to being a beer geek.

Beer snob. A beer geek to a higher degree. These are the people who seem overly concerned with the minutiae of brewing and beer. Sure, that's a fine quality for a brewer or a beer judge to have, but beer snobs are eager to show off their knowledge to the beer geek crowd or anyone else who will listen. Sometimes they know what they are talking about, but often they are full of something that is not beer.

Beer styles. I will borrow the definition from the Beer Judge Certification Program (BJCP) website (www.bjcp.org/bjcpfaq.php#s01): "Styles are a convenient shorthand for discussing beer. They allow all those who are tasting and describing a beer to use a common framework and language. Style Guidelines are designed to assist organizers, entrants and judges participating in beer, mead and cider competitions by providing a standardized set of descriptions of beer, mead and cider styles." Some of the more popular styles are defined in this glossary, but there are dozens, and the lists vary with different groups and competitions. The BJCP website is a great tool for learning more.

BMC. Acronym for Bud, Miller, Coors, the most widely sold beers made and, some say, the least imaginative. Once U.S.-controlled companies, all three are now owned by foreign conglomerates. Beer geeks sometime use the term in a derogatory manner; beer snobs always do.

Bottle conditioning. The process of adding live yeast to a beer at the bottling stage. Bottle-conditioned beers are sometimes called "living beers" because the added yeast keeps the fermentation process going, sometimes for years or decades, meaning that the taste of a beer in a properly stored bottle will evolve over time.

Brettanomyces, or brett. A wild yeast that most breweries guard against because its introduction into the beer can cause undesirable off flavors. Some breweries, however, especially those seeking to duplicate certain European styles, deliberately introduce brett to add tart and sour flavors.

Brewer. A maker of beer. Technically, it does not matter where the beer is made physically, but those who don't brew at commercial operations use the term "homebrewer."

Breweriana. Collectible items related to beer, especially cans, bottles, signs, glassware, and other items that advertise the older, "classic" breweries. Most collectors look for these items for fun, but some do it for investment purposes. Be warned, however, that most breweriana does not command high prices.

Brewhouse. The area and equipment used to brew beer, primarily the mash tun, lauter tun, and brewkettle. This book gives the capacity of each brewery's brewhouse in barrels. Annual volume produced varies.

Brewpub. As defined by the Brewers Association, "a restaurant-brewery that sells 25% or more of its beer on site." Some apply this term to any brewery that sells most of its beer on the premises. In Florida, it usually refers to one of those that also sells food. In the past few years, reinterpretation of existing regulations has resulted in some Florida brewpubs also producing beer for distribution.

Carbonation. The fizzy stuff in a beer. It's the bubbling effect from the carbon dioxide (CO_2) produced during brewing and what gives the beer its head—the layer of foam on top. Often, especially in draft beer, the CO_2 is injected.

Cask. A vessel designed to serve beer through manual pumping or gravity rather than gas pressure. Some beer geeks love it; others prefer more carbonation.

Cask-conditioned beer. Unfiltered beer that is put into a cask to finish fermenting. This produces a tricky balancing act in which the beer must be tapped at the ideal time and consumed within a few days to avoid having it develop off flavors. Also called "real ale," it's generally served at 55 to 65 degrees Fahrenheit, or cellar temperature. People sometimes think it is served at room temperature. That is wrong, especially in Florida, where most of the year you'd need to really crank the air-conditioning to make the room that cool.

Cicerone. The equivalent of a sommelier in the wine industry; basically, someone who is expert on the ideal serving temperatures, appropriate glassware, and food-pairing possibilities for various beers. Cicerones are considered guides for those who want to learn more about beer, and they advise bars and restaurants on proper serving and sanitation techniques. Founded in 2007, the Cicerone Certification Program (cicerone.org) offers training and exams for three levels: Certified Beer Server, Certified Cicerone, and Master Cicerone. As of this writing, there are only seven master cicerones in the world.

Contract brewer. A brewer who makes beer at an existing brewery rather than his or her own facility. Sometimes the brewer wants to generate income to open a brewery; other times the brewer has run out of capacity. Some maintain that contract brewing can produce inferior beer, but as long as proper sanitation and techniques are used, it doesn't make much difference in taste. Another, perhaps more valid, argument faults brewers for calling their products "local beers" when they might be made in another state.

Craft brewery. You still hear the term *microbrewery* thrown around a bit, but it has largely been replaced as an overall descriptor by *craft brewery*, defined by the Brewers Association (BA) as "small, independent and traditional." *Microbrewery* fell out of fashion as a general term with the growth of the industry, as some breweries became not so micro, though the BA still uses the term for breweries producing fewer than 15,000 barrels per year. The Boston Beer Company, makers of Samuel Adams, for instance, currently produces more than 2 million barrels per year, which prompted the BA a few years ago to raise the production limit to be considered a craft brewery from 2 million to 6 million. Still, the entire craft beer industry in 2012 accounted for only 6.5 percent in volume and 10.2 percent in sales in the U.S. beer industry.

Draft or draught. Beer that is poured from a tap. This can be beer from either a keg or a cask, poured in a bar or at home. It is the most economical method by far for beer drinkers who have a personal draft system.

Dry-hopping. Adding hops to the beer after the initial fermentation to give the final brew more flavor, aroma, or bitterness.

ESB. Extra special bitter, a rich malty beer with, despite its name, minimal hops bitterness. Often dark and full-bodied.

Esters. Fruity, flowery, or spicy aromas and flavors produced during fermentation, usually because of the yeast strains used and not the addition of natural or artificial flavors.

Fermentation. The chemical process that makes beer what it is. Yeast devours starches and sugars and turns them into alcohol and carbon dioxide. It's a wonderful thing.

Final gravity. See *gravity*.

Firkin. A 9-gallon keg or cask designed to be poured through hand pumping or gravity.

Flagship. The beer that a brewery produces the most of or is best known by. This beer is usually the most widely available outside of the brewery, if it distributes.

Florida Weisse. A local version of Weisse that's not an official style but is being made by an increasing number of Florida brewers. To a base of the lower-alcohol, lighter-tasting Berliner Weisse, a cloudy wheat beer that originated in northern Germany, the brewers are adding tropical fruit flavors, often locally produced ingredients. The result is a tart, thirst-quenching ale that can have an ABV as low as 2 to 3 percent.

Gastropub. A fancy term for a restaurant or pub that serves gourmet-style food along with high-quality craft beers.

Gravity. A technical term that's important to understand. *Specific gravity* is a chemical term that measures the density of a substance in relation to the density of water. In brewing terms, *original gravity* is the specific gravity of the wort prior to its being fermented, measured on a scale that starts at 1.000. *Final gravity* is the specific gravity of the finished beer after fermentation, when the fermentable sugars have been converted to alcohol and carbon dioxide. The amount of sugars fermented can be calculated through a formula that determines the final ABV. Generally, the higher the original gravity, the higher the alcohol content will be.

Growler. A reusable container that can be filled from a tap line at a brewery, brewpub, or other location where it's allowed for later consumption at home or elsewhere. In most of the country, the 64-ounce growler is the standard, equivalent to 4 pints. In Florida, a quirk in the statutes forbids the sale of that size but allows 32- or 128-ounce growlers. A lot of people are working with the state legislature to change this so businesses can sell the more popular half-gallon size.

Guest taps or guest beers. Beer from other breweries sold on tap or in bottles in addition to a brewery's own products. Most breweries offer guest beers on tap to support the local craft beer community.

Handpump. A device used to manually pump beer from a cask or keg. Also called a *beer engine*.

Homebrewing. What it sounds like—making beer at home. The law does not allow you to sell it, but you can certainly drink it and share it with friends.

Hops. An essential ingredient in brewing that gives beer aroma and flavor and acts as a preservative. The scientific name of hops is *Humulus lupulus*. The female plant produces flowers, or cones, that are harvested for flavoring beer. There are more than a hundred hops varietals in the world, with more being developed.

IBUs. International Bitterness Units, which provide a measure of a beer's bitterness on an established scale. Generally, the higher the IBUs, the bitterer the beer.

Imperial. A term for a superhigh-ABV beer, applied to various styles. Because some brewers, especially in the United States, have been increasing alcohol content and bitterness, a term was needed to distinguish "regular" beer from the stronger ones.

IPA. India pale ale, a style developed by the British in the nineteenth century with more hops to help preserve the beer on its way to British beer drinkers in India. The craft beer movement in the United States took this style and added even more hops, creating a radically bitterer brew.

Keg. A cylindrical container for transporting beer, usually steel or plastic. A wooden keg would be a cask. The common sizes in the United States are 15.5 and 7.75 gallons, though more breweries are embracing the sixth barrel, or sixtel, approximately 5.2 gallons. A barrel is 31 U.S. gallons.

Kräusening. A traditional method of brewing in which a small amount of unfermented wort is added to a fully fermented beer to create a secondary fermentation and more carbonation.

Lager. Unlike ales, lagers are made with bottom-fermenting yeast, which does its work at the bottom of the fermenting tank. Lager yeasts thrive at temperatures colder than ale yeasts and ferment more slowly. In general, lagers are cleaner, clearer, and less bitter than ales. Lager styles include pilsners, bocks, and American adjunct lagers such as Budweiser and Miller.

Lambic. A beer style brewed mainly in Belgium that is spontaneously fermented by wild yeast. Traditional lambics have tart and sour flavors that some beer drinkers find unpalatable. But it's worth a try, because those who enjoy this style rave about it.

Macrobrewer or megabrewer. A big brewer that makes more than 6 million barrels a year, such as those that brew Budweiser, Miller, and Coors beers.

Malt. See *barley*.

Mash. A mixture of malt and hot water that is strained to form wort, the liquid concoction produced early in the brewing process. Other grains, such as wheat or rye, can be used, but most often the mash is made from malted barley.

Microbrewery. A brewery defined by the Brewers Association as producing less than 15,000 barrels of beer annually, with 75 percent of its sales off-premises. See also *craft brewery*.

Nanobrewery. There is no exact definition, but generally a brewery with a tiny system, sometimes as little as 5 gallons.

One-off. A beer produced by a brewery only once, sometimes to commemorate special occasions or events, though some breweries take pride in being experimental and producing one-offs for nearly all their taps.

Original gravity. See *gravity*.

Pasteurization. Named for French microbiologist Louis Pasteur, who invented this process, which involves heating beer to destroy any microorganisms. Though it will give the beer a longer shelf life, it affects its taste.

Pilsner. A pale lager developed in 1842 in Czechoslovakia that eventually became the world's most popular beer. Because it's neither too hoppy nor too malty, it can be quite a refreshing drink.

Pitching. Adding the yeast to the wort once it has cooled to the ideal temperature.

Prohibition. The period from 1920, when the Eighteenth Amendment to the U.S. Constitution essentially banned the sale and use of alcoholic beverages in the nation, to 1933, when the Twenty-first Amendment repealed it. Hundreds of breweries failed to stay in business during that time, and it was the start of a decades-long consolidation in the breweries, which was reversed by the craft beer movement.

Regional brewery. Defined by the Brewers Association as producing 15,000 to 6 million barrels per year.

Reinheitsgebot. The German Beer Purity Law, which in 1516 barred the use of any ingredient in beer other than barley, hops, and water (the role of yeast in brewing had not yet been discovered). This was to protect the citizenry from poorly made—or even poisonous—brew. It has since been amended, but many German breweries pride themselves on adhering to the original law, though they now know about yeast.

Saison. A complex, flavorful brew that originated in the French-speaking region of Belgium. Modern saisons have a higher ABV than the original, believed to have been 3 to 3.5 percent. They are also known as farmhouse ales, as they were brewed in farmhouses during the cooler months and stored for the farm workers to enjoy during the summer. Saisons can have fruity or spicy flavors and are highly carbonated.

Session beer. Some people have strict definitions, but commonly used for a beer that you can drink several of over the course of an afternoon or evening without getting plastered. After a lot of brewers competed for years at producing more and more alcohol in their beers, there's been a backlash, and more session ales of 5 percent ABV or lower are finding their way to the market.

Sixtel. See *keg*.

Three-tier system. A system set up after the repeal of Prohibition to stop alcoholic beverage producers from selling directly to consumers, which had previously led to abuse and corruption. The way it works is that producers can sell only to distributors, who sell it to retailers, who are the only ones who can sell it to consumers. There has been some loosening of the regulations over the years, but it remains the dominant system of beer distribution in the country.

Wort. The liquid resulting from the boiling of malted grains and hops, to which yeast is added after cooling. The yeast starts the fermentation process that results in beer.

Yeast. The little microscopic buggers that turn the fermentables in wort into beer. Brewers use different yeast strains to produce various flavors and aromas.

Zwickel. A tiny spout on the side of a brewing tank that lets the brewer pull samples from the beer as it ferments. This is important because sometimes an off flavor can be corrected by various methods during fermentation.

Index